For Rosellen Callahan

"Everybody's Favorite Country":
A Word About This Book

Italy A to Z embraces the major destinations on most visitors' itineraries. By that I mean Rome (the first and, understandably, the longest chapter) and—in alphabetical order—Florence, Milan and Lake Como, Naples and the Bay (including the Amalfi Drive resorts, Capri and Ischia), and Venice. As in the ten companion A to Zs, I start at what I consider the beginning in any new place, with a briefing on what has gone before. Then I move along into specifics, as a result of my own explorations and samplings.

Within each city, the opener is a carefully considered compendium of requisite destinations—of special value to the short-time visitor. Then I go on to capsule evaluations of what I believe to be the most visit-worthy churches (in Italy more than in any other country, these double as art galleries), museums, palaces, excursions, and other treats—with the range wide, from opera at La Scala in Milan and a tour of a still-inhabited Renaissance palace in Rome, through to the two-thousand-year-old treasures of Pompeii, outside Naples, a visit to the church where Amerigo Vespucci worshiped in Florence, and to a vast hall in Venice upon whose ceiling and walls Tintoretto painted half a hundred frescoes more than four hundred years ago.

Creature comforts are dealt with in quite as much detail. In each of the five cities (and at the bay resorts in the Naples chapter and Lake Como in the Milan chapter), I evaluate hotels that I've lived in or thoroughly inspected, in the principal categories—luxury, first class, moderate. There are equally extensive mini-reviews of restaurants in which I've eaten—expensive, moderate, and inexpensive, with rundowns of the best buys of the local wines. These are followed by suggestions on shops, category by category, that I have personally scouted.

The subject territory is Everybody's Favorite Country. The early-eighteenth-century Grand Tourists—earnest young Englishmen sent to the Continent to complete their educations—never omitted Italy from itineraries. Contemporary counterparts rarely do, either. Which is quite as it should be. Still, there is a new dimension to Italian travel: it has become more complex and less casual. I don't mean to imply that today's traveler is faced with anything like the overwhelming confusion of his eighteenth-century predecessor. But today's Italy is a considerable distance removed from the Italy of a quarter-century ago, when I first came to know and love it. While the traveler still is warmly welcomed—no people are more naturally gregarious or better at making friends—officially and otherwise, the apparatus of the visitor industry has become more sophisticated and, in the process, less open-arms-effusive. It could not have been otherwise, during this period in which the Italian worker took long-needed steps to improve conditions of labor in ways that had been undertaken earlier in other countries. The days of the excessively large grin and the bonhomie of the slapped back are largely gone. Relations between client and waiter, concierge, reception clerk, shopkeeper, guide, and taxi driver are more businesslike, much as in neighboring countries. No longer are churches open at all hours for the occasional dropper-in; they close for lunch much as do the shops. As for museums and art galleries, recent seasons have seen them keeping abbreviated hours, sometimes with staff enough to admit visitors to only certain of their exhibit rooms. Getting about can take longer, especially in cities like Rome and Naples, where traffic in the central sectors sometimes barely moves. And, until the government sees its way clear to mint more coins and print more low-denomination notes, minor financial transactions continue a problem, because of the shortage of small change.

Italy is, in a word, harder work than it was. Which is not to say that this country—with more diversity in the range of what it has to offer visitors than any other in Europe—need be a whit less rewarding. That is where this book comes in. By means of specific recommendations in the major areas of visitor concern, its aim is to help the reader get value received for his investment of time and money, whether the budget be luxury, middling, inexpensive, or as is often the case, a blend of the three, depending on the type of expenditure.

The idea has been to chronicle my researches with a view to providing just enough nitty-gritty—not so much as to be encyclopedic— to make Italy as exciting in the late nineteen-seventies as it was a couple of centuries back. But without the hassle.

ROBERT S. KANE

Contents

"Everybody's Favorite Country": A Word About This Book   vii

I *Rome*   1
  To Know   1
  To See   5
    Lay of the Land   5
    The Essential Rome   7
    Behind Museum Walls: A Selection of Favorites   13
    Treasures of Art and Architecture: Selected Churches   20
    A Roman Miscellany   30
  To Watch   37
  To Stay   40
  To Eat and Drink   50
  To Buy   60
  To Note   70

II *Florence*   74
  To Know   74
  To See   76
    Lay of the Land   76
    The Essential Florence   78
    Behind Museum Walls: A Selection of Favorites   83
    Florentine Palazzi: A Sampler   85
    Treasures of Art and Architecture: Selected Churches   86
    A Florentine Miscellany   87

	To Watch	89
	To Stay	90
	To Eat and Drink	94
	To Buy	99
	To Note	107
III	*Milan*	109
	To Know	109
	To See	111
	Lay of the Land	111
	The Essential Milan	112
	Behind Museum Walls: A Selection of Favorites	119
	After the Duomo: Selected Churches	121
	A Milanese Miscellany	122
	To Watch	123
	To Stay	124
	To Eat and Drink	128
	To Buy	133
	To Note	140
IV	*Naples and the Bay*	142
	To Know	142
	To See	145
	Lay of the Land	145
	The Essential Naples	146
	Behind Museum Walls: A Selection of Favorites	152
	Treasures of Art and Architecture: Selected Churches	153
	A Neapolitan Miscellany	155
	Cultural Countryside: A Trio of Excursions	156
	The Resort Islands: Capri and Ischia	157
	To Watch	161
	To Stay	161
	To Eat and Drink	163
	To Buy	167
	To Note	170
V	*Venice*	172
	To Know	172
	To See	175

Lay of the Land 175
The Essential Venice 177
Behind Museum Walls: A Selection of Favorites 182
Treasures of Art and Architecture: Selected Churches 184
A Venetian Miscellany 187
To Watch 190
To Stay 191
To Eat and Drink 197
To Buy 202
To Note 206

VI *Italy: A Mini A to Z* 209
Addresses 209
Advance Bookings 209
Breakfast 210
Climate 210
Clothes 211
Currency 211
Customs 211
Driving 212
Electric Current 212
Language 213
Museum Passes 213
Open Hours 213
Telephoning 214
Tipping 214

Acknowledgments 215

Index 217

I

Rome

Rome: To Know

For the generation I have known it, Rome has been the most changeless of the capitals. Return when you will, and the skyline as seen from the Pincio, in the Borghese Gardens, is quite as you have always remembered it, with the dome of St. Peter's dominating, as it has for centuries, and as surely it will for many centuries more. The municipal authorities—whose oft-seen symbol, "SPQR" (Senatus Populusque Romanus), dates back to a Senate that met twenty-five hundred years ago—have not had the success they would like in restricting the automobile from the core of the city. (The traffic continues horrendous.) But they have kept the skyscraper out in the newer peripheral sectors. Central Rome remains, rather miraculously, the Rome of the Caesars, of the great Renaissance-era *quattrocento,* of the beautiful Baroque centuries, even of the later nationalists' *Risorgimento* that resulted in the city becoming capital of a modern, united Italy.

It is not necessary in Rome, as in other cities, to make special excursions to an "old town." You are already there. Your hotel is within walking distance of where your Roman hosts' ancestors lived more than half a millennium before Christ was born. The rather gruesome Romulus and Remus legend having to do with the founding of Rome is no more than that: legend. You may remember that these twins were brought up at first by a female wolf on whose breasts they fed, later by a shepherd, and that Romulus, after doing in his sibling twin, set about founding the town that took its name from his, populating it with local passers-by whom he mated with ladies of the neighboring Sabine tribe, these last having nothing to say in the matter.

THE ETRUSCANS' ROME

There is more sense in the historians' reports that it was the ancient Etruscans who gave the settlement its name—the very same *Roma* it is called today—in the seventh century B.C. The Roman Republic was formed in 509 B.C., and by 272 B.C. Rome had the whole Italian peninsula under its control; then came Carthage, whose ruins still are to be seen on the Tunisian coast, across the Mediterranean. All of the Hellenistic states fell to Rome. Asia Minor, Egypt, Greece, Spain, and Gaul followed, so that by the time Julius Caesar (102–44 B.C.) took over as dictator, Rome controlled the entire Mediterranean world. Caesar intelligently reformed what had become a strife-ridden state, with a program that ranged from the granting of citizenship rights to the Spaniards and Gauls to intensified public building on the home front. But his good works ended with his assassination, and within decades the republic had become the empire.

Its first emperor, Octavian Augustus, was extraordinarily competent; he set a course of peace and prosperity that lasted for two centuries. Rome, despite the stigma of the institution of slavery, had long since accepted the culture of the Greeks whom it had conquered, and had continued to extend its frontiers. This was the period of such emperors as the high-living but nonetheless efficient Nero, whose reign ended with his suicide; of Hadrian, the sophisticated administrator and reorganizer; of Marcus Aurelius, at once a fine ruler and a philosopher-teacher.

THE SPLENDOR OF IMPERIAL ROME

Imperial Rome—visualized today from its remarkable core-of-town remains—was a luxurious and architecturally splendid city of a million population whose life revolved around the market center that was the Forum, and the entertainment center that was the Colosseum, and whose upper classes knew central heating, efficient sanitation, and running water.

Both republic and empire were studded with immortals—Lucretius (poetry), Caesar (history), Cicero (author of the first Latin prose, with his *Orations*), Virgil (poetry as exemplified by the *Aeneid*), Horace (poetry and satire), Livy (history), and Pliny the Younger (prose).

It ended in 476—the fateful year when a barbarian upstart named Odoacer was able to dethrone Romulus Augustulus—for a variety of reasons, the barbarians' strength but one of them. Politically, Rome was overlarge and overwieldy. Spiritually, there was the conflict of the new Christianity with the old Roman religion. Morally, there was the spectacle of a slavery-dependent society, sloppy-rich at the top, and with the masses at once morale-poor and economically impoverished.

Which is hardly to write classical Rome off as a decadent bust. We are still, a couple of millenniums later, greatly in its debt. We learned from the enormous empire Rome administered for centuries how sophisticated governments are organized and run. We inherited legal codes that were the first to espouse the principle that better a guilty man go free than an innocent man be adjudged guilty.

The Latin language, from which all of the Romance languages sprang—not to mention other languages with Romance connections, like our own—is a major Roman legacy. And so, for that matter, was the rich culture—embodying art, architecture, philosophy, and literature—that the Romans adopted from the Greeks and passed along to posterity.

THE ROME OF THE GREAT POPES

Rome, as an empire, moved east to the Byzantium that the Emperor Constantine renamed Constantinople, after himself. But within the city the power that was increasingly to be reckoned with was that of the leaders—or pontiffs—of the rapidly growing Christian Church, who gave Rome an eminence in the area of religion that it had lost in matters political. Still, the early medieval centuries saw tremendous decline. Gregory I, the sixth-century Pope who was one of the greatest Romans of them all, started the city back on the road to greatness. The later establishment of the Holy Roman Empire, with the German emperors assuming their crowns in Rome, gave the city a renewed prestige, if not the political power it once knew. But the Middle Ages were not Rome's proudest. There were incessant squabbles between factions vying for the papacy that resulted in periodic turmoil and a variety of types of government.

Coincident with the arrival of the fifteenth century, moral standards in the papal court sank to a level that made easy the appeal of the Reformation. Withal, this period—the fifteenth century or *quattrocento*—was the Golden Age of the arts in Italy, of popes like Sixtus IV, Innocent VIII, Leo X, Clement VIII, whose patronage of the arts, possibly not always with spiritual motivations, resulted in the employment of such geniuses as Michelangelo and Raphael in the papal courts. They created much of the Rome that we know today; and their successors, in the Baroque period of the seventeenth and early eighteenth centuries—Bernini, for example—added to the city's still-evident splendor.

KINGDOM OF THE SAVOYS AND MUSSOLINI

By the time Napoleon invaded Rome at the end of the eighteenth century, its papal rulers had made of it one of the great cities of the world. Intervening decades saw popes in and popes out. At one point Mazzini—one of the three great leaders of the Risorgimento movement for Italian unity, along with Garibaldi and Cavour—headed a short-lived Italian republic. But in 1870, Rome became the capital of a united Italian kingdom under the House of Savoy. King Victor Emmanuel II that year moved into the Quirinale Palace, displacing Pope Pius IX, who retreated to the Vatican to complete the longest pontificate in history.

From that year until 1929, the Vatican and the Italian Government were angry with each other, the popes not recognizing during all that period the loss of their temporal sovereignty. (With the 1929 Lateran Treaty, they agreed to sovereignty only over Vatican City.)

Fascism marched into Rome—and Italy—in 1922 in the person of Benito Mussolini, who promptly took over the government (leaving the little King Victor Emmanuel III a puppet and creating for himself the title of Il Duce). Mussolini became at once an imperialist (snatching Ethiopia in the face of the League of Nations' condemnation), racist (emulating the anti-Semitism of fellow-dictator Hitler), Axis partner (with his admired Hitler), and supplier of troops to Francisco Franco's insurgent Spanish Civil War troops.

Italy joined Germany in World War II, to suffer losses so severe that Mussolini's own people overthrew him, executed him in 1945 at Lake Como, and ended the war on the Allied side. At war's end

King Victor Emmanuel fled the country for Egypt (where he died a few years later), leaving the throne to his son Umberto. Umberto's reign was not long—from May 19 to June 13, 1946. A referendum voted the monarchy out of existence.

TODAY'S REPUBLIC

Republican Italy, in the north at least, has made remarkable economic progress. The long-impoverished south remains way, way behind the rest of the country in many economic and social areas. The seventies saw the beginning of a southern development fund, and reforms in education and housing. But the same decade saw agitation in the city that is the seat of the worldwide Roman Catholic Church, for divorce, birth control, and legal abortions. Added to that was a commendable, albeit short-lived, experiment—the first in the world—of free, no-fare public transport, the sensible idea being to get Romans to leave their street-clogging, air-polluting cars at home. Contemporary Romans are as partial to strikes as their ancestors were to circuses. All the while, governments change with a frequency not unlike that of pre-de Gaulle France.

But this is a city that has known Octavian Augustus and Julius Caesar, Virgil and Horace, Napoleon and Mazzini, the Victor Emmanuels and Mussolini, Gregory I and John XXIII, Michelangelo and Bernini. It can take work-stoppings and challenges to spiritual dogma, and the comings and goings of late-twentieth-century premiers: Rome remains the Eternal City.

Rome: To See

LAY OF THE LAND

The wise visitor to Rome walks until his feet kill him and he can go no farther. He then relaxes over an espresso in a caffè, and resumes.

There is always the door of a newly discovered church to open, with who knows what great art or architecture within. Or a newly noticed shop to case. Or a caffè in a previously unexplored quarter. Or a restaurant that looks inviting. Rome is at once the Romans themselves—attractive, animated, amusing—and the Rome they and their ancestors have created. The combination is unbeatable and unsurpassed anywhere on the planet.

Nowhere have I come across a map of Rome as good as the map of Paris that the French Government Tourist Offices have for years distributed free to all who ask. The map of the Ente Provinciale per il Turismo di Roma is adequate, though, and one comes across others with certain advantages. Take a look at whatever map you have and find the north-south thoroughfare called *Via del Corso*. It is Rome's principal street, and its extremities are both easy-to-remember landmarks. At the north is *Piazza del Popolo,* with a central obelisk, trio of churches, and a situation just beneath the *Pincio Hill* of the *Borghese Gardens*. The southern extremity of Via del Corso is *Piazza Venezia*. You cannot miss it because it is dominated by the massive nineteenth-century wedding cake that is the *Vittorio Emanuele Monument*. *Palazzo Venezia,* onetime home of Mussolini and now a museum, is opposite the monument, and *ancient Rome—* or what is left of ancient Rome—is just behind it: the *Forums, Capitoline Hill,* and, more distant, the *Colosseum*.

Retrace your steps on Via del Corso about two thirds of the way back to the Piazza del Popolo, until you come to *Via Condotti,* on your right. It is at once the heart of the smartest shopping area in town, and leads to *Piazza di Spagna*—the Spanish Steps area— which is where you're likely to bump into Cousin Jane or your college classmate or the couple you sat with on a bus your first day in town. There are flower vendors in the lovely plaza, and the splendid steps leading up to the *Church of Santa Trinità dei Monti* are congested the summer long with hirsute, incense-burning souvenir-selling youngsters from various points of the planet.

From Piazza di Spagna, you may proceed to Piazza del Popolo by *Via del Babuino,* the main antiques-shop street of Rome, or along *Via Margutta,* another fashionable thoroughfare running parallel with Babuino. You are wondering, about now, how to get from Piazza di Spagna to *Via Vittorio Veneto,* another street of which you've heard. You're close. Walk up the Spanish Steps to *Via Sistina,* on which earlier-mentioned Church of Santa Trinità dei Monti faces. Take Sistina (another interesting shopping street) downhill a bit to *Via Francesco Crespi,* turning left on that street until you reach *Via Ludovisi* and the Eden Hotel on its corner. Walk down Via Ludovisi a couple of short blocks, and you've reached Via Veneto. Continue to its summit, and you bump smack into the *Borghese Gardens*. Walk downhill on Via Veneto and you pass a number of hotels as well as the ex-royal palazzo that serves as the *American Embassy;* follow Via Veneto's curve and you are at *Piazza Barberini* with its lovely *Triton fountain* by Bernini.

Just beyond is *Palazzo Barberini,* and one of the city's great museums. From Piazza Barberini, you may take shop-lined *Via del Tritone* westward to Via del Corso—where you began. Or you may walk south on *Via Quattro Fontane* to the massive *Basilica of Santa Maria Maggiore,* thence a few blocks to its right and *Stazione Termini,* the main railway station that is perhaps the finest example of modern architecture in the city (the British Embassy is another).

St. Peter's and the *Vatican* are across the Tiber. You may take either of two bridges, one leading directly to the circular fortress-landmark that is *Castel Sant' Angelo.* The other is closer to *Via della Conciliazione* which leads directly to *Piazza San Pietro* and the basilica, with the *Vatican Museums* to the right of St. Peter's as you approach it. On this same side of the river, but considerably below St. Peter's and the Vatican, is the mellow *Trastevere* quarter, which you will want to amble about, perhaps in connection with a lunch or dinner.

THE ESSENTIAL ROME

One man's Rome is not necessarily another's. Still, based on visits and revisits over the years, these dozen destinations are counseled, to the short-time visitor, the newcomer not tarrying for long, as the essence—or at least as *an* essence—of the city.

The Vatican—St. Peter's and the Sistine Chapel. Who knows, if the Pope were to commission a headquarters today for the Catholic faith, what might be the result? Italy is not without its distinguished contemporary architects, artists and artisans. Nor are other areas of the planet. Still, the likelihood is that the result might have been an inverted shoebox, with a travertine face. There is no disputing the good luck of the church to have built when it did, reaping the genius of the Renaissance.

No great global monument is more easily distinguished, more a part of its environment. Interminable spats with the Vatican over the centuries notwithstanding, the Roman city fathers have left St. Peter's dome to dominate the skyline. One sees it from almost everywhere in town. And as you walk or even drive to it from the Tiber, along Via della Conciliazione, you realize that you cannot separate it from the piazza fronting it and bearing its name. One's spiritual faith, or even a total lack of it, is not all that important, when it comes to the world's largest church occupying disproportionately excessive space in the world's smallest country. St. Peter's Basilica, laying aside its function as No. 1 Catholic place of worship (only the Pope may officiate at mass from the high altar), is Rome at its most reassuring, its most stable, yes—even more so than the core-of-town remnants of the ancient empire—its most eternal.

It took well over a century to build. By the time it was consecrated by Pope Urban VIII in 1626, collaborators had included Michel-angelo (the still-ascendable dome and the marble *Pietà*—the Virgin with Christ descended from the Cross—which crossed the Atlantic to the 1964–65 New York World's Fair and made news again in 1972 when it was damaged by a Hungarian fanatic), Bernini (the brilliant altar canopy or baldachin, and the piazza, without), and Raphael (the façade). From stem to stern, the length exceeds 600 feet. The dome is almost 400 feet high. There's a lot to take in—richly decorated chapels (daily masses are said in the Capella del Coro), papal tombs, monumental sculpture, and, more impressive than any of the component parts, splendid scale.

There is a Treasury, with relics and ornaments, and, in the Grotto, entered from the left of the basilica, a maze of tombs spanning the history of the church, from St. Peter to John XXIII. Both basilica and piazza—the colonnaded oval that is a mid-seventeenth-century Bernini creation—are impressive enough empty, or nearly so. Still, both deserve attendance in the course of a papal-led mass, ceremony or audience (100,000 in the square is not an unusually high figure).

The Sistine Chapel, a part of the Vatican Museums complex (of which more later), goes back to the early sixteenth century. It is the site of the meetings of the College of Cardinals, when a new Pope is elected. If your visit is a summer one, prepare for a mob scene in the Sistine. Indeed, every part of it except the ceiling—which Michel-angelo began painting in 1508—will be occupied. Have a good look around. The end wall is Michelangelo's interpretation of the Last Judgment, while the ceiling embraces his *Creation* and *Prophets*. The right and left walls are by other artists—Botticelli most especially, but also Luca Signorelli, Pintoricchio, and Ghirlandaio. But the Sistine is, more than anything else, Michelangelo, a masterwork that even upon repeated revisits remains one of the great interiors of a city where great interiors are commonplace. The crowds are understandable.

Ancient Rome—The Colosseum and the Pantheon. There is no question but that strolls through the Forums are rewarding. Still, there are two absolute requisites of the old empire. Both are enough of a piece, these many centuries later, for the nonarchaeologist visitor to immediately perceive this city as it was some two millenniums past. The Colosseum is sufficiently intact to be appreciated for what it was: the seat of the action, with gladiators vs. lions and other fun and games, dating back to the first century, and with a seating capacity of some fifty thousand—which was not all that large, if you consider that ancient Rome had a population of about a million.

It is difficult to believe that work was begun on the Pantheon almost three decades before Christ was born. It is the only 100 per cent shipshape ancient Roman building. Its domed, colonnaded exterior is in such good shape that it could be *neo*-classic. But it's the real thing. The unusual proportions of the dome are not fully appreciated until one steps inside. The Pantheon is now a church, and contains the tombs of the painter Raphael and of monarchs of the House of Savoy.

Two of the Four Major Basilicas—Santa Maria Maggiore and San Paolo Fuori le Mura. "Basilica" is the title given to certain churches by the Pope as a special honor. (It is not to be confused with "cathedral," a church—which may or may not be a basilica—that is the seat of a bishop.) Rome has a higher proportion of basilicas than any other city. Of these four, after St. Peter's, are considered top-rank, for a variety of reasons—historical and ecclesiastical. The interiors of the lot are formidably severe, immense, and virtually chairless. (Do not plan on resting weary feet.) Of this quartet, two—San Giovanni in Laterano, or St. John Lateran, and San Pietro in Vincoli, or St. Peter in Chains—are later described. The other two are up here in this honor group of requisite Roman attractions. One, Santa Maria Maggiore (St. Mary Major), is called to the reader's attention at this point for several reasons. First is that it is the major (*maggiore*) church in Rome named for St. Mary, of many, many, many. (There are more St. Mary's churches in Rome than those by any other name.) The second is that it is so heart-of-town, fronting Piazza Santa

Maria Maggiore, as central a Rome landmark as, say, the nearby railway station, which is close only geographically; in age, some fifteen centuries separate the two. Santa Maria Maggiore goes back to A.D. 431, although it has been several times remodeled. It's a mix of styles, with a Baroque façade, a Renaissance campanile (the tallest in town), and a multiperiod interior with a magnificent coffered ceiling, fine mosaics, a number of chapels, and, as in the case of all the major basilicas, tremendous size.

San Paolo Fuori le Mura (St. Paul's Outside the Walls), on Via Ostiense, is special for two reasons. First is size. This is the largest church in town after St. Peter's. Second is beauty. This is the loveliest of the four major basilicas, with a Romanesque cloister that frames a garden of quiet charm, and a mosaic frieze of all the popes, from St. Peter to John XXIII. Though originally ancient, most of the church one sees today is mid-nineteenth century, a meticulous restoration that took two and a half decades after an 1823 fire.

A Pair of Requisite Museums: Museo Nazionale Romano-Baths of Diocletian and Galleria Nazionale d'Arte Antica-Palazzo Barberini. Thanks to the global repute of the Vatican Museums—which persist, even in the late twentieth century, in covering the genitals of nude sculptures with fig leaves, but which are otherwise estimable—the museums of Rome proper are among the most undervisited of any capital in Europe. They are also among the Continent's very best, and, I might add, devoid of fig leaves. I am fond enough of them to have singled out a good score of favorites that are dealt with in later pages. At this point, though, I single out two representatives as requisites. They have been selected not only because of their exhibits —one deals with ancient Rome, the other mostly with the Italian Renaissance—but because of absolutely smashing settings.

Museo Nazionale Romano-Baths of Diocletian (Piazza della Repubblica) comprise the baths themselves—a complex of high-ceilinged, splendidly proportioned halls and patios, built seventeen centuries ago (when it accommodated some three thousand bathers); and a remarkable collection of classical art that ranks with that of the National Archaeological Museum in Naples: mosaics, frescoes, sarcophagi, and sculpture—both busts and full figures, ranging from a *Satyr Looking at His Tail* to an *Amazon Leaping on a Fallen Gaul.* Take note, too, of the odd group, *Gaul Killing Himself After Having*

Killed His Wife, of the head of a gorgeous goddess who may or may not have been Aphrodite, of a geometric mosaic simply called *Whirling Disc,* of a seated pugilist. It is worth noting in advance (nobody in the museum is going to tell you) that also created out of the ancient baths—or at least from one of the baths' immense halls—is the Church of Santa Maria degli Angeli (later described). Its architect was Michelangelo himself. Museum and church have completely separate entrances and there are no signs directing the visitor from one to the other.

Galleria Nazionale d'Arte Antica-Palazzo Barberini is but one of two component parts of the national ancient-art museum. (The other— in a dazzlingly beautiful palazzo called Corsini—is Rome's best kept museum secret and is recommended on a later page.) Barberini is conveniently heart-of-town (13 Via Quattro Fontane). It is sumptuous Baroque (Carlo Maderno and, later, Bernini were its designers and the great builder-Pope, Urban VIII, was its original occupant). The paintings are sumptuous too—mostly Renaissance and mostly Italian (with seventeenth- and eighteenth-century Italian works among others, in Palazzo Corsini). The Barberini's treasures are abundant—Tintoretto's *Jesus and the Adulterous Woman,* Lotto's *Portrait of a Young Man,* Raphael's seductive lady, *La Fornarina;* Piero di Cosimo's exquisite *La Maddalena;* Titian's *Venus and Adonis;* a Holbein of *Henry VIII.* But paintings on the walls are not all. The ceiling of the immense ballroom, called *Il Trionfo della Gloria,* and painted by Pietro da Cortona, is a glorious triumph indeed, and surely the No. 2 ceiling in town, after that of Michelangelo in the Sistine Chapel.

A Renaissance Palace—Palazzo Farnese. Aside from those palazzi now doing duty principally as art museums—Palazzo Barberini, above, is a sublime example—there are others to be regarded principally for their architecture and decoration. Palazzo Farnese (Piazza Farnese) is one of the great town houses of the world. It has for a long time served as the residence of the lucky French ambassadors to Italy, and we are in their debt for traditionally allowing us one hour each Sunday (11 A.M. until noon—unless a new ambassador changes the schedule) to pop in and see some of the interior. Even with the place out of bounds the rest of the week, the piazza on which the palace fronts is in itself a major Roman destination. The building was begun in 1514 by Antonio Sangallo the Younger—using building materials from the Colosseum, of all places. But it was completed by Michelangelo. The French think enough of it to have commissioned Jean Cocteau to write a preface to a French-language guidebook to the palace and to the illustrious Farnese family. The entire structure is a work of genius—architectural proportions, arched entrance vestibule, superhigh ceilings, frescoed and tapestried reception rooms. It may not be shown, but one room, the White Room, was where Sweden's Queen Christina lived after her abdication in the mid-seventeenth century, when she left Sweden for Rome and became a Catholic. (Two area churches, later described—Santa Brigida and San Girolamo della Carità—are easily taken in, in conjunction with a Palazzo Farnese visit.)

A Square and a Fountain—Piazza Navona and Fontana di Trevi. No Italian city, indeed no European city, is more beautifully endowed with these beloved appurtenances of urban life. Piazza Navona is the most romantic in town. Bernini's glorious Fontana dei Fiumi dominates, but there are seventeenth-century palaces and churches (including Sant'Agnese in Agone, later described), good restaurants and relaxing caffès. Until a little over a century ago the square was flooded on summer Sundays, becoming Rome's—if not Europe's—No. 1 swimming pool.

Fontana di Trevi is the richest such in the world, ever since the world learned from a film, *Three Coins in the Fountain,* back in the 1950s, of the old legend decreeing that if you threw a coin into Trevi (presumably with your back to it) you were bound to return to Rome. On one visit, I happened by about ten in the morning. The water had been turned off and the fountain's pool drained, while sanitation men (bank tellers, they should be called) gathered up the previous day's haul. There appeared to be enough to keep a visitor in Rome for an entire season. Coins or no, the mid-eighteenth-century fountain is Rome's most dramatic, with its exuberant, Baroque, chariot-drawn Neptune surrounded by playing gusts of water.

A Suburban Excursion—Villa d'Este at Tivoli. Despite the spectacular crenelated towers of its fifteenth-century fortress and a few mellow churches, the town of Tivoli would not be worth the boring twenty-mile drive eastward from Rome. It is Villa d'Este that makes it an exceptional excursion destination. What happened was that an ambitious sixteenth-century cardinal named Ippolito d'Este (whose mother was Lucrezia Borgia) thought he had enough money and power to land himself the papacy. While still a young man, he had served at the court of François I, in France. Back home after the death of King François, he found himself Governor of Tivoli, whose official residence was—at least for this man whose home had been the French royal court—a relatively plain ex-monastery. What he did, then, was build Villa d'Este, with the collaboration of a brilliant team —architect Piero Ligorio and a slew of designers, artists, artisans, and—not to be overlooked—landscapists. It was these last—the garden planners—who are responsible for Villa d'Este's lasting fame. The house is a fine Renaissance country villa, no argument here. But in and of itself, it would never draw the crowds that come. They want to see the fountain-filled formal gardens. If one excepts Petrovorets, Peter the Great's horticultural fantasy at his country palace outside Leningrad, there is nothing else—anywhere—that can touch them.

One does not need a great deal of time—half a day all told will do it, preferably with the sun shining. (Or, perhaps, an evening when the fountains are illuminated.) There is a great central Fountain of Dragons, or Girandole, a walkway, verdant and sparkling, bordered by no less than a hundred fountains; grottoes and fishponds, grand stairways and sprinkled sculpture. And masses of visitors, domestic as well as imported. (The public washrooms are the most disgusting that I have encountered anywhere in Italy.) Go as early in the day as possible, lunching if you like at Ristorante Villa Gregoriana (Via Ponte Gregoriano 33), and staying on for a look at the restored villa-complex of Emperor Hadrian, anticlimactic after Villa d'Este, and dealt with on a later page.

BEHIND MUSEUM WALLS:
A SELECTION OF FAVORITES

Earlier on in this chapter I have included two Roman museums— National Gallery-Palazzo Barberini and Roman National-Baths of Diocletian—as among requisites for even the most abbreviated of Roman visits. In that same honor group the Sistine Chapel—actually a part of the Vatican Museums complex—is also included. Now come a score more, of which I am fond, and which are as recommendable for their settings—palaces, villas, town houses, even a castle—as for their contents.

Unless conditions improve appreciably, the museum-goer must brace himself for obstacles. He must be prepared for occasional "closed" signs even on open days. (The excuse is usually lack of staff or "restoration.") Even in museums that are technically open it is no longer unusual to find extensive sections shuttered, again for lack of staff or "restoration." The same goes for stalls selling post-card reproductions of the exhibits and illustrated booklets; they are closed more often than open. (At certain museums there are nearby outdoor newsstands that oblige in this regard.) Last but not least, there are the absurdly abbreviated open-hours, especially at museums controlled by the national government, of which Rome—the capital— has a higher proportion than any other major city. Unless and until these hours are expanded, visitors must plan museum-going care-fully and in advance, noting that, by and large, afternoons are out of the question for this important visitor occupation. Consider, too, each museum's official closing day. These vary, with Monday and Tuesday the most popular. That said, here—alphabetically—are my appraisals of the most worthwhile museums in one of the great museum cities of the planet.

Castel Sant' Angelo (Lungotevere Castello) is a Roman surprise package, at least to the many visitors who believe that the ancient circular mausoleum-*cum*-fortress-*cum*-papal palace on the right bank of the Tiber near the Vatican, is today no more than a historic land-mark, to be admired for its derring-do façade. Well, step inside. Up you go on the ramps that connect the various levels, in which are housed exhibits ranging from armor, guns, and swords to Renaissance paintings and frescoes, with a series of sumptuous papal apartments the real treats, most especially the so-called Cupid and Psyche Room with its Del Vega frieze, and a carved and gilded ceiling of unusual beauty.

Galleria Borghese (Viale del Museo Borghese) houses a remarkable group of paintings and sculpture collected by Cardinal Borghese in the seventeenth century—not long after most of these works were created. The beautiful gallery was designed for the purpose for which it is still being used, except that when it went up the Borghese Gar-dens were vineyards rather than a public park. The cardinal knew how to pick painters whose works and whose fame would last through the centuries—Raphael's *Deposition from the Cross,* Titian's *Sacred* *and Profane Love,* Caravaggio's *Madonna dei Paladrenieri,* Botticelli's *Three Angels Singing,* Bernini's *Self Portrait,* a Carpaccio *Courtesan,* a Bellini *Madonna, St. John the Baptist* as interpreted both by Veronese and Bronzino. Sculpture, too. Very special.

Galleria Farnesina (Via della Lungara) occupies an exemplary early-sixteenth-century mansion whose interior decorators included Raphael and Il Sodoma (both of whom painted striking frescoes), not to mention other ravishing works. To be combined with Palazzo Corsini, just opposite and below described.

Galleria Nazionale d'Arte Moderna (Viale delle Belle Arti) is hardly in a league with New York's MOMA, Paris's Musée National d'Art Moderne, Amsterdam's Stedelijk, or even Milan's or Stockholm's lesser known modern-art museums. On hand are representative works of such foreigners as Braque, Cézanne, Courbet, de la Fresnaye, Degas, Mondrian, Van Gogh, and Utrillo. There are several galleries devoted to their Italian contemporaries—mostly unknown to visitors from abroad, but not without interest. And there are occasional short-term shows. The setting is bright and relatively contemporary.

Goethe Museum (Via del Corso 18) is worth a brief inspection, even to non-Goethe fans, if only because it provides one an opportunity to see inside a central Rome town house of considerable vintage. Goethe was in residence for two years starting in 1786, and the place is crammed with objects relating to his stay and its influence on his work.

Keats-Shelley Memorial House (Piazza di Spagna 26) is perhaps of more interest to English-speaking visitors than the Goethe house, above. Still, aside from its architecture (it went up in 1725) and limited furnishings, it is mainly for Keats, Shelley, and Byron buffs, with memorabilia of all three English poets, each having lived in Rome. Although only Keats was in residence in this house, it was where he died in 1821, while on an extended visit with painter Joseph Severn. Unless it changes, the admission fee sets some sort of record as the steepest in town; postcards are similarly costly. But the view of the Spanish Steps from the terrace is agreeable enough.

Museo Barracco (Corso Vittorio Emanuele 168) embraces a curious variety of periods. It occupies a sixteenth-century palace which, if hardly exuding warmth and charm, is nonetheless soberly grand. It is named for a late-nineteenth-century baron who gathered together its exhibits, which are mostly sculpture of Egyptian, Roman, and Etruscan times, paling in contrast to the Barracco's high point: its coffered ceilings. The City of Rome is the landlord.

Musei Capitoline (Piazza del Campidoglio) are, as you may have guessed from the spelling, *musei,* which indicates plural, a pair of museums, one facing the other on the elevated, Michelangelo-designed Piazza del Campidoglio, in the heart of ancient Rome. The third of the square's trio of structures—lying between the museum-duo, Palazzo del Senatore, is Rome's Town Hall, and not open to visitors. Still, its exterior double staircase is a sight in and of itself, and so is the statue in the center of the square of Emperor Marcus Aurelius; it goes back some eighteen centuries, during which time few equestrian sculptures have surpassed it. One ticket admits the visitor to both museums, operated by the City of Rome. To the left, as one approaches, is Museo Capitolino (but the building, to confuse, is known as Palazzo Nuovo). To the right is Museo dei Conservatori, in Palazzo dei Conservatori. Both museums' exhibits are essentially ancient sculpture. Indeed, the Capitolino (with the ticket office for both museums) is primarily so, with its *Statue of the Dying Gaul* the most memorable single work, along with a lovely Venus. Across the court, in the Conservatori, standouts are a dazzling salon with giant frescoes; a sculpture from Etruscan times (some twenty-five centuries ago) of the notorious she-wolf who mothered Rome's legendary founders, Romulus and Remus; and—not to be missed—an upstairs *pinacoteca,* or picture gallery, with such gems as a Michel-angelo self-portrait, a Bellini *Youth,* Titian's *Baptism of Christ,* and —again relating to Rome's founding—Rubens' *Finding of Romulus and Remus,* in the midst of taking nourishment from their wolf-mother's breast. When you've absorbed these two museums, and if the day is fine, sit for a spell on one of the stone benches of the piazza, and gaze at the panorama of Rome, spread out below.

Museo Nazionale d'Arte Orientale (Via Merulana 248) occupies the second floor of a somber palace-like structure, not far from Santa Maria Maggiore. Many Western cities—New York, Toronto, Paris, London, Stockholm, Amsterdam, to name a few—have far more sub-stantial Asian arts collections. Still, if you are in the neighborhood, climb the staircase and have a look. (The guards, who have very few customers, cannot help but be perked up by your visit.) There is good early Persian pottery, Indian and Nepalese sculpture, Thai Buddha heads, and, occupying most of the space, considerable Chinese work —paintings, ceramics, statues, textiles.

Museo Nazionale delle Arti e Tradizioni Popolari (Piazzale Giuseppe Marconi 10) is a considerable distance from central Rome, in the so-called E.U.R. section, named for the international exposition Mussolini intended to mount in 1940. Although there is later construction in the area, built for the 1960 Olympics and including Nervi's Palazzo dello Sport, the neighborhood is essentially Mussolini Modern, which, no matter what else one thinks of this lasting manifestation of Italian fascism, is substantial. The museum is devoted to Italian folk art, region by region—furniture, clothes, ceramics, rugs, needlework, woodenware, paintings and prints, religious articles, toys and dolls. And there is a larger-than-life Venetian gondola. On my long-delayed first visit, the sole guard was a rather formidable lady, who had jurisdiction over a not inconsiderable area—the museum goes on and on and on—but no other visitors save myself. This one is for a visit only if you're in the neighborhood, or with special interest in the field. (That, however, is more than can be said for the impressively titled *Museo dell'Alto Medioevo*—just across the way and with nothing more than a guard or two protecting exhibits which are mostly blown-up photographs of medieval buildings.)

Palazzo Braschi (Piazza San Pantaleo 10) is the Museum of the City of Rome, chockablock full of paintings and pottery and sculpture, with other objects—ranging from mosaics to a papal throne—all having to do with the history of the city. Still, the setting supersedes the exhibits. Palazzo Braschi is a late-eighteenth-century house that was built to house a papal nephew. The main stairway is grand and neo-Renaissance, but the various rooms put one in mind of eighteenth-century England's Robert Adam. Every salon has frescoed ceilings and walls, massive eighteenth-century paintings, and fine eighteenth-century furniture. Lovely.

Palazzo Corsini (Via della Lungara 10) is Rome's best-kept museum secret. And one of its most lavish palazzi. Located on the right bank of the Tiber near Trastevere, it went up in the early eighteenth century for Pope Clement XII's family, replacing an earlier palace that had been the principal Roman home of Sweden's Queen Christina in the seventeenth century. (A plaque outdoors advises that *"La Regina Christina di Svezia mori in questa stanza il 19 avrile 1689"* and is accompanied by the same text in a Swedish translation.) At any rate, the Corsini—or at least a dozen or so of its splendid chambers—has been for some years now the "temporary" home of the mostly seventeenth- and eighteenth-century paintings of the Galleria Nazionale d'Arte Antica, the bulk of which is housed in the earlier-recommended Palazzo Barberini. The idea is to eventually house the whole collection in the Barberini, but with budgets for national museums skimpier than ever in recent years, the move does not appear imminent. Still, the guardians of the remaining paintings at the Corsini appear not to want customers. Upon arrival, one must make one's way through its cavernous inner courtyards, up and over grand stairways, and finally into an unmarked administrative office, there to beg, practically on bended knee, for a bit of time to look at the exhibits. It is all worthwhile. I counted five Caravaggios, including his matchless *St. John the Baptist,* a whole room full of Canalettos, and more foreign art than one often sees in Italian museums—Van Dyck, Rubens, Hooch, Murillo, Breughel. Not to mention the palace itself, its painted ceilings in themselves a major Roman treat. (And earlier-recommended Galleria Farnesina is just across the street.)

Palazzo Doria Pamphili (Piazza del Collegio Romano 2a) has some exquisite paintings—most especially a Velásquez of Pope Innocent X and Titian's *Herodias*—but is of even more interest because of the setting itself—a treasure of a rococo palace, containing a chapel whose worshipers sat in elegant eighteenth-century armchairs; and a hall that is smaller than that at Versailles, but not a whit less beautiful, with frescoes and Venetian chandeliers and gilded settees.

Palazzo Spada (Piazza Capo di Ferro 3) does anything but encourage visitors. Indeed, it may or may not have enough guards on duty when you arrive to man the galleries. What you must do in this case is find the administrative office and humbly request admission, for the briefest of periods. If your plea is honored, a staff member will be detached from office duty to accompany you. Even before reaching the office you'll have seen the elaborately stuccoed courtyard of the palace. Within are a quartet of splendid rooms, containing paintings

—Del Sarto, Bassano, Tintoretto are among the artists—frescoes, furniture. Room No. 3 is the most elaborate; every inch of it is brilliantly decorated.

Palazzo Venezia (Piazza Venezia 3—opposite the wedding-cake Vittorio Emanuele monument) is possibly the most bypassed major museum in Rome. It is pointed out as a fine specimen of fifteenth-century architecture and as a former home not only of some Renaissance popes and later Venetian ambassadors, but of this century's Benito Mussolini—who harangued the Romans from a balcony. Within, though—once one finds the entrance, which is not easy—is one of Europe's best museums of the decorative arts: furniture, tapestries, ceramics, metalwork, even armor, mostly all Italian Renaissance but with foreign work, too. And with the fine arts—paintings and sculpture—hardly overlooked.

Musei Vaticani (Viale Vaticano). The Vatican Museums complex (all gained by the sole entrance on Viale Vaticano) can overwhelm if one lets it. To some visitors, a look at the paintings in its *Pinacoteca* represents the Rome museum scene in toto. To others, too many of its component parts are undertaken at a single time, with the resulting museum fatigue of the worst kind. Ideal tack is to divide the Vatican Museums into several inspections. The Sistine Chapel, a part of the group, is earlier recommended as a Roman requisite. It and the Pinacoteca evince the most visitor interest. The latter dates to the late eighteenth century, when Pope Pius VI began to systematically collect and group together paintings from various parts of the Vatican. Much later, in the early 1930s, Pope Pius XI built a modern building for the collection, which now numbers some 500 paintings, representing Italian art through the centuries. There are exquisite Giottos and Fra Angelicos, Bellini and Da Vinci, Titian and Raphael, Caravaggio and Bordone, and as a bonus a surprising group of French Impressionists and Post Impressionists. The *Raphael Rooms* (*Stanze di Raffaello*) are not so well known as the Sistine Chapel but are quite as special. They house a series of frescoes on various themes—mostly biblical and classical. The adjacent *Rafael Loggias* are a gallery full of religious-theme paintings based on designs by the master but executed by his students. *Museo Pio-Clementino* is a treasure trove of classical sculpture, with that of *Laocoön and His Sons*—being gruesomely strangled by snakes—perhaps the outstanding piece. *Museo*

Chiaramonti's highlights are busts of the Roman emperors, in a sumptuously decorated gallery. The *Library* is elaborately frescoed, full of
fascinating old manuscripts and globes. The *Borgia Apartments* are
a suite of handsome rooms that for long constituted the papal residence; the chief decorator was the artist Pintoricchio (who painted
his series of frescoes in the late fifteenth century). The *Papal*—or
Nicholas V—Chapel had no less a master than Fra Angelico as its
decorator. There are a *Tapestry Gallery,* an *Egyptian Gallery,* and an
Etruscan Gallery. And in the *Pauline Palace,* adjacent to the Pinacoteca building, are the quartet of museums—mostly theological in na-
ture—that had for long been situated in the Lateran Palace, adjacent
to the historic Basilica of San Giovanni Laterano.

Villa Giulia (Piazza di Villa Giulia 9) is of dual interest. The handsome house itself had been the sixteenth-century summer retreat of
Pope Julius III. In and of itself, it is a delight of no mean aesthetic
value. The exhibits, on the other hand, are of quite another era—
mostly pottery from the pre-Roman Etruscan period, indoors, with a
gem of a meticulously reconstructed Etruscan temple in the capacious
garden.

TREASURES OF ART AND ARCHITECTURE: SELECTED CHURCHES

It is to its everlasting credit that the Catholic Church, in its headquarters city, has never considered art and architecture incompatible
with its dogma. Quite the contrary. Even the earlier medieval
churches, of which some remain, set aesthetic standards. Then, with
the Renaissance, and upon the return of the seat of the papacy to
Rome from France's Avignon, the city began to blossom as a great
artistic as well as spiritual center, under art-minded pontiffs like
Sixtus IV, Julius II, and Leo X in the fifteenth and sixteenth centuries. There was no stopping, though, with that era. Roman church
construction continued under popes like Urban VIII in the seventeenth century, and Benedict XIV in the eighteenth. Rome today is,
as a consequence, a veritable maze of churches, from the biggest and
grandest extant, St. Peter's, through to charming albeit uncelebrated
Baroque parishes in every corner of the older precincts. (Of contemporary churches in the suburbs the less said—aesthetically, at least—
the better.) So as to give the newcomer to town an idea of the magni-

tude of the church plant, if that it may be called, I have suggested as Roman requisites earlier on in this chapter, not only St. Peter's, but two of the four so-called major basilicas. Each of this quartet could easily serve as the sole principal place of worship in any leading city. But in Rome this group is but frosting on the cake. There are hundreds more churches that are artistically, architecturally, and historically worthwhile. From this overwhelming total, I have singled out twoscore, of a group of many more that I have visited. Included are two lovely old churches operated by American priests, as well as the chapel in the downtown outpost of the North American College at the Vatican. In every case, the location is central Rome.

That said, let me add this word: Simple exteriors can conceal opulent interiors. Pop into whatever churches you pass by. Relatively few of those in the central city will disappoint; more often than not they are exemplary on architectural lines, with art treasures as well. You may enter when masses are being said, but *quietly* and *unobtrusively*. (That is not the time for an inspection of the main altar.) At other periods, don't hesitate to query priests or sacristans for details, in whatever languages are at your disposal. (Many clergy speak English, French, or German.) The era when Catholic churches in Rome, as in all Italy, were open all day, nonstop, and well into the evening is long past. Contemporarily, they close for long midday breaks. These correspond roughly to shop-closing hours but at times vary, church by church. It can make for frustration. Still, when a church is open, one can count on a priest or sacristan being on duty, if not in the church proper, then in the sacristy (*sacrestia*), where—in more cases than with today's museums—postcards and even guidebooks of the subject structure are on sale. (Look for postcards in automatic wall dispensers, too.) As to the location of sacristies, there is no hard and fast rule. They are usually behind closed—albeit unlocked—doors to either side of the main part of the church, or to the rear; don't be afraid to snoop about. Only rarely are there signs directing one to them. For that matter—and of more import—only occasionally are there easily discernible, clearly legible signs on the exteriors of churches, identifying them. Too often, posters advising of special activities in *other* churches are what strike one's eye. To ascertain the name of a church, step into its vestibule, the tiny passage that no Italian church is without, through which one proceeds to the interior. Most vestibules have bulletin boards on which the church's name and the times of masses are indicated. In Italian, of course.

Which is why I give the Italian names of churches first, there being little gained in translating, say, Santa Maria del Popolo into St. Mary of the People, or Trinità dei Monti into Trinity of the Mountains. Order is alphabetical.

Sant' Agnese in Agone (Piazza Navona). If you are not up on St. Agnes's tribulations, it's worth noting that she is said to have been forced to disrobe on Piazza Navona just before her execution. She was saved from humiliation only by Providential aid, with her long hair unfurling and curtaining her naked body from the stares of the assembled curious. This Baroque church commemorating her agony is handsomer without; two side towers frame a central dome, the lot beautifully blending into the beautiful square. Inside, look up at the frescoes lining the cupola.

Sant' Agostino in Campo Marzio (Via di San Agostino), is originally fifteenth century and was rebuilt in the eighteenth, with a façade embracing both Renaissance and Baroque motifs. The interior dazzles, with a dozen side chapels, beautifully decorated cupola and high altar, and paintings by Caravaggio (*Madonna dei Pellegrini*) and Raphael (*Isaiah*)—among others.

San Andrea al Quirinale (Via del Quirinale), bearing the name and in the shadow of the presidential (and ex-papal) palace, does not disappoint. It's a little gem of Baroque, the work of no less a master than Bernini.

San Antonio de Portoghesi (Via de Portoghesi) is the Portuguese national church in Rome, welcoming Baroque in style, with a pair of striking angel-trumpeters atop its façade, to herald one's entrance.

San Bernardo alle Terme (Piazza San Bernardo) is an architectural standout: a circular structure, severely but smartly neoclassical and dating to the start of the eighteenth century.

Santa Brigida (Piazza Farnese) is for viewing in conjunction with a visit to earlier-recommended Palazzo Farnese. It has a blue ceiling dotted with gold stars, and there is an exquisite gilded sunburst over the altar.

San Carlo al Corso (Via del Corso) gives one a clue as to its importance with the towering dome (the work of Pietro da Cortona) behind its Baroque façade. Within, though, one is overwhelmed by tremendous size—high and long and wide—and ceaseless decoration, the chief delights of which are sculpted angels at every turn.

San Carlo alle Quattro Fontane (known also as San Carlino and a neighbor of San Andrea al Quirinale, above) is at the intersection named for its quartet of Baroque fountains, one on each corner. It's a case of big things coming in small packages—Baroque, with an unusual oval-shaped dome, and a winsome galleried patio.

Santa Cecilia in Trastevere (Piazza di Santa Cecilia) embraces a variety of styles, and they all come together nicely, from early mosaics to Baroque sculpture, most certainly including frescoes by Pintoricchio, a Romanesque campanile, and a joyfully tranquil courtyard.

San Clemente (Piazza di San Clemente), a near neighbor of the Colosseum, is called after the fourth Pope, who died toward the end of the first century, only a few decades after the first, St. Peter. The two-level Basilica of San Clemente is somewhat newer. It embraces a beauty of a twelfth-century street-level church, and a fresco-decorated fourth-century subterranean church as well. Gifted New Zealand-born mystery-novelist Dame Ngaio Marsh barely disguised it as the setting for her Inspector Alleyn thriller, *When in Rome* (1972). It's a treasure trove of sculpture, mosaics, and frescoes, among the more remarkable churches in town. Irish Dominicans have operated it for almost three centuries; nowhere in Rome does one hear lovelier English spoken, although there are more Irish priests, of another order, at San Silvestro in Capita (see below).

SS. Cosma e Damiano (Via in Miranda, adjacent to Foro Romano) is a basilica at once boasting great age and great art. It goes back to the fourth century, with later additions. The standout work is a sixth-century mosaic, over the apse, of Christ, Sts. Peter and Paul and two martyrs. But there are half a dozen side chapels with fine paintings, and a Renaissance frescoed ceiling. The adjacent monastery is the mother house of that branch of the Franciscans known as the Third Order Regular of St. Francis—and has been since 1512.

Il Gesù di Roma (Piazza del Gesù) is the world headquarters church
of the Society of Jesus. It is a masterful sixteenth- to seventeenth-
century work that has served as prototype for Jesuit churches around
the world. The Baroque interior is one of the most elaborate—and
beautiful—in Rome, with quantities of gold and jewels in the décor, a
lapis-lazuli-embellished tomb with the remains of St. Ignatius Loyola
(the Jesuits' founder) and splendid frescoes.

San Giovanni in Laterano (Piazza di San Giovanni in Laterano)—
or St. John Lateran—is one of the four major basilicas of Rome,
along with Santa Maria Maggiore, San Pietro in Vincoli, and San
Pablo Fuori le Mura, the lot comprising a group that follow just
after St. Peter's in ecclesiastical importance. St. John Lateran dates
to the first Christian emperor, Constantine. (Although its façade is
eighteenth century, with a lot within from other epochs.) It's the core
of a complex that includes the palace wherein was signed the 1929
Lateran Treaty between the Vatican State and the Italian Government. The church itself—immense and formal and formidable—was
the very seat of the papacy and remains the Cathedral of Rome. The
gilded wood ceiling and the mosaic-decorated apse highlight the interior, but what one wants most to see is the thirteenth-century
cloister, among the handsomest in town. (What one may—or may
not—want to see is the nearby *Scala Santa,* a staircase in a Renaissance building that is supposed to contain the actual steps—twenty-
eight of them—used by Jesus when he went before Pontius Pilate for
sentencing. For this reason, the faithful climb the Scala Santa, or
Holy Staircase, on their knees; there is a relic-filled chapel at the top,
closed to the public but visible through windows, and gained also by
a second, unsanctified stairway.)

San Girolamo della Carità (Via di Monserrato) adjoins church-dotted
Piazza di Santa Caterina della Rota, near Piazza Farnese and its
earlier-recommended palace. Its interior, with marble employed as
you may not have seen it elsewhere, is among the more richly
sumptuous in Rome.

San Luigi dei Francesi (Piazza di San Luigi dei Francesi) identifies
itself also as St.-Louis-des-Français. As well it might, for it is the
French national church in Rome. (You may hear mass *en Français,*

tous les Dimanches à 1030.) Its Renaissance façade is uncommonly striking. So, for that matter, is the interior, whose special treasures are a trio of massive Caravaggio paintings in the last chapel on the left; and a series of Domenichino frescoes—the subject is St. Cecilia—in the second chapel on the right. *Vive la France!*

Santa Maria degli Angeli (Piazza della Repubblica) is a part of the earlier-recommended Museo Nazionale delle Terme—Baths of Diocletian—the part of these ancient Roman baths that Pope Pius IV commissioned Michelangelo to turn into a church. And a remarkable church it is, with an immense, high-ceilinged, colonnaded Renaissance interior that remains very grand—if hardly very warm or inviting. (Even though both museum and church are carved out of the old baths, each has a separate entrance, and there are no signs to help one get from one to the other. If you've inspected the museum first, the church entrance is to the museum's left.)

Santa Maria dell'Anima (Via della Pace 20) is known also as the Chiesa della Pace, and is to my knowledge the only Catholic church in town that keeps its doors locked during official open hours. This may or may not have to do with the fact that it's the *Deutsche Nationalkirche* in Rome. (Masses are said in German.) At any rate, after one finds the bell, the German-speaking Italian sacristan opens up. (The price of his postcards is *per stück*.) There is a little gem of a courtyard, filled with lovingly tended plants. And, within, the smallish interior yields treasures, including Raphael frescoes, a papal tomb (Hadrian VI), and a rather super high altar.

Santa Maria d'Aracoeli sul Campidoglio is notable for its location (on the Capitoline Hill just next door to the earlier-recommended, Michelangelo-designed Musei Capitoline and Senato), its façade (somberly striking, virtually unadorned buff-colored brick), the main approach to it—up a dramatic flight of 124 steps that were built in 1348, its essentially Renaissance interior (with a memorable ceiling of that era), and works of art by Donatello and Bernini, among others. All told, this basilica goes back fifteen centuries. (The name *Aracoeli* means Altar of Heaven.) Franciscans have run it since the thirteenth century, and so that I don't frighten you away by my mention of those steep 124 steps, there is another entrance on Piazza del Campidoglio.

Santa Maria in Cosmedin (Piazza della Bocca della Verità) is on a square named for its best-known appurtenance, the decorative cover of a drain hole in its entryway. Bocca della Verità translates as Mouth of Truth. The sculpted cover is of a man's face, with a big opening for the mouth. Legend has long decreed that anyone holding his hand in the mouth while swearing to tell the truth but not so doing would find himself minus a hand; the mystically endowed jaws of the mouth would chop them off. The church's gift shop—one of the best stocked of any such in Rome—sells little ceramic boxes with the man's face on their lids. And countless postcard reproductions. But the church has so much more to recommend it—an essentially Byzantine interior, with exquisite frescoes and floors, framed by an essentially Romanesque exterior. Very beautiful.

Santa Maria Maddalena (Piazza della Maddalena) is gorgeous, almost giddy Baroque. There are angels framing the front door, in the choir, over the main altar. A white dove hovers in the cupola. Walls are of pink marble. Sculpture is in blue niches. And the paintings are first rate.

Santa Maria Nova (Via Sacra) is in the heart of ancient Rome, goes back to the tenth century, but except for its medieval campanile is now mostly Baroque, with a multicolored and gilded coffered ceiling its outstanding feature; and a fifth-century painted Madonna and Child its most charming surprise. Alternate name: Santa Francesca Romana. Near neighbor: the ruins of Basilica di Costantino.

Santa Maria del Popolo (Piazza del Popolo) is one of the trio of churches on this great oblong of a square (later described). Of the three it is the oldest and the finest, thanks to the great art within. This is an essentially Renaissance structure, but there are Baroque additions. To be especially noted are frescoes by Pintoricchio in two chapels and the main-church ceiling; the Raphael-designed Chigi Chapel, a Nativity by Piombo and two Caravaggios in still another chapel. While you're in the piazza, pop in, also, to the Baroque near-twins—*Santa Maria dei Miracoli* (the one with the *round* dome) and *Santa Maria in Montesanto* (with the *oval* dome).

Santa Maria in Traspontina (Via della Conciliazione) is a Baroque beauty on the street leading to St. Peter's—in case you were wondering if the world's largest church has any competition in its immediate neighborhood. The answer is yes. This is but one of a number, with a finely coffered ceiling, imposing dome, and crown-topped altar.

Santa Maria in Trastevere (Piazza Santa Maria in Trastevere) is a landmark whose Romanesque façade is known to countless diners in restaurants across the square it fronts. Go in. The lures are a coffered ceiling, busy Byzantine altar, and a nave delineated by chunky neo-Ionic columns.

Santa Maria dell'Umiltà (Via dell'Umiltà 30) is the chapel—a lovely, beautifully embellished Baroque chapel—of the onetime seventeenth-century Dominican nuns' convent that was turned over to the American Catholic bishops in the mid-nineteenth century by Pope Pius IX. Until 1953, it was the principal site of the North American College in Rome; in that year, a much larger college building was opened on Janiculum Hill, in the Vatican, to house the college's undergraduate students. The smaller graduate group now use the Via dell'Umiltà building as headquarters. It also contains the Bishops' Office for United States Visitors to the Vatican, operated by the U. S. Conference of Catholic Bishops. For Catholics, this is the address where parish priests write in advance for tickets to the weekly papal audiences (traditionally they take place on Wednesday) adjacent to St. Peter's Basilica. Others may write directly to this office in advance, or call there in person, to arrange for tickets (they are free), or simply, for that matter, to see the chapel.

Santa Maria in Vallicella (Piazza della Chiesa Nova), known also as Chiesa Nova, is a place of special charm. Pietro da Cortona painted the ceiling, cupola, and apse frescoes with grace and style. Rubens painted three pictures; other artists and artisans contributed fine work; even the marble floor is noteworthy.

Santa Maria della Vittoria (Via XX Settembre) is surpassed in the exuberance of its décor by no other Roman Baroque church. It is mostly the work—as regards interior design—of Carlo Maderno, with a major exception of frescoes by Domenichino and a breath-taking sculpture—St. Theresa in Ecstasy—by Bernini, in a chapel of his design. There is a sumptuous ceiling fresco framed by sculpted angels, and a gleaming gilded sunburst dominates the high altar.

San Pietro in Montorio (Piazza San Pietro in Montorio) is atop Janiculum Hill, adjacent to Trastevere, with absolutely super views of the Vatican and Rome. The church is Renaissance with a quartet of paintings by Sebastiano del Piombo, a noteworthy chapel by Bernini, and, in its little courtyard, a little charmer of a circular classic-style temple by Bramante.

San Pietro in Vincoli (Via degli Anibaldi) is the major basilica of St. Peter in Chains, so named because it is the repository of the chains of St. Peter's Jerusalem and Roman imprisonments; they are contained in a glass-walled bronze casket in front of the main altar. The pewless, multiperiod sanctuary is severely handsome and is dominated by Michelangelo's oversized, powerful statue of a stern, long-bearded Moses—the principal reason for a visit.

Santa Pudenziana (Via Urbana) is a bit of Early Christian Rome. In other words, a rarity. Parts of it date to the fourth and fifth centuries, including, from the latter, a still-graphic mosaic. The campanile is Romanesque, but most of the church was restored in the sixteenth century and is still essentially as it was then. Special.

Quattro Coronati (Via del Querceti) is an away-from-the-center combination church-convent that sees few contemporary visitors. One enters as callers have since medieval times. You knock at the entrance of a convent of cloistered nuns. A revolving metal box—surely as old as the church itself—is silently turned outward to meet your gaze. You open it and, bending to look within, find an equally venerable key, with the veiled face of a silent nun in the darkened background. The key opens the church, which in turn leads to a serene garden-cloister that (along with one of the chapels—San Silvestro) is one of the most memorable of Roman destinations. On leaving, one returns the key in the same way.

San Rocco (Largo San Rocco) has a handsome Baroque façade-cum-guardian angels and an interior mellow with lovely paintings; this church is a fine halting spot in the course of a busy central Rome afternoon. Likewise, its next-door neighbor (they both face the

Tiber), *San Girolamo degli Illirici,* a.k.a. San Girolamo degli Schiavoni—which means Slavs, this being the national church of Catholic Yugoslavs in Rome. It dates back to the sixteenth century and it's a beauty.

San Silvestro in Capita (Piazza San Silvestro in Capita) is a Baroque enchantment. One enters through an unexpected front yard, with carefully tended plants and flowers, and fragments of ancient artifacts scattered about. The church itself, under a ravishing ceiling fresco, is walled in faux-marble, and fringed by half a dozen side chapels. The first chapel on the left has paintings by Francesco Travasani, which the Irish Pallottine priests—a detachment of them along with Italian students runs the place—regard as the principal treasures. Mass is said in English, with an Irish lilt to it.

Santa Susanna (Via XX Settembre). What one most remembers about Santa Susanna—apart from the not unimportant fact that it is operated by American Paulist fathers, whose mother church is the big, gray, neo-Gothic St. Paul the Apostle on New York's Ninth Avenue—is a pair of absolutely enormous frescoes on either of its principal inner walls by the painter Baldassar Croce, who is responsible for a number of other luminous works as well. But chief credit for this excitingly beautiful Renaissance masterwork of a church goes to Carlo Maderno, who was in charge of its stem-to-stern restoration in the late sixteenth century. Masses are said in Yank-accented English, and there's a worth-knowing-about bulletin board used by resident Americans to buy, sell, swap, rent, or whatever.

San Teodoro (Via di San Teodoro) is in ancient Rome, beneath the Palatine Hill and is itself appropriately ancient. Santa Sabina is even older, and Santa Pudenziana, too. Still, this church—strikingly circular in design—dates to the seventh century, but only partially. An important mosaic excepted, it is mostly Renaissance restoration.

Santa Trinità dei Monti (Viale Trinità dei Monti), atop the Spanish Steps and with twin campaniles, is a classic Rome landmark, and has been French-controlled since it went up some four centuries ago. There are some good frescoes, but by and large Trinità dei Monti is best appreciated from without.

A ROMAN MISCELLANY

Arco di Costantino is the triumphal arch to beat all triumphal arches —ancient ones, at least. (What, after all, can compete with the nineteenth-century Arc de Triomphe in Paris?) The Arch of Constantine went up seventeen centuries ago to commemorate a military victory of the forces of Emperor Constantine. It remains almost completely intact, beautifully carved and inscribed, with its bas-reliefs variations on a theme of valor in battle. Location is opposite the Colosseum.

Castelli Romani—Roman Castles—is the collective name of a group of picturesque little towns in the Alban Hills, southeast of town. They make for a nice half-day—or, if you like, full-day—excursion in the warm weather months, when the Pope is invariably in residence at his summer palace in *Castel Gandolfo.* Traditionally he holds mass audiences on Wednesday, along the lines of those held the rest of the year in the Vatican. If I had but two choices to make on a Castelli Romani outing, the first would be to Castel Gandolfo, for a walk round the pretty little square, a look at the Baroque papal palace (by the same Carlo Maderno who designed St. Peter's) from without its walls, and a view of the immense water-filled crater that goes by the name of Lago Albano, way below. There are agreeable little caffès all about for refreshment, most especially the local wine—white, crisp, and fruity. And the little domed cathedral on the square— designed by Bernini and with plaques commemorating papal visits —is special. I would return to Rome, then, by means of the road through other regional towns, stopping at *Frascati,* which gives its name to the most celebrated of the region's white wines. There is a bustling central sector—you might want to walk about, investigate the shops and caffès, and pop into the cathedral. And there are a number of elaborate Renaissance mansions, most especially Villa Aldobrandini, in an open-to-visitors terraced park.

Catacombs of San Callisto. Catacombs, nothing more than the fancy name for underground cemeteries, are not everyone's idea of fun. Still, they are not without historic, theological, or, for that matter, architectural interest. There are four major groupings in and about Rome. Most important are those of San Callisto, out on the ancient

Appian Way. They go back to the second century and are named for
a Pope who suffered martyrdom in the Trastevere quarter of the
city. A band of priests are the contemporary custodians of San
Callisto, guiding small groups from a ground-level reception area
(with a chapel) into the depths. What you see is an extraordinarily
elaborate maze of chambers, decorated with antique frescoes and
containing the tombs of about a dozen early popes. There is, as well,
a niche marking the site where St. Cecilia was originally buried, along
with a copy of the statue by Carlo Maderno that stands alongside her
current burial place at the Basilica of St. Cecilia in Trastevere, in
town; current, that is, since the ninth century.

Contemporary Architecture. The *Parioli* sector, north of the
Borghese Gardens and home to the Foreign Affairs Ministry—is
Mussolini Modern, that is, overscaled and built-to-last (if not necessarily to please aesthetically). In this same northern area is *Foro
Italico,* postwar name for the prewar Foro Mussolini, with a range of
buildings including the immense Olympic Stadium and the much
smaller and adjacent sculpture-encircled *Stadio dei Marmi.* Still more
souvenirs of the Mussolini era are to be found south of town, in the
E.U.R. area, the initials standing for Esposizione Universale di Roma,
Il Duce's planned 1942 Fascism Fair, which, because of the war,
never came off. Still, the buildings in the exaggerated style of the
period remain, most especially the Palazzo della Civiltà del Lavora,
with its façade a maze of arched windows set in white marble. Two
museums earlier described are here too. The architecture of the
period has a heavy-handed, no-nonsense look that if not felicitous
at least says a lot more for its designers than much of the plastic-like
construction of our own period, which is represented in this area by
Palazzo dello Sport built for the 1960 Olympics.

The Forums (Roman and Imperial) and Palatine Hill. I have
earlier recommended the Colosseum, Pantheon, and Arch of Constantine as the best of ancient Rome because they are the most intact
of its souvenirs, the easiest to come to grips with, at least for the
lay visitor. The Forums, Roman (the original) and Imperial (its successor), are ruins of the ancient city, many of them in part restored.
Many visitors content themselves with vistas of the contiguous area
they occupy, from a distance. A better way to take in this beautiful
area is to walk down Via dei Fori Imperiali, linking the Colosseum

and Piazza Venezia, with the Roman Forum on one side, and the Imperial Forums on the other. Each forum area keeps specific open hours, museum-style, for visitors who would like to amble about. *Foro Romano* (Roman Forum) requisites, in my view, are what remains of two once-lovely temples—Antonino e Faustina and Castore e Polluce. *Fori Imperiali* (Imperial Forums) basics are the remains of Basilica dei Massenzio, especially its trio of magnificent arches and the hundred-foot column, Colonna Traiano, that dominates the Foro Traiano area. History-studded *Palatine Hill,* from which there is a splendid panorama of the forums, is not without substantial monuments. See the frescoes in the Casa di Livia, what is left of a once-vast stadium, and, just above it, Domus Flavia, the remarkable Imperial Palace.

Fontane (*Fountains*). Rome is the most fountain-filled of cities. *Fontana di Trevi* is earlier recommended in The Essential Rome. *Fontana dei Fiumi* (Fountain of the Rivers) is the Bernini masterwork—actually a trio of fountains with a central obelisk—that dominates Piazza Navona. One of its two neighboring fountains, *Fontana del Moro* (Moor's Fountain), whose central figure of a Moor, dolphin in hand, is also by Bernini. So, for that matter, are the *Fontana del Tritone*—surely the most dramatic of the smaller Roman fountains—on Piazza Barberini, and the less celebrated *Fontana delli Api* (Bees' Fountain) at the Via Veneto intersection. *Fontana delle Tartarughe,* a sixteenth-century treasure by a sculptor named Landini, on Piazza Mattei, is called after the bronze turtles drinking from its waters. *Fontana Naidi* is the circular attention-getter in Piazza della Repubblica (still also called by its former name, Piazza dell'Esedra). *Le Quattro Fontane* are located at the intersection of Via del Quirinale and the street called Quattro Fontane. The fountains are Baroque conceits, one each on the side of the buildings flanking the crossing.

Isola Tiberina is a much-ignored island of some little beauty smack in the waters of the Tiber, near Piazza Venezia and the forums. It has been inhabited since ancient times. Today, the approach is by bridge from either riverbank. Have a look at the *Church of San Bartolomeo,* on the site in one form or another for a millennium; and *Torre della Contessa,* a medieval tower.

Ostia (less than twenty miles from town) means two things to Romans. First, and the oldest by a couple of millenniums, is Ostia Antica—the excavations (begun near the turn of this century) of a remarkable ancient port-city. The other is Ostia Lido, Rome's No. 1 seaside resort. *Ostia Antica* operates with specified hours. My suggestion is to start out in its museum, with documentation as well as objects—including some handsome frescoes—that explain the ancient city's significance. Then amble about, taking in the mosaic-decorated baths, the once-imposing forum, the mosaic trademarks of various ancient merchants in Piazzale delle Corporazioni, and the theater, used for contemporary performances each summer. *Ostia Lido,* jammed by Romans in the warm-weather months (they reach it in half an hour by train from Stazione di Piazzale or by subway), embraces beaches and facilities for changing, eating, drinking, and otherwise relaxing, including the Kursaal complex, with amenities including swimming pool and evening dancing. There's no more typical way to do as the Romans do (and with them) on a steamy summer day.

Palazzi (Palaces) are frequently put to good public use in Rome, and a number so employed are called to your attention elsewhere in this chapter. Others, not necessarily open to the public but worth an inside peek if you can manage it, and certainly an exterior appraisal: *Palazzo della Cancelleria* (Piazza della Cancelleria) is a Renaissance masterwork built under papal auspices and still Vatican property, of especial style and elegance, both as regards its colonnaded façade and its inner courtyard; *Palazzo Chigi* (Piazza Colonna), severely handsome, beautifully proportioned, late-Renaissance in era, currently houses Italian cabinet offices; *Palazzo Madama* (Piazza Madama) was the Roman outpost of the powerful Florentine Medici, who rarely stinted on building budgets. It is seventeenth-century outside, eighteenth within, and is now the Senate, or Upper House, of the Italian Parliament. *Palazzo Montecitorio* (Piazza di Montecitorio) is now the seat of the Lower House of Parliament, immense, formidable, and dating back to Bernini (mid-seventeenth century) but with an unfortunate early-twentieth-century façade on one side. *Palazzo Margherita* (Via Veneto) is an elaborate neo-Renaissance beauty out of the late nineteenth century that once housed a queen but is now the embassy of a republic, to wit, the United States of America. *Palazzo del Quirinale* is the history of Rome for the last four centuries all in a single building that went up in 1574 as a papal summer palace, remaining the Pontiff's home until about a century ago when Rome became the capital of the unified Kingdom of Italy. Savoyard monarchs then replaced popes until after World War II, when the current republic succeeded the monarchy and the palace became the seat of the presidents of Italy, with interiors—completed over a period of several centuries—magnificent, most particularly the high-ceilinged, fresco-walled Sala Regia. It is possible that Palazzo del Quirinale may be open on a limited basis during the time of your visit; this has been the case in the past and may be once again. At any rate, try popping into its across-the-square neighbor, eighteenth-century *Palazzo della Consulata*. It has been a papal ministry as well as the Foreign Ministry and the Ministry of African Affairs during the period when Italy controlled Ethiopia, part of Somalia, and Libya. It's now a law court.

Parks. There are a number on the fringes of town—*Monte Mario,* in the north (its landmark for travelers is the Cavalieri Hilton Hotel), is a good example—but for most visitors the misleadingly named *Villa Borghese* best exemplifies verdant Rome. It is a vast green (Borghese Gardens, in English) named for the seventeenth-century cardinal whose estate it was. In and of itself, it makes for pleasant walking or driving territory in fine weather. But it is for more specialized pilgrimages as well. Within it are three earlier-recommended museums of import (Galleria Borghese, Villa Giulia, Galleria de Arte Moderna) as well as *Giardino Zoologico* (Rome's·zoo and a delightful destination for half a sunny day). It is also the site of *Villa Medici,* a splendid Renaissance palace that has long been the French Academy, oldest of the study centers for nationals of various countries in Rome. Its *Pincio Gardens* sector is entered from Piazza del Popolo. One may also enter from the Church of Santa Trinità dei Monti atop the Spanish Steps, and from Porta Pinciana, atop Via Vittorio Veneto.

Piazzi (Squares) not otherwise brought to your attention are many. Let me concentrate on a handful. *Piazza Barberini* is so near Via Vittorio Veneto that many visitors get to know it—and its earlier-recommended Bernini-designed Fontana del Tritone; the palazzo bearing the square's name is now a major art museum, also earlier recommended. *Piazza Colonna* straddles busy Via del Corso—Rome's main street—and is distinguished by the Marcus Aurelius Column in its center, earlier described Palazzo Chigi, and colonnaded Palazzo Wedekind, now a newspaper office. *Piazza della Repubblica,* still also called by its former name of Piazza dell'Esedra, is graced by the earlier-mentioned Fountains of the Naiads, with the also-described Terme Diocleziano-Church of Santa Maria degli Angeli and Stazione Termini near neighbors. *Piazza del Popolo* is one of the city's great Baroque squares, at the terminus of Via del Corso, just beneath Pincio Gardens, and with no less than three first-rank churches, earlier recommended. *Piazza del Quirinale* is dominated by the presidential palace, not to mention neighboring palaces as well as churches, a number of which are earlier described. There is a central obelisk and, thanks to the elevation, splendid vistas. *Piazza di Spagna* is, along with Via Vittorio Veneto, the most visitor-trod territory in town. The 137 magnificent steps—*Scalinata della Trinità dei Monti*—that lead from the square to the Church of Santa Trinità dei Monti and the Via Sistina, above, are today mostly occupied by hirsute young travelers selling handmade jewelry, incense, and other trifles. The steps are eighteenth-century and the lovely fountain in the square is more than a century older. *Piazza Venezia* is also of requisite visitor interest. First, because of the sore-thumb landmark, a turn-of-century mock-classic horror that is a monument to King Victor Emmanuel II and is known locally as the Vittoriano; second, because of earlier-recommended Palazzo Venezia, now a first-rank museum; third, because the square is a terminus of important Via del Corso; and fourth, because it is the entry point to Capitoline Hill and to ancient Rome—the Forums, Palatine Hill, and the Colosseum. *Piazza di Santa Maria in Trastevere* is the heart of the across-the-Tiber Trastevere quarter, substantially working-class—but drawing modish Romans to its old houses—with a disproportionate quantity of restaurants, earthy night-spots, and venerable monuments, including earlier-described Museo Palazzo Corsini and the church for which the fountain-centered piazza is named. *Piazza del Campidoglio* was designed by Michelangelo and houses a trio of exquisite palaces, two of which are now distinguished museums, earlier recommended. The third is Rome's Town Hall; they all surround an equestrian statue of Marcus Aurelius that is at once ancient and forceful. The views of Rome from this on-high square of many delights are memorable.

Stazione Termini (Piazza Cinquecento). It is a pity that the Italians did not take post-World War II architecture more seriously; the

ugly modern apartment buildings similar to those the world over
excepted, there has been little important public construction—nothing
to match the output of Mussolini Modern in the 1930s. Stazione
Termini, the main train station, is modern Roman design at its most
striking—long, sleek, and of a piece, an immense marble rectangle
whose exterior is an easily identifiable landmark and whose interior
is at once coolly severe and utterly functional.

Vatican City (Città del Vaticano) is essentially, for the visitor at
least, tours of St. Peter's Basilica and the Vatican Museums, earlier
recommended. At this point it might be worth noting that this compact enclosure of just under 109 acres (even tiny Monaco is four
times larger), with a population under a thousand, is a sovereign
state, under terms of agreements with Italy, most especially the Lateran Agreement signed in 1929 and incorporated into the Constitu-
tion of the postwar Italian Republic in 1947. The concordat defines
Vatican City to include St. Peter's, the Vatican Palace (the papal residence to the right of St. Peter's as you approach it), the museum
complex, the gardens, and adjacent structures, as well as a group of
thirteen buildings outside the Vatican, including the Basilicas of St.
John Lateran, St. Paul's Outside the Walls, and Santa Maria Maggiore
(see Selected Churches, above), and the summer papal palace at
Castel Gandolfo (see Castelli Romani, above). Vatican City ex-
changes diplomats with some seventy countries (there has never
been an exchange of ambassadors with the United States, but Presidents Franklin Roosevelt and Nixon had personal representatives).
Visitors in search of embassies in Rome must always ascertain
whether they want the embassy to the Italian Republic or the Vatican; many countries have both and the latter are located in Rome
proper, just as are the former. Tiny resident populace notwithstanding, there are Vatican laws, postage stamps, coins, newspaper
(foreign press and diplomats watch papal trends in *Osservatore
Romano*), trains, and—most apparent of all to visitors—soldiers.
These last are the Swiss Guards (they come mostly from the French-
speaking part of Switzerland), who still wear—at least for dress—the
uniforms designed for them half a millennium ago by no less distinguished a couturier than Michelangelo. Hats are iron helmets
with scarlet pompons; tunics and trousers are in wide vertical stripes
of blue and orange, with leggings to match. Hands are white-gloved;
one invariably holds a long wrought-iron halberd, with a battle-ax at

its extreme end. But it's not all pomp and glitter. Actual work of administration of the state, in matters temporal, is entrusted to the Secretary of State; he serves under the Pope on behalf of the Pontifical Commission, whose members are cardinals. Spiritual affairs are the business of the Roman Curia, a group of boards headed by cardinals, each with its own specialty, and all under the direction of the Pope, who is elected to office by the College of Cardinals (they hold their elections in the Sistine Chapel) and remains in his post for life. The Pope (*Il Papa,* in Italian) has but a single temporal title: Sovereign of the State of Vatican City. But his spiritual titles are considerable: Bishop of Rome, Vicar of Jesus Christ, Successor of St. Peter, Prince of the Apostles, Supreme Pontiff of the Universal Church, Patriarch of the West, Primate of Italy, Archbishop and Metropolitan of the Roman Province. Pope No. 1 was St. Peter (he arrived in Rome A.D. 42), and Paul VI was crowned in 1963; in between were nearly 300 popes and antipopes. There are two principal Vatican languages—Italian, the language of the state, and, more important because it is the language of papal encyclicals and other major documents, Latin, the official language of the Holy See. The populace, which includes some actual citizens of the Vatican state holding Vatican passports, is mostly Italian in origin but includes imported clergy from many countries, as well as the Swiss Guard.

Villa Adriana, Tivoli, is frequently but not always combined on excursions out of the capital to Villa d'Este in the same town of Tivoli, and honored, in this chapter, as a requisite of The Essential Rome grouping of destinations. Villa Adriana (Hadrian's Villa) dates back to the second century, occupies a vast, sprawling estate, and embraces a remarkable enough assortment of ruins, as well as a museum recommended for orientation in advance of touring about. Withal, unless one is a scholar, the magic that should emanate from any imperial palace is absent.

Rome: To Watch

Opera. Like other major Italian cities, Rome disappoints late-spring through early-autumn opera buffs who would like to hear their favorites sung in its opera house. Principal seasons for this performing art are traditionally late November through May. There are sup-

plementary seasons, of which more later, but in winter the locale is
the beautiful late-nineteenth-century red-and-white décor *Teatro dell'-
Opera* (Via Viminale)—multitiered, elaborate, elegant. The Rome
Opera has long had political, financial (losses of about $1.5 million
per annum), and artistic problems. And it is without the international
repute of Milan's La Scala, or for that matter Naples' San Carlo.
Which is hardly to counsel nonattendance if one is on hand during
the season. Far from it, and for either a ballet (the company has its
own troupe) or an opera evening; the repertory is heavy on Italians
—Verdi, Puccini, Donizetti. But foreign works are performed too.
Note also that during the summer the company moves itself, with
considerable flair and imagination, to the *Terme di Caracalla* (Via
delle Terme di Caracalla), the immense and ancient Baths of Caracalla, which date to the third century, when they could accommodate
a whopping total of some 1,600 bathers. A performance there,
under summer Roman stars, is quite as memorable as its downtown
winter counterpart.

Take note, too, of the relatively unheralded supplementary opera
season—*Stagione Lirica Tradizionale*—in June and September-early
October. The locale, traditionally, has been *Teatro Eliseo* (Via
Nazionale 183). This is an Art Deco house out of the 1930s, still
smart and smartly maintained. Its stage is too small for opera. But
no matter: singers' voices are usually very big and frequently very
good. I know of no orchestra pit in the world into which more musi-
cians—and first class ones at that—are crammed, and to good
advantage. The repertory is a traditional one.

Concerts. The first-rate *Rome Philharmonic* generally plays at
Teatro Olimpico (Piazza Gentile da Fabriano 17)—late fall through
early spring. In the summer, try to take in a concert at *Basilica di
Massenzio* in Fori Imperiali, a magnificently proportioned fourth-
century souvenir of Emperor Constantine. Chamber music concerts
take place at *Accademia Santa Cecilia* (Via dei Greci 7). Atmospheric *churches* often double as concert halls, too.

Movies. Rome is headquarters to a globally celebrated film industry
and has no dearth of cinemas; some fifty are first-run houses, but at
almost all the sound tracks of imported films are dubbed into
Italian. A notable exception, where imported movies are shown with

the original sound tracks (and with printed Italian titles), is *Cinema Archimede* (Via Archimede 71).

Legitimate Theater. The capital is the national center of the thriving Italian theater. Plays are, of course, presented in Italian, but language is never a barrier for true theater-lovers who are curious about details of production like sets, costumes, music when present, direction, acting. Principal theaters are the earlier-mentioned *Eliseo* (Via Nazionale 183), *Quirino* (Via Marco Minghetti 1), and *Valle* (Via del Teatro Valle).

Sound and Light (or *Son et Lumière,* to use the term in the French, who invented this combination of drama, narrative, and architecture at historic sites) have traditionally taken place in summer at *Villa Adriana* in suburban Tivoli, and *Foro Romano* in town.

Papal Audiences. Traditionally, the Pope holds a mass audience Wednesday afternoons in the modern Audience Hall adjacent to St. Peter's Basilica (to the left as you approach on Via della Conciliazione). In summer, these move to the papal palace at suburban Castel Gandolfo, earlier described. Admission is by gratis ticket *only*. Audiences are arranged and operated by the Prefettura della Casa Pontificia, at the Vatican. Americans who are Catholics may arrange in advance for admission through their parish priests. Americans, Catholic and otherwise, may also apply for tickets upon arrival in Rome, through a facility operated by the Conference of American Bishops. It is the *Bishops' Office for United States Visitors to the Vatican,* and is located in the earlier-described Casa dell'Umiltà, Via dell'Umiltà 30, a splendid Renaissance palazzo-cum-chapel, in central Rome. (If you know what Wednesday you would like to attend, write in advance; the postal zone is 00187, Roma.) To say that these audiences are the greatest show in Rome is not to be disrespectful. One's religious faith or lack of same notwithstanding, attendance at a papal audience provides one with a grasp of the extraordinary universality, the multinational, multilingual, multiracial composition of the Catholic Church. The Pope, in scarlet cape and white biretta, traditionally welcomes—and later briefly addresses—his visitors in Italian, French, English, German, Spanish, and Portuguese after his entrance and a tour around the hall during which he bestows his blessing. Invariably, there is a good sprinkling of vividly costumed

cardinals—representing every major racial group—in attendance.
Adding more color is a complement of helmeted Swiss Guards, wearing the uniforms Michelangelo designed for them half a millennium
ago. I repeat: It's quite a show. But if you can't make it, bear in mind
that traditionally the Pope, when in residence, greets Sunday morning visitors, from the balcony of his palace, overlooking Piazza San
Pietro; about 11 A.M.

Horse Racing. Join the fans at *Ippodromo delle Capannelle* (Via
Appia) for standard racing, and *Ippodromo di Tor di Ville* for
trotting.

Convention Facilities. *Palazzo dei Congressi,* out at the earlier-
described E.U.R., is the principal hall, but hotels have facilities too;
those of the Cavalieri Hilton are probably the largest.

Sightseeing Tours. Local agencies—*Carrani Tours* (Via Vittorio
Emanuele Orlando 95), *Appian Line* (Via Vittorio Veneto 171), *Via*
(Via due Macelli 105) are a few—run a variety of half-day, day-long,
and Rome by Night bus tours, as well as out-of-town excursions to
points like Naples, Pompeii, Capri, Florence, and Assisi. More unusual, and worthwhile if one can understand some Italian, are the
guided visits (traditionally offered without charge and by experts)
of various Roman historic districts and museums, operated by *Amici
dei Musei di Roma* (Friends of the Museums of Rome); telephone
67-82-862 weekdays, from 11 A.M. to 1 P.M.; or on Sundays and
holidays, 65-68-704, between 9:30 and 11:30 A.M. (These phone
numbers are subject to change, and you must not blame me
if no one answers.)

Rome: To Stay

If Roman hotel-keeping standards are not quite what they were,
even as recently as half a decade back, neither are most other cities'
—Italian and otherwise. The service-cum-smile that was a hallmark of
hotel staffs in the capital and throughout Italy is now more appreciated than heretofore, if only because it is not always encountered.
Still, appraising Rome on a world scale, it remains among a handful
of leading cities as regards standards of operation and, equally im-

portant, range of categories—from simple through very grand. There are score upon score of hotels and pensiones conveniently located in the city's central sectors. Herewith, my personal evaluation of half a hundred plus, in which I have either lived, dined, drunk, or, at the very least, thoroughly inspected. The presentation is alphabetical, with the price range—*luxury, first-class, moderate*—indicated in each case. Air-conditioning is standard in luxury and most first-class places; most of these hotels also equip rooms with frigo-bars stocked with drinks and snacks for purchase.

Hotel Alexandra (Via Vittorio Veneto 18) is well situated, and a delight, with a nifty green and yellow lobby and comfortable rooms. *First class.*

Hotel Alicorn (Via Scosscavalli 11) is smallish (50 rooms) with only a dozen-odd private baths, bar and breakfast service, but no restaurant. This is worth knowing about if one is on a budget and wants to stay in the neighborhood of the Vatican. *Moderate.*

Ambasciatori Palace (Via Vittorio Veneto 70) has a smart location just opposite the American Embassy. The lobby (note the 1920s murals) is among the most beautiful in town; the restaurant moves to a canopied terrace in summer, there is a convenient late-hours coffee shop in the basement, and the level of luxury is such that more than half of the double rooms have *two* baths, with refrigerators —stocked with drinks and snacks—in all 152 rooms and suites. Skilled and smiling management. Very special. *Luxury.*

Hotel Anglo Americano (Via Quattro Fontane 12) is an elderly 120-room house with an inspired central location—some rooms overlook Palazzo Barberini—that has been completely modernized. All rooms have bath, and the lobby is welcoming. Breakfast only. *First class.*

Hotel Atlantico (Via Cavour 23) has a cheery lounge and the advantage of a lobby passage connecting it to next-door luxury-class Hotel Mediterraneo (they are both part of the well-run Bettoja chain), whose restaurant and bar it shares. All 77 rooms are perky-modern-functional, and with bath. Situation is near Stazione Termini. Very pleasant. *First class.*

Atlas Hotel (Via Rasella 3) has a heart-of-everything location and behind its traditional façade are nearly half a hundred rooms with bath, pretty lobby-lounge-bar, and a super roof garden for sun-cum-views. Breakfast only. *First class.*

Bernini Bristol Hotel (Piazza Barberini 23) is the modern building that backs Bernini's Triton Fountain, from which it takes the first half of its name. Rooms and suites—132 in all—are luxurious and taste-ful, and those on the top two floors are kitchenette-equipped. There's a summer roof restaurant with a socko view, and an agreeable bar-lounge. *Luxury.*

Hotel Bologna (Via Santa Chiara 9a) occupies a fine eighteenth-century house, very central, that has been converted into an excep-tionally good-looking moderate-category hotel, with an antiques-filled lounge, bar, compact but comfortable rooms. Breakfast only. *Moderate.*

Hotel Boston (Via Lombardia 47), in the Veneto area, has been thoroughly updated, with especially attractive bedrooms, 121 in all, a handsome lobby, restaurant, and bar. And agreeable service. *First class.*

Cavalieri Hilton Hotel (Via Cadlolo 101) is out in the smart Monte Mario residential section, a considerable distance from central Rome. (There is gratis hotel-operated bus service to Piazza di Spagna.) But it is not without advantages: 400 modern rooms, many with sump-tuous views, a variety of places to dine, drink, dance, hold meetings, and shop, and a honey of a pool in the beautiful garden that is a distinct bonus in summer. Among the better-looking of this quality chain's properties around the world—and I know most Hilton Inter-nationals, from Barbados to Manila.

Columbus Hotel (Via della Conciliazione 33) is a fifteenth-century cardinal's palazzo turned hotel, and within the shadow of St. Peter's. The public rooms are museum-caliber—one, for example, with a ceiling painted by Pintoricchio, others with magnificent wall frescoes. Still, the category is not luxury; 80 of the 100 relatively plain bedrooms have baths, however, and there are both restaurant and bar. Popular with visiting clerics, but all are welcome. *First class.*

Pensione Daria (Via Sicilia 24) is just off Via Vittorio Veneto, with fussily but amusingly decorated public rooms (pictures occupy every available inch of wall space), kind management, an absolutely spot-less look, and 27 rooms, all with bath or shower. Breakfast only. *Moderate.*

Hotel De la Ville (Via Sistina 67) is a few steps from the Church of Santa Trinità dei Monti, atop the Spanish Steps. The De la Ville is traditional-style beautiful, with a smart lobby, engaging restaurant (that moves to the garden in summer), bar-lounge, and lovely guest rooms, some of which have panoramic views. *Luxury.*

Hotel Dinesen Bellavista Milton—what other hotel's name embraces Denmark, Italy, and England in a single mouthful?—is at Via Porta Pinciana 18, near the Veneto, and has 84 rooms, half of which have their own baths. There's a restaurant but no bar, and a loyal British repeat-clientele who appreciate its good location and value. *Moderate.*

Hotel d'Inghilterra (Via Bocca di Leone 14) is just off Via Condotti and a step from the Spanish Steps. It's an early Roman home of mine and has been refurbished in recent years to the point where about half of the 100 pleasant if mostly unelaborate rooms now have baths. Lounges are rather giddy Italian-Victorian, and there's a congenial bar. Astute management. Breakfast only. Fiercely loyal international repeat-clientele of individuals only—no groups. *Moderate.*

Hotel d'Italia (Via Quattro Fontane 150) is just opposite Palazzo Barberini in central Rome, with 50 rooms, half with private facilities. Breakfast only. *Moderate.*

Hotel Eden (Via Ludovisi 49) is among the smaller of the grander hotels; its ambience is intimate and relaxing. There is a pair of restaurants, including a rather special rooftop one affording fine vistas; cozy bar, too, as well as 115 attractive rooms and suites. The location, on Via Ludovisi midway between Via Vittorio Veneto and Piazza di Spagna, is inspired. Lots of repeaters. *Luxury.*

Hotel Excelsior (Via Vittorio Veneto 125) is the larger of the top-rank CIGA chain's pair of Roman hotels (the other is the Grand, see below), with elaborate public spaces that include restaurant, bar, and Veneto caffè, and 378 fully equipped rooms and suites with capaciousness generally the rule. The location is superb. *Luxury*.

Hotel Flora (Via Vittorio Veneto 191) is near the top of the Veneto hill, and is an absolute charmer of an old-timer—dignified and correct but at the same time friendly and warm. Rooms and suites—200 in all—tend to understatement rather than excess in décor, and many offer dazzling views. There's an attractive restaurant, and a convenient caffè-snack-bar-cocktail lounge in the basement. *Luxury*.

Hotel Forum (Via Tor de' Conti 25) is not large—there are 82 rooms and suites all told—but it is attractive, not only because of its tasteful décor but because of its ace-in-the-hole location just opposite Foro Romano, which makes its Forum-view rooms and restaurant (dealt with on a later page) quite special. A treat, especially in fine weather, is the roof-garden bar-lounge. *First class*.

Hotel Genio (Via Zanardelli 28) has private baths in 47 of its simply furnished rooms. Nothing fancy here, but location is central. Breakfast only. *Moderate*.

Grand Hotel (Via Vittorio Emanuele Orlando 3) is an elderly beauty with more style in one room than many others have in a dozen. It would be difficult to find hotel interiors where color and traditional-style decorative detail have been more imaginatively used. Bedrooms and suites—there are only 175 with no two precisely alike—are absolute beauties. Lobbies and lounges could easily rank with some of the palazzi as sightseers' attractions. Location is central. Le Maschere Restaurant is one of the most eye-filling in Rome, with an extensive menu including pasta specialties—in 38 variations. (It is elegant even at breakfast—a difficult ambience for a restaurant to achieve so early in the day.) Le Rallye, the Grand's grill, is worthy of special comment on a succeeding page. The cocktail lounge is among the more winning in the capital. Clientele is at once attractive and multinational. Management is skilled. No question in my mind: queen bee of the CIGA chain. *Luxury*.

Hotel Hassler (Piazza Trinità dei Monti 6) has an advantage with its location: atop the Spanish Steps. There are just over a hundred elaborately decorated rooms and suites (those with front views, looking out over the city, are choice, especially if they have terraces), a restaurant, and a bar which branches out into the garden in summer, becoming quite the nicest part of a hotel that, in other respects, appears to patronize its rich, heavily American clientele. *Luxury*.

Hotel Imperiale (Via Vittorio Veneto 24) is a well-situated, good-looking house that is not so big (there are only 84 rooms, many of which are oversized) that it can't provide pleasant service. Restaurant, bar. *First class*.

Hotel Internazionale (Via Sistina 79) was where I put up on a long-ago Roman trip during a time when it was clean but very simple. Recent seasons have seen it handsomely refurbished; 33 of its 36 snappy rooms now have private baths. There's a bar and breakfast room. The location, as always, is perfect—just down Via Sistina from the head of the Spanish Steps. *Moderate*.

Jolly Hotel (Corso Italia 1) is the relatively recent representation in the capital of the Italy-wide Jolly chain. And worth waiting for: 200 ultramod rooms, all with rather super bathrooms, a great big lobby, a cocktail lounge that seems even bigger, an attractive restaurant, a façade that is among the better of Rome's modern exteriors, and a convenient location not far from Via Vittorio Veneto. Polished Jolly know-how is reflected in management and service. *First class*.

Pensione delle Legazioni (Via Barberini 11) is very central and with a considerable number of rooms (87), all of which have private shower or bath. Bar and breakfast. *Moderate*.

Hotel Leonardo da Vinci (Via dei Gracchi 324) went up in the late 1960s. It's handsome—big lobby and adjacent lounges, good restaurants, and bar, inviting rooms, including singles, doubles, and suites. And big bouquets of fresh flowers in all the public areas. The location is interesting. It's just a few minutes' walk across Ponte Regina Margherita from central Piazza del Popolo, on the Vatican side of the

Tiber, in a quiet residential quarter. Zippy, smiley management. *First class.*

Hotel Majestic (Via Vittorio Veneto 50) is a traditional-style winner, with a quiet ambience. The lobby, with a frescoed ceiling, is handsome, and there is a summer terrace-restaurant. Nice rooms, too; 100 all told. *First class.*

Pensione Maria Teresa (Via Sicilia 66) has none of the eighteenth-century opulence associated with the Hapsburg empress for whom it is named. Its thrust is good value: 18 spotless albeit simple rooms, all with bath or shower, and 14 with running water only. Alfresco terrace. Choose from bed and breakfast, half- or full-pension plans. *Moderate.*

Hotel Massimo d'Azeglio (Via Cavour 18) is No. 2 in the Bettoja chain, just after the luxury-category Mediterraneo. Thoroughly refurbished, it is also the oldest, dating back to 1875, with a restaurant—later described—that is exceptional, a convivial bar, spacious lobby and lounges, 210 pleasant rooms, and that friendly Bettoja service—thanks in large part to direct personal, always-on-the-scene direction of President Angelo Bettoja, second-generation head of the five-hotel chain who knows America and Americans well, in part because Signora Bettoja is American-born; the Bettojas make regular trips to visit the in-laws in Georgia. (Connects with the San Giorgio, another Bettoja house, next door.)

Hotel Mediterraneo (Via Cavour 15) is the biggest and most elaborate of the quintet of Bettoja hotels, with 367 bright rooms and suites (some with terraces), a rather grand marble lobby, the first-rate 21 Restaurant (with really good Italian fare), and a comfortable cocktail lounge. I've always found the service at once professional, warm, and gracious. *Luxury.*

Hotel Michelangelo (Via Stazione San Pietro 14) is a modern 200-room house whose distinctive feature is location: it's in the very shadow of the dome of St. Peter's—which was designed by the genius for whom the hotel is named. Rooms are light and bright, public rooms—including restaurant and bar—capacious. *First class.*

Hotel Minerva (Piazza della Minerva 69) is a lovely, unabashedly old-fashioned house that takes its name from the Church of Santa Maria Sopra Minerva, which is just opposite; the Pantheon is another near neighbor. Seventy of the 180 rooms have bath or shower, all quite as venerable as the hotel itself. The lounges are a joy, and there's a bar. Breakfast but no restaurant. *Moderate*.

Hotel Nazionale (Piazza Montecitorio) fronts the splendid broad square named for the palace housing the lower chamber of the Italian Parliament. It is small enough—there are 78 rooms—to be intimate, and there's an air of elegance, too, in the traditional-style lobby, the blue-brown-and-white-hued lounges; restaurant and bedrooms are in the same color scheme. *First class*.

Hotel Nord (Via Giovanni Amendola 3) is a functional, up-to-date 200-room house, the least elaborate of the Bettoja Rome quintet. Which is not to say that it's not nice. Just that it's not fancy, and is without restaurant or bar, as are so many in its category. Location is the Stazione Termini area. Breakfast only. *Moderate*.

Hotel Pace Elvezia (Via IV Novembre 104): Any hotel whose name translates as Swiss Peace has to have something going for it. The Pace Elvezia's is a central location near Piazza Venezia, cozy public spaces, and 64 rooms, most of which have private baths but could do with a bit of brightening up, or at least could when I last saw them. Breakfast only. *Moderate*.

Hotel Parco di Principe (Via G. Frescobaldi 5) is quite the most imaginatively designed of the newer Roman hotels—mid-sixties Italian Modern at its severe, understated best. The dominant color is green and the setting is a capacious green garden—with a broad terrace and outdoor pool—on the Via Mercadante side of the Borghese Gardens, which is a fairish walk to the Via Veneto but is close enough so that it can be walked. One whole window wall of the restaurant overlooks the garden and pool. There are just over 200 comfortable rooms and suites. *Luxury*.

Pensione Paisiello Parioli (Via Paisiello 47) is functional, no-nonsense, with private baths in 24 of its simple 35 rooms, and a bar-restaurant-lounge on the street floor. In a nice residential district. *Moderate.*

Hotel Plaza (Via del Corso 126) was built in 1860 with what must then have been the most knock-'em-dead public rooms in Rome, and it has maintained them well ever since. The main lounge, with its great crystal chandeliers and neo-Renaissance ceiling, must surely have first served as a very grand ballroom. The entrance hall and adjacent smaller lounges are equally dazzling, and there's a handsome restaurant with an adjacent bar. Bedrooms—there are 240 with bath—are less elaborate but inviting; many have brass beds. A super period-piece, with an equally super location. *First class.*

Hotel Quattro Fontane (Via Quattro Fontane 149) is nicely situated between Palazzo Barberini and Palazzo Quirinale. There are 50 rooms with bath or showers; doubles are small, but the value is good. Pretty lounge with a coffered ceiling. Breakfast only. *Moderate.*

Hotel Quirinale (Via Nazionale 7) is just off Piazza della Repubblica and a hop and a skip from the Opera, with which it is connected by both tradition *and* a tunnel—heavily trafficked after performances by patrons en route to the Quirinale for refreshment. The hotel, dating back to 1865, is graced with a quiet inner garden where lunch is served in summer. There are 189 pleasant rooms and suites, restaurant, bar. *First class.*

Hotel Raphael (Largo Febo 2) is near Piazza Navona, in one direction, and the antique shops of Via dei Coronari, in another. It's a fine old building, converted with exceptional imagination into a 100-room hotel in the 1960s. The look is provincial-traditional, blended with contemporary touches. Fine antiques are scattered about in lounge, restaurant, and bar. Rooms are a joy, and so is the roof garden, where guests may have drinks and even breakfast in summer. Directly next door is the venerable Church of Santa Maria della Pace; rooms on the church side overlook its exquisite cloister. *First class.*

Hotel Regina-Carlton (Via Vittorio Veneto 72) is diagonally opposite the American Embassy, and has been skillfully refurbished; the updated bedrooms—they total 134—are among the more desirable in town; and there's a striking, high-ceilinged lobby. Restaurant, bar. *First class*.

Hotel San Giorgio (Via G. Amendola 61) is a gem of a period piece, the period being the 1930s. There are a handsome high-ceilinged lobby, lounge, bar, breakfast room, and nearly 200 attractively furnished rooms. A passage leads into earlier-recommended Hotel Massimo d'Azeglio, with its exceptional restaurant (later described). Both of these houses are part of the Bettoja chain. *First class*.

Hotel Savoia (Via Ludovisi 5), with its Via Veneto-corner-of-Via-Ludovisi location and a stylishly refurbished plant, is a pleasure; good-looking, high-ceilinged, scarlet-and-white restaurant and cocktail lounge, inviting guest rooms and suites—110 all told; and bold neo-Renaissance façade. *First class*.

Hotel Sistina (Via Sistina 136), located on convenient Via Sistina, near the Spanish Steps, is small and unpretentious; just 27 rooms (all, though, have bath). Breakfast but no restaurant or bar. *Moderate*.

Hotel Sitea (Via Vittorio Emanuele Orlando 90) is just across the street from the esteemed luxury-category Grand. It has a neat, neo-Renaissance façade, attractive lounges (one up on the roof), breakfast service, and a snack bar. There are 40 neat rooms, all with bath. *Moderate*.

Pensione Suisse (Via Gregoriana 56) is an absolutely spotless little place, as well it had better be, given its name. It is near both Piazza di Spagna and Via Sistina. There are 29 rooms, 10 of which have private baths. Nice lounge and a capacious guest-terrace as well. Breakfast only. *Moderate*.

Pensione Terminus (Piazza della Repubblica 47) is upstairs in one of the curved, arcaded buildings of this central square (also known as Piazza dell'Esedra). Mind, now, this is hardly fancy. There are 20 rooms, 11 of which have bath. They are clean and adequate but I would not call them cheery. Breakfast only. *Moderate*.

Pensione Texas (Via Firenze 47): That's what I said, pardner:

Texas. The ownership is part American, which explains the name.
And the popularity is explained by warm and effortless service and
by the fact that 13 of the 17 rooms have private facilities. Antiques
are scattered throughout, especially in the lounge, with a wood-
burning fireplace that makes it popular at cocktail time in the cool
months. Breakfast only. *Moderate.*

Pensione Trinità dei Monti (Via Sistina 91) has a score of rooms,
all with bath, agreeable lounge, and a restaurant serving all meals;
rates are quoted, however, on a bed-and-breakfast basis. This is a
simple place; lures are the central location and the low prices.
Moderate.

Hotel Visconti Palace (Via Federico Cesi 37) is herein described
principally because it is clean, modern, and with 250 rooms with
bath or shower that might be useful to some group-organizer. However, beds that I inspected were narrow and saggy. There are both
restaurant and bar. Location is the Vatican side of the Tiber, about
midway between Ponte Cavour and Ponte Margherita, not far from
Piazza Cavour and not the most central in town. *First class.*

Rome: To Eat and Drink

As with other matters, one eats in Rome as do the Romans. Which
means à la carte. Table d'hôte has never caught on in Italy. One occasionally sees a so-called tourist menu, but they're rarely exceptional
buys and not popular. Unlike the French, not to mention other
Europeans and Americans, too, Italians prefer selecting the component parts of meals by themselves. They'll order an opening course
—antipasto (cold hors d'oeuvres), soup, pasta, or even (and this is
of interest to dieters) a vegetable—spinach, green beans, broccoli—
interestingly prepared: served cold. These vegetables—*contorni*—are
usually displayed along with the antipasti, on appealing cold tables.
A main dish—meat, poultry, seafood—will follow. The wine, invariably, will be a carafe (or a half or quarter if one is alone) of the dry,
crisp, and fruity Frascati or a variation thereof from the nearby
Castelli Romani area. (Romans drink whites with all types of food,
but reds in copious variety are everywhere available.) Like most
Italians, Romans make relatively little of desserts—fresh fruit and

cheese (especially the delicious, hard, crumbly Parmesan) are usual, but most restaurants also feature *profiterole,* puff pastry filled with custard or whipped cream and topped with chocolate sauce, a cake or two or three, and a few species of ice cream and/or sherbet, which are no better in any country in the world. It is worth noting that one need never feel compelled to order a large meal. Roman restaurateurs respect customers' wishes, eccentric as they may be; feel free to order as little as you want to eat or, for that matter, drink. (No one will urge you, for example, to order wine, if you would rather not, and Italians are not nearly as averse to serving water as, for example, the British.)

Terminology. Not to worry. Most eating places are *ristoranti,* but there are *trattorie,* too. A trattoria is simply a restaurant less elaborate in menu and décor than the ristorante. Caffès serve sandwiches, hot snacks, coffee, tea, hot chocolate, soft drinks, wines, and hard drinks, ice-cream dishes, too. And places called bars are a variation on the caffè theme, with just about as much variety; indeed, many Italian city dwellers take their breakfast—rolls and coffee—in them. A special pleasure of dining in the Eternal City is that its restaurants embrace the specialties of the various regions of the country, most especially culinarily distinguished Bologna and Tuscany. But Rome has its own food specialties: *gnocchi alla romana*—semolina-base dumplings; *spaghetti alla carbonara* (with bacon and eggs), *all'Amatriciana* (with bacon), *cannelloni*—wide canal-shaped pasta with an appropriate sauce and melted-cheese topping; the deep-fried seafood mélange called *fritto misto,* the veal, cheese, and ham entree known as *saltimbocca;* the richly sauced *fettuccine alla romana, straciatella*—a delicious egg-drop soup; chicken either *alla diavola* or *alla cacciatore;* roast suckling pig; novel ways of preparing veal and lamb (*abacchio al forno* is the delicious local lamb roast), and vegetables like artichoke and broccoli.

Most restaurants open for lunch at noon, serving until about two; dinner service starts at seven, although most Romans dine from about eight until about ten, after which it's not easy to get served. Advance reservations are advised, through one's hotel concierge or by oneself.

Here is a select—a very select—group of restaurants that I enjoy. They have been picked so as to afford the visitor variety—different parts of town, different price ranges, different specialties. There are proper restaurants, elegant and near so; a vast middle group extending into *trattorie;* and some exceptional caffès for coffee and specialties like ice cream. The order is alphabetical. And I've categorized each as *expensive, moderate,* or *inexpensive.*

Alemagna (Via del Corso at Piazza Colonna) is a great big cake-bakery-confectionary-caterer kind of establishment, run by the people who make the sweet *panettone* bread widely exported to the United States at Christmas (along with that of their major competitor, Motta). Go for a quick lunch, midmorning coffee, afternoon snack, whenever. The species of *gelati* (ice cream) and sherbet are limitless and magnificent. There are candies boxed as only Italians can box them, tiny frosted cakes, little sandwiches and mini-pizzas, and great counters of antipasti. Pasta dishes take up another cafeteria-style counter. And, best of all, there is the drink called *frullati di fruta:* strawberries, peaches, bananas, pears, apples, apricots, lemons, oranges, and grapefruit are combined in a blender with milk, sugar and maraschino liqueur. Think of me when you order one. *Inexpensive.*

Alfredo alla Scrofa (Via della Scrofa 104) is one of the "original" Alfredo's which made *fettuccine alla romana*—pasta in a rich cream-and-butter sauce, tossed at table—into a world-renowned dish. It's called *fettuccine al triplo burgo* here, and it's delicious. So is just about everything else, especially the chicken-breast preparation called *petto di pollo all' Cardinale,* and roast lamb—*arracchio arrosto.* There's a good *fritto misto*—mixed fried seafood—too. Photos of luminary customers line the walls, but ordinary mortals are treated rather haughtily, albeit with dispatch. The outdoor terrace, on the street, is recommended in warm weather. *Moderate.*

Antico Moro (Viccolo delle Bollette 13) appeals from the moment one enters. Walls are white and garnished with strings of garlic bulbs and onions. The place hums with modish Romans who know where to go for Roman specialties served with panache. Ignore *spaghetti al Moro* (the surprise is bacon and eggs) at your peril; grilled veal chops are super, too; so are veal with tomato sauce and *prosciutto*—a specialty. And nowhere in Rome is the Parmesan cheese more deliciously crumbly or served with better bread. *Moderate.*

Babington's Tea Room (Piazza di Spagna 23) is an across-the-square neighbor of the house in which Keats lived, and it may well be almost as old. Despite, or perhaps because of, the Anglo name, clientele is mostly Roman—youngish, good-looking couples obviously with money to spare. Cash in quantity is required here, to sample the very good cakes and pastries, the tea and *cappuccino*. Go at 5 or 6 P.M. and you would think they were giving the stuff away. It's fun. But with the exception of a fancy tea-spot in Paris called Angelina, it appears to me to set a world record when it comes to steep tabs for places of its type. For what you get: *Expensive.*

Dal Bolognese (Piazza del Popolo 1): The lure here is the wickedly rich, cream-based cuisine of Bologna. Sit under the big green canopy outside and watch the crowds in the Baroque piazza, or dine within, observing contemporary art on wood-paneled walls. A framed telegram is from the late King Frederick IX of Denmark, thanking the management for a delicious meal, upon returning to Wonderful Copenhagen from a Roman holiday. The royal compliment was deserved. And the service is as kind and expert as the fare. Try the specialties: *misto di pasta*—a combination plate with *tortellini, canolliccini, tortelli,* and *lasagne verde; maccheroncinialla crema e prosciutto*—macaroni in a ham sauce; *giambonetti cremolati*—veal in a typically Bolognese cream sauce; and *polpettone de vitello*—balls of minced veal subtly sauced. *Granita,* a type of sherbet (try the raspberry or the lemon) makes a lovely, light dessert. There's a good red house wine. *Moderate.*

Caffè Berardo (Piazza Colonna) is heart-of-town and a Roman institution. The ice creams are special. So are the whole glacéed oranges. Good pizza, too. And candies to purchase so unusual as to include mini-salamis made of almond paste. Romans love the plum cake—English-style and English-spelled. *Inexpensive.*

Caffè di Colombia (Piazza Navona): A top-notch Piazza Navona restaurant is later counseled. But for a snack, coffee or—especially —an ice-cream break, this is a nice, traditional-style place in a glorious setting. *Inexpensive.*

Caffè Giolitti (Via del Uffici del Vicario 40) is, more than anything else, a *gelateria*. By that I mean that after you've eaten its ice cream (especially the chocolate) not even the brownie-fudge back home at

Baskin-Robbins is going to mean much to you. The sherbets—
particularly the lemon—are matchless, too. There are ravishing pastries, as well as sandwiches and drinks. *Inexpensive.*

Caffè Greco (Via Condotti 80), which had passed its sixteenth
birthday the year our Declaration of Independence was signed, remains, decade in and decade out, the most convenient locale in
town for the study and observation of beautiful Romans. Coffee,
snacks, drinks, what-have-you. Wonderful-looking, too. *Inexpensive.*

Caffè Pellacchia (Via Boncompagni 49) is typical of any number of
quite ordinary—but quite nice—caffès near, but not *on,* the tourist-
trod Via Vittorio Veneto that are so much nicer than the Veneto's
—with kind staff and fair prices. *Inexpensive.*

Caffès on Via Vittorio Veneto—they line it from the top of the hill to
its base—are ideally regarded only as places that must be resorted to
when it's not convenient to go elsewhere for coffee, a drink, or a
snack. Prices are generally higher than in any other area of Rome,
and service rarely charms. For what you get: *Expensive.*

Della Campana (Vicolo della Campana 18, almost next door to
earlier-recommended Alfredo alla Scrofa) calls its quarters the oldest of any restaurant in town; the building housing this typically
Roman, solid, and unpretentious place goes back to the sixteenth
century. The staff, so far as I can ascertain, speaks not a word of
English. Still, the waiters communicate. Everything comes to table
the instant it has been prepared and it's all delicious, especially
such dishes as *fettuccine con funghi* (mushrooms), the grilled fish
of the day, roast lamb, veal in a number of ways. Desserts are
fancier than one might expect; try the *torte di marmellata,* which
in this case translates as plum jam. Fun. *Moderate.*

Cannavota (Piazza San Giovanni in Laterano 2) typifies bourgeois
Roman dining: too fussily decorated perhaps, with a staff that takes
itself too seriously and rarely smiles. One goes for the food and the
good value. The cold table is a honey; try one of the *contorni* (a
choice of spinach, peppers, chicory, or mushrooms) or open with a
pasta specialty like *rigatoni alla Rigore* or *bucatini alla Cannavota,*

which is thick spaghetti in a seafood sauce. *Scallope alla verbena,* lemon-flavored veal, is delicious. A bonus is the location: the Basilica of St. John Lateran is across the square. *Moderate.*

La Capricciosa (Largo dei Lombardi 8) is a convenient spot, just off Via del Corso, and especially appealing in summer, thanks to a capacious outdoor terrace. It makes a specialty of pizza, but the menu runs a wide gamut. Pleasant service. *Moderate.*

Cesarina (Via Piemonte 109) is a big, busy, noisy, immediately likable place, minutely and expertly supervised by Mamma Cesarina. A delectable house specialty is a tripartite pasta plate—*tortellini, lasagne,* and *ravioli verde. Misto Cesarina*—deep-fried *fritto misto* of vegetables and hot stuffed tomatoes—is inspired. So is sautéed veal *piccata* with lemon butter sauce. Mamma is bigger on desserts than much of the competition; her *Semifreddo Cesarina* embraces soft vanilla ice cream, *zuppa inglese* (trifle), and chocolate sauce. *Moderate.*

Al Chianti (Via Ancona 19) dishes up such relative rarities as *pappardelle sulla lepre*—a pasta concoction with hare sauce, out of Tuscany; *vitello tonnato*—the cold veal-tuna specialty that is so good on a hot summer day, and a variety of Tuscan dishes. *Moderate.*

Flavia (Via Flavia 9) draws as smart a crowd as one is likely to encounter in Rome, unpretentious décor notwithstanding. The lure is absolutely super food—such as vegetable soup (*zuppa di verdura*) and *saltimbocca romana.* And note the Italian bread transformed via the grill into hot toast. *Moderate.*

Fontanella (Largo Fontanella di Borghese) is a delicious touch of Tuscany in the capital. One's fellow-diners are invariably upper-class Romans, talky and enthusiastic—as well they might be. There's a great mosaic mural of Florence dominating the décor within, and an outdoor terrace for summer meals. Service is unobtrusive but expert. Good things to eat include *salame toscano*—a plate with several types; *pappardelle alla toscana*—noodles under a pair of sauces; *tacchino modo nostro*—turkey "our style"; *anitra*—or duck—cooked with olives; and the classic Tuscan standby, broiled steak. *Moderate.*

Forum Hotel Roof (Via Tor de' Conti 25) has nothing less than Foro Imperiali as the subject matter of the panorama offered lunchers and/or diners, enclosed in winter, alfresco in warm weather. There are good-value *piatti del giorno*—daily blue plates—but a considerable selection; of the pasta, try *cannolicchi alla Forum;* of the meats, the *Scaloppine alla Forum.* And of the sweets, I would opt for *pera alla bell' Elena,* ice cream-cum-chocolate sauce topping over pears. And that view! *Moderate.*

Francesco Perilli (Via Piemonte at Via Boncompagni) could not be more elegant, thanks to the Art Nouveau walls that set it off. A candlelit summer dinner in the garden is pleasurable. Good antipasti, veal and lamb specialties. Range is from *moderate* to *expensive.*

Galeassi (Piazza Santa Maria in Trastevere) is smack in the heart of Trastevere, on its finest square, facing its finest church. In summer you eat under a canopy on the piazza, and you eat well. Consider such unusual pasta dishes as *penne all' arabbiata* or *agnolotti,* house-style fish specialties like *spigola dorata,* or fried *calamari*—the squid so beloved by Romans. *Moderate.*

Giggi Fazi (Via Lucullo 22) is Rome's answer to New York's Mamma Leone—a vividly decorated place with a high decibel count, agile waiters, animated clients. This is a good place to see Roman families—Mamma, Pappa, Granny, and the kids—enjoying a meal. The entire hierarchy—maître d', captains, waiters—makes a point of chatting with guests. Don't be surprised at the odd-appearing menu; you're looking at Roman dialect. Start with *antipasto romano*—a plate of green olives followed by plates of salami, eggplant, *prosciutto,* sausages, and black olives. *Pollo spezzato co'li peperoni* (chicken with peppers) and *fiji de lapecona a lo spido* (lamb chops with chicory) are both good. The house wine is a coarse chianti served in a vast opened bottle. You're charged for what you drink with the waiter taking the measurements. A better buy might be an unopened bottle ordered from the wine card. *Moderate.*

Hostaria dell'Orso (Via Monte Brianzo 93). One goes to the Hostaria neither for the food, which is pedestrian, nor for the service, which can be patronizing. (Affluent steak-and-baked potato Americans have a way of demoralizing restaurant staffs.) Tabs are high, but one looks upon a dinner as an expensive evening, with something to eat and drink, at a magnificent antique house. The Hostaria dell-'Orso or Inn of the Bear, goes back more than half a millennium and embraces three sumptuously furnished levels—bar-lounge as you go in; restaurant up a flight; and *boîte,* topside. Inspect the furnishings, objects, and paintings of all three. *Expensive.*

Marte (Piazza in Campo Marzio) is a sensible heart-of-old-Rome choice for an alfresco lunch or dinner in warm weather, or a cozy meal at other times of year. The soups are good—try the minestrone, and so are any number of pasta choices. Smiling waiters. *Moderate.*

Massimo d'Azeglio Hotel Restaurant (Via Cavour 18). This century-and-more-old hotel and restaurant (a part of the Bettoja chain) are a Roman institution, the atmospheric restaurant especially. Businessmen in the area like to stop in for lunch. Pasta is inordinately tasty; try the *spaghetti all' amatriciana,* here flavored with ham and truffles. Grilled fresh trout is another house specialty. The *piatti del giorno* are invariably good bets: *ossobuco con risotto* and *scaloppine al vino bianco,* for example. Grills are always available, and of the desserts the banana flambé is exceptional. Agile service. *Moderate.*

Mastrostefano (Piazza Navona 94) starts out with an inspired location on one of the great Baroque squares of Europe, continues with décor—the comparison is to a docked Art Deco ship of the 1930s— concludes with delicious food and skilled service. Meals start with an on-the-house fresh vegetable dip. *Cannelloni* and *fagotto* (spinach-filled ravioli) are delicious pasta choices; so are such entrees as *paillard*—a veal steak; and the roast veal as well. You may buy the little brown jugs in which the house Frascati is served. In warm weather, sit on the terrace for vistas of the earlier-recommended Church of Sant' Agnese in Agone and a masterful Bernini fountain. *Moderate.*

Da Necci (Piazza dell'Oratorio 50) is a typically old-fashioned, typically Roman place; a brick fireplace dominates its arched, stuccoed interior. In summer, dinner on the piazza is indicated. Food is

unexceptional but generally tasty; pastas are nicely sauced, and the
veal dishes—especially veal with peppers—are good bets. Delightful
service. *Moderate.*

Passetto (Via Zanardelli 14) is a rather smart old-timer that has,
happily, never gone out of fashion. You enter on Via Zanardelli,
but if it's summer aim for a table at the rear on the covered terrace
overlooking Piazza Sant'Appolinaire. *Spaghetti all' amatriciana*, made
here with bacon, tomato, and white wine, is a specialty. So is the
tacchina novellia con cipolline—a turkey dish. *Abbacchio d'Abruzzi*
is tasty baby-lamb. *Expensive.*

Piccadilly (Via Barberini at Piazza Barberini) is something of a confusion in images, with that Anglo name, a late-hours pizzeria section,
still another area with a counter-restaurant, a self-service cafeteria as
well; drinks, too. And surely as many Italian as English-speaking
customers. Open very late and convenient when one is on the run,
or alone, or both. *Inexpensive.*

Piccolo Mondo (Via Aurora 39), just off Via Vittorio Veneto, is
no-nonsense delicious. *Tortellini* is the house pasta specialty. So are
veal scaloppine and spaghetti with clam sauce. The roast lamb is
super. In summer you lunch or dine under a canopy on the sidewalk;
it's a pleasure. *Moderate.*

Piperno (Monte Cenci 9) was established in the mid-nineteenth
century by one Pacifico Piperno, on a mini-square near a Renaissance palace. The area, long the core of the Roman ghetto, is also the
site of eight-century-old San Tommaso Church. There is, in other
words, no lack of atmosphere, as regards setting. Food specialties include Roman-Jewish *carcioffi alla giuda*—artichokes Jewish-style,
deep fried in batter, crispy, crunchy, and delicious; one may sub-
stitute zucchini or order a platter of several deep-fried vegetables.
Abbacchio al forno—roast jumbo chunks of baby lamb—is tasty; so
are *gnochetti alla piperno*—potato dumplings in a delicate tomato
sauce; and *angnolotti di vitello ripassati*—a sort of ravioli stuffed with
minced veal. Super service. And a summer meal on the terrace, with
the façades of San Tommaso and Palazzo Cenci as backgrounds,
is a treat. *Moderate.*

Le Rallye (Grand Hotel, Via Vittorio Emanuele Orlando 3) is the elegance of Rome—Europe's most elegant capital—compressed into a single restaurant. Stop first for a drink—this is the spot to indulge in homesickness for a dry martini in the small adjacent cocktail lounge. The meal can be as genuinely international or as authentically Italian as one wishes. Grills—steaks, roasts, fish, chicken—are first rate. But so are more typical meat preparations, like *saltimbocca alla romana,* veal *piccata, abbacchio alla romana.* Pasta is available in quite the profusion of the same hotel's Le Maschere Restaurant, where chefs pride themselves on nearly twoscore varieties—*trenette al pesto, carbonara, pansoti al latte di Noci,* perhaps the most special of the lot. At meal's end, ask to have the dessert trolley wheeled over. Service? As impeccable as is to be found in Rome. *Expensive.*

Ranieri (Via Mario dei Fiori 26) is a step from Via Condotti, near the Spanish Steps. It's another old-timer—smallish, intimate, and with a history that goes back to the middle of the last century. The place is named for a onetime chef of Queen Victoria who took over the restaurant only after his subsequent employer, Queen Carlotta of Mexico, lost her husband to a firing squad—and her own reason. The *cannelloni all'casalinga*—the house's own—is four-star; so is the veal dish called *costoletta di vitello all'imperiale,* and the chicken, Massimiliano style. *Torta deliziosa,* a cake enveloped with chocolate cream and bitter chocolate shavings, is indeed *deliziosa. Expensive.*

Sabatini (Vicolo di Santa Maria in Trastevere 18) is a Trastevere landmark, facing the Church of Santa Maria in Trastevere, on its broad piazza. The look is substantial—natural brick walls supporting venerable beamed ceilings. What one wants to order here is the seafood; fish as fresh as is to be found in Rome, and it's delicious simply grilled, preceded by soup or a pasta, and followed with a crumbly chunk of Parmesan cheese. Agreeable service. *Moderate.*

El Toula (Via della Lupa 29) is a good looker with a nice sense of style and fare mostly emanating from the Veneto region of the north. Which means that this is a good source of *risotto,* to mention but one tasty possibility. *Expensive.*

31 al Vicario (Via Uffici del Vicario 31) has one of the handsomest restaurant interiors in town; one lunches or dines in any one of a

number of modish gray-walled rooms, each hung with good contemporary paintings, one with a bar. Everything tastes good: *minestrone* or *tortellini* to start; *fegato*—liver—of veal, or *petti do polla
alla vodka*—a chicken-breast triumph—to follow. Elaborate desserts.
Cool but correct service. *Moderate* if you're careful; otherwise
expensive.

Rome: To Buy

Of course bargains are to be had, in Rome as in other great world
shopping centers. But the point for the shopper to bear in mind is that
this is the most stylish of all the European capitals, where one seeks
smartness, quality and design. And finds it.

Here are some personally scouted shops in those categories at
which Rome excels. The order is alphabetical, for the various
categories, and for shops within each.

ANTIQUES

Unless you know old things, it is not a bad idea to make the rounds
with someone who does, for there are many ingeniously executed
copies of Italian antique furniture, not to mention paintings; Italians
are extraordinarily skilled in these areas. Have whatever you buy
authenticated by means of a written notation from the seller. (You
will want this for U.S. customs, in any event, to qualify your purchase of anything more than a century old, for duty-exemption.) No
matter how fancy the shop, it is always wise to ask if the price quoted
is indeed the final price. It also pays to ask questions about age,
origin, workmanship, and the like. Good dealers are glad to answer,
and you learn a lot in the process. Main antiques shopping areas are
Via del Babuino, Via Giulia, Via Margutta, and Via dei Coronari—this
last mostly with English and French eighteenth-century wares rather
than with Italian things.

Antichità la Colonna (Via dei Coronari 17): Mostly mid-nineteenth-
century French and English objects, with some old paintings.

Antiquaria (Corso Vittorio Emanuele 141) deals in eighteenth-century Italian furniture, paintings, and *boiseries*—antique wood paneling.

Antiquitas di Nepi (Via del Babuino 87) sells fine old oriental rugs and very good antique paintings.

Alberto di Castro e Figlio Franco (Via del Babuino 102) is top-drawer for furniture and paintings, much of it eighteenth century.

Il Cenacolo (Via dei Coronari 190) specializes in Renaissance carved and gilded pieces and fragments; paintings, too.

Enzo Costantino (Via del Babuino 89a)—exceptional antique paintings.

Fallani (Via del Babuino 58a) specializes in ancient Roman and Greek coins, and Italian medieval coins, too; objects of archaeological interest as well.

Flea Market. Rome's flea market is a Sunday-morning institution, at Porta Portese, between Viale Trastevere and the Tiber River. It is almost frighteningly immense to the first-timer. Ideally, one has several hours to spare and is prepared to wade through masses of junk and lots of new merchandise including clothing, to find the occasional antique. Used objects—some not yet elderly, some antique—can be fashioned of any number of materials—glass to mahogany, semiprecious stones to silver. The order of the day is no-nonsense bargaining.

Gasparini (Via Fontanella di Borghese 56) is known for old paintings, tapestry, and furniture.

E. Gelardini (Via del Babuino 114) is small but generally with choice furniture and paintings, mostly Italian.

Old London (Piazza di Campo Marzio) is an amusing source of elderly things and doodads, mostly nineteenth-century English, on into Art Nouveau.

Olivo (Via del Babuino 136) is for mostly eighteenth-century furniture (small-scale pieces) and fine paintings.

Il Pozzo (Via dei Coronari 180) vends stylish furniture—Italian eighteenth and nineteenth century mostly.

Marcello & Carlo Sestieri (Piazza di Spagna 81) specialize in antique decorative objects and paintings.

V. & L. Veneziana (Via Frattina 16) are for Italian faïence and other antiques.

BOOKS

Libreria Rizzoli (Largo Chigi, off Piazza Colonna) is the very same that New Yorkers know from a smart Fifth Avenue outlet. The Largo Chigi store is enormous, and with big selections of art books, which the Italians print beautifully; good prices.

CHILDREN'S CLOTHES

La Cicogna (Via Frattina 136) is full of good-looking duds for small fry.

Leri-Baby (Via Barberini 50 and Piazza Colonna) has appealing baby and infant wear. Expensive.

Ida Simonelli (Via Sistina 31) sells what are perhaps the most imaginative kids' togs in town.

CHINA AND GLASS

Dom (Via Condotti 73): stylish selections, also in Milan.

Richard Ginori (Via del Tritone 177 and branches) is Italy's leading designer-manufacturer of porcelain and dates to the eighteenth century. Quality is first rate, and designs—especially those that go back a century or two—can be lovely, with the variety tremendous, and prices lower than in the U.S. and abroad. Dinner services are the major specialty.

Venini (Via Condotti 59) is a retail outlet of an old-established Venetian glass house, with considerable style; steep-tabbed except for some kicky little gifts—paperweights, ashtrays, and the like.

Arte 70 (Via Sistina 19) is smart Italian Modern—plastics, china, pottery, housewares. Expensive.

DEPARTMENT STORES

Italians have never quite accepted department stores, at least as anything other than sources of relatively inexpensive merchandise. This concept is changing in progressive Milan more than in Rome. But one must not expect anything like London's Harrods or Paris's Galleries Lafayette.

La Rinascente, especially in its principal store on Piazza Colonna, is the smartest of the department stores, occupying several levels. Depending on when you're there, there may be bargains in clothing and accessories—men's, women's, and children's—as well as in housewares.

CIM's main outlet is a big building on Via XX Settembre. The merchandise level is budgety, but the basement is interesting because of its china department and an excellent supermarket with a wine section; a good place to stock up on drinks and nibblies for your hotel room or train rides. Ask for the store's own gratis map of Rome.

UPIM and **Standa** are other inexpensive department store chains, with stores all over town.

FOODSTUFFS

CIM (Via XX Settembre) is a department store with a top-notch basement supermarket. (See above.)

Perugina (Via Condotti, other locations) is a celebrated Perugia candymaker whose wares—particularly the chewy chocolate-almond *bacci,* or kisses—you see all around the world, including in their own New York shop. The packaging is as noteworthy as the contents.

Alemagna (Via del Corso at Piazza Colonna) is recommended as a restaurant-caffè-*gelateria* on an earlier page, and is here called to your attention as a take-away source of chocolate, baked goods, and all manner of perfectly delicious comestibles.

Street markets are a joy of Rome, as of all Italy. Here are several that I defy you to walk away from without making a delicious purchase, or two or three. *Mercato Rionale* occupies the vast square called Campo dei Fiori—super fruits and vegetables, as well as fresh-caught fish and other items of interest. An ideal place to study the ingredients of the Italian table. *Piazza San Cisimato* is a people-packed, food-filled Trastevere market—lots of fun. Still another open market is that on *Via della Pace,* near Piazza Navona.

GLOVES

Italian gloves remain good buys and perfect gifts; they're invariably beautifully made. Good sources include:

Anticoli (Via Barberini 70)

Gloves (Via Barberini 78)

The Glove Shop (Via Vittorio Veneto 106)

Amedeo Perrone (Piazza di Spagna 92, with a Cavalieri Hilton branch)

HANDICRAFTS

Bella Copia (Via dei Coronari 8): Leave it to a clever Rome-based American couple—Mr. and Mrs. Kellogg Smith, ex-Cleveland *Press* —to step in to fill the gap in this area. Rome had needed a quality retail source of Italy's superb handicrafts, and Bella Copia is it: pottery, textiles, woodwork, from all regions of the republic. And with charm and style.

JEWELRY AND SILVER

Mario Buccellati (Via Condotti 30), which has a Fifth Avenue outlet in New York, specializes in hammered Florentine-style silver—heavy, ornate, and often handsome; old pieces and gold jewelry, as well. Expensive.

Bulgari (Via Condotti 10) has a New York outlet; high-style jewelry fashioned of gold, silver, platinum, and precious stones. Expensive.

Menichini (Piazza di Spagna at Via del Babuino) is an old-timer vending jewelry—much of it handsome—watches, and silverware.

LEATHER AND LUGGAGE

Ceresa (Via del Tritone 117) is a good source of luggage and leather accessories in Gucci-style designs but with lower prices; suede men's and women's coats, too.

Val Corso (Via del Corso 151) is for well-priced leatherware, luggage and otherwise.

Gucci (Via Condotti 8 and a branch in the Cavalieri Hilton) conveys the impression, from the hordes of Italian, American, and Japanese customers, that it's giving its merchandise away. Far from it. But the style and quality make people want to buy, buy, buy—baggage, wallets, briefcases, shoes (both men's and women's), women's handbags. Prices are lower than in the U.S. outlets. Stocks may vary among the Rome, Florence, and Milan branches, so that if you see a bauble at the Rome Gucci's that you really covet, buy it there; it may not be in stock at the other stores.

Gherardini (Via Bocca di Leone—and also in Milan and Florence) is a very smart source of leather—luggage, handbags, briefcases, wallets.

Leandro (Via Sistina 21): high style, and with leather coats.

Metius (Via del Tritone 195) has attractively styled and priced luggage and handbags.

Righini (Via Condotti): well-done Gucci-style luggage and accessories.

LINENS AND EMBROIDERY

Emilia Bellini (Via Condotti 77) has linens of surpassing beauty; a Florentine firm.

Mamma Galassi (Via Condotti) has big stocks, good quality.

Pratesi (Piazza di Spagna) has a Madison Avenue branch in New York; its bed linens are contemporary high style and expensive.

MEN'S CLOTHES AND ACCESSORIES

In a word: Europe's smartest. Herewith, a sampling of sources.

Angelo (Piazza della Trinità dei Monti): elegance plus.

Comandini (Via Frattina 83) is for imaginative ties and accessories.

Cucci (Via Condotti)—that's spelled with a capital C—is a conservative haberdasher with emphasis on quality things that last.

G. Battistoni (Via Condotti 61a—through courtyard) is at once a source of exceptionally good-looking clothes and leatherware, too. Made-to-order suits are a specialty; they can be made up in less than a week for rushed customers.

Emilio (Via dei Crociferi 30, near Fontana di Trevi) is for high-style furnishings, including nifty swimsuits.

Fabio (Via Sicilia 14) has gorgeous albeit expensive ties.

Ibbas (Via Barberini 16) is for conservative, custom-made shirts of impeccable quality.

Piatelli (Vias Condotti, del Corso, Nazionale) is a fine tie source but—as has long been the case with Italian ties—they look better than they tie.

Prisma (Via del Corso at Piazza Colonna) is for shirts, sport and dress; good prices.

Rudy (Via del Corso 10, at Piazza del Popolo) has interesting men's accessories.

Fabrizio Runci (Via Condotti 93) is a handsome shop with equally handsome clothes.

Angelo Sermonetti (Via Frattina): very smart suits, custom made overnight if you're in that much of a hurry.

Spagnoli for Men (Via Barberini 84): Luisa Spagnoli women's shops blanket Italy. This Spagnoli shop, though, for men only and with stylish clothes and accessories, is noteworthy.

Stuart (Via del Babuino 105) is small but the shirts, ties, belts, and other accessories are choice.

Testa (Via Frattina 87): offbeat, inventive resort and casual duds.

Uomo (Via Frattina 91): an exceptionally mod-look shop with exceptionally mod-look merchandise.

Valentini (Via Frattina 110): in a word, elegant.

PAINTINGS

Alinari (Via del Babuino 98): posters and graphics, new and old.

Antiquaria Romana (Via del Babuino 90): eighteenth-century paintings are a specialty.

Eugenio di Castro (Via del Babuino 92a-b): antique paintings of considerable quality.

Galleria Russo (Piazza di Spagna 1): contemporary paintings, mostly Italian.

La Vetrina (Via del Babuino 97): contemporary paintings, mostly Italian.

PRINTS AND ETCHINGS

Olga Bruno (Via del Governo Vecchio 38): lovely old and rare books, venerable engravings, fascinating maps; a treasure trove in an area full of very explorable shops vending antique prints and paintings.

Plinio Narcecchia (Piazza Navona 25) is a maze of good etchings, many with considerable age. Fun for browsing.

Slam (Via del Babuino 153) may not sound like a print shop, but it is—and a good one.

RELIGIOUS ARTICLES

Via della Conciliazione—a street, not a shop—leads from the Tiber to St. Peter's and is Religious Goods Row with one shop after another full of this kind of merchandise, with little discernible difference, one from the other, at least to an inexpert eye.

Lelli Garey (Piazza Farnese 104) is an Italian with an English husband, and her shop is patronized by English-speaking visitors from both sides of the Atlantic; she is experienced in shipping to the United States and Canada.

SHOES

It is possible to get stung on Italian shoes, their global reputation for quality notwithstanding. And prices are no longer so appealing that one must feel constrained to buy a pair while in the country of origin. As for design, there are none smarter.

Michele di Ceglie (Via Sistina 93) himself makes beautiful handmade shoes for both men and women.

Salvatore Ferragamo (Via Condotti) is noted, with good reason, for his high-style women's shoes; in New York, too.

Fragiacomo (Via Condotti) sells both men's and women's moderate-priced shoes and sandals; branches in other Italian cities.

Gucci (Via Condotti) is earlier recommended for leather goods and luggage. Shoes based on the brass-bit design that is the firm's trademark are a major Gucci manufacture, too—for both men and women. Cheaper than in the U.S. but still expensive.

Mariam's (Via del Gambero 12) is a good source for good-looking, moderate-priced women's shoes.

Nickol (Via Barberini 32): very stylish men's and women's shoes and boots; medium-priced.

Raphael (Via Vittorio Veneto at Via Sicilia) has smart men's and women's shoes at reasonable tabs, and by well-known makers.

Saddlers' Union (Via Condotti 26): handmade, costly, and beautiful.

TASSELS AND FRINGE

Giuseppe Mici (Via Frattina 57a) is a long-time leader in this centuries-old Italian specialty.

WOMEN'S CLOTHES AND ACCESSORIES

Batilocchi (Via Sistina) is a source of smart boutique clothes and costume jewelry.

Eleanora Garnett (Via Sistina) is still selling her own quiet but lovely and costly clothes.

Filippo (Via Condotti): modish, original designs for both women and men.

Max Mara (Via Frattina 28): very high-style clothes and accessories.

Mila Schön (Via Condotti, near Caffè Greco) is one of Italy's top couturiers; here she sells her own very individual designs; accessories, too.

Pannani (Via Sistina): an amusing, camp boutique.

Roberta di Camerino (Piazza di Spagna): Rome outlet of this Venetian firm—smart clothes and accessories; also in New York.

Rome Alta Moda—the seasonal *alta moda* fashion showings of the industry, for clothing buyers and fashion press; information from Camera Nazionale della Moda Italiana, Via Panama 26, 00198 Roma, Italy.

Schubert (Via Condotti) is at once conservative and elegant.

Valentino (Via di Bocca di Leone, in Hotel Inghilterra)—bold and *alta moda*.

WOMEN'S HANDBAGS

Frattegiani (Via Sistina 50): very smart bags, and shoes as well.

Pova (Via Frattina 64): an always reliable collection of up-to-the-minute bags.

Rome: To Note

Access. *Air.* There is daily air service from points throughout Europe and Italy, as well as from the United States and Canada, via Alitalia, Italy's international carrier; Alitalia flies from New York, Boston, Toronto, and Montreal. TWA and Pan American fly from New York; CP Air flies from Toronto and Montreal. Leonardo da Vinci International Airport at Fiumicino—twenty-two miles from town—is best reached by cheap airport buses; note that it does *not* have duty-free shops, although there are gift shops with Italian goods. Ciampino, the older, smaller airport, is used for certain shorter flights.
Rail: Stazione Termini, the main station, is so outstanding architecturally that it is accorded space on an earlier page. It is at once central, attractive, and functional. As for trains, one is advised to

travel first class on the major, crack, very-best-available expresses in and out of Rome, *always booking seats in advance—or risk standing, even in first class*. Porters usually meet trains on platforms: note their number, meet them inside, and tip the current set fee. Concierges and travel agencies can make advance bookings. To do it yourself, go to Stazione Termini, and descend to the basement to the large room labeled *Pre Notázioni*—and in summer, blessedly air conditioned, unlike the rest of the station. Clerks with airline-style computers and some command of foreign languages will take care of you.

Driving into and out of Rome is not the problem that driving *within* the traffic-clogged city presents; there are modern *autostrade,* the north-south Highway of the Sun in particular. There are good long-distance *bus* services, including that of the Italians' own CIAT, which combine sightseeing with getting there.

Getting About. Within Rome, *taxis* are metered and plentiful, except, of course, at rush hours, when they can be extremely rare; fares are low, but it is rare that one can take a ride without being soaked for some extra or other; there are extras for baggage, extras for being summoned by phone (Telephone 117), extras for riding after the wickedly late hour of 10 P.M., extras for traveling on holidays, extras for airport rides to cover the driver's journey back to town. And inevitable screaming if the tip does not appear adequate. Which it usually doesn't. The *subway,* grandly called the *Metropolitana,* is actually a rather modest proposition—a one-line railway that runs on a north-south direction between Stazione Termini in town, to Ostia-Antica and Ostia-Lido (earlier described) with intermediate stops including Via Cavour, the Colosseum, Porta San Paolo (St. Paul's Outside the Walls) and the E.U.R.

Buses. There is an extensive public bus system; touristically popular routes include No. 33, which goes to places like the Olympic Village, Stazione Termini, and Basilica Santa Maria Maggiore; No. 4, which takes in Basilica San Giovanni in Laterano; No. 32, which includes Foro Romano; No. 60, which covers the core of central Rome; No. 75, which includes the Trastevere quarter; and No. 118, which goes out the Appian Way via the Baths of Caracalla and Colosseum to the Catacombs of St. Calixtus (earlier recommended).

Sightseeing. The species of bus tour, both local and to points throughout Italy, is virtually limitless, from a half-day or Rome-by-night, in town, to destinations north and south—some of them too distant for comfort in the time allotted.

Currency. The lira, for some years, has been in inexplicably short supply as regards small-denomination notes and coins. For as long as this disagreeable situation exists, count on being given postage stamps or even hard candies for change and, in some instances, being told the transaction you desire to undertake—like buying a museum ticket—cannot be completed, there being no change for the bill you present. Best exchange rates are obtainable at the exchange departments of banks, and at commercial *cambios*—change-making firms; it is essential that one have one's passport along. Hotels always change money, at lesser rates.

Climate. The summer can extend into mid-autumn, on occasion—by that I mean October. Have plenty of warm-weather togs along, and worry not about dressing formally on daytime sightseeing excursions; the point is to keep as cool as possible, there being not all that much air-conditioning. Autumn (late October and November) and spring (April and May) are mild and can be beautiful, with high-fifties and low-sixties temperatures. Winter—December through February—sees days in the forties; March is low-fifties; summer is at its hottest and most humid in July and August, when every Roman who can clears out; June is the preferred summer visiting time; the locals are still on hand, and the city retains an air of normalcy.

Clothes. Roman clothes sense, both male and female, is unequaled. This is the best-dressed capital in Europe. Be as informal as you like during the day, but dressy—at least in the better places, and when the weather is not too hot or humid—after dark.

Tipping. One has the feeling that this is where it all began and where it will never end; keep pockets full of change handy at all hours. (At least when it's available—see Currency above.) Although restaurants add a 15 per cent service charge, waiters expect 5 per cent—or so—in addition. Hotel bellhops expect 100 lire per bag (150 lire to station baggage porters); chambermaids look forward to a daily tip, but it's not necessary if they do nothing special for you. Likewise, room service. Hotel concierges should be tipped a few hundred lire a day but only if they have been of special service. Washroom ladies—they are inescapable—get 50 lire ransom; bootblacks the same. I could go on, but suffice it to say that taxi drivers get 15 per cent of the metered fare—and invariably complain that it's not enough.

Business Hours. Shops open at 9 to 9:30 A.M., close at about 1 P.M., and reopen from 4 to 7 P.M. in winter, and from 4:30 to 8 P.M. in summer; these are Monday–Saturday hours. Hairdressers and barbers generally shutter Mondays. Museum hours, in recent years, have been considerably curtailed; keep your fingers crossed that they will improve; generally, it is the Italian Government-operated museums that have the shortest hours; Rome being the capital, the proportion of such museums is higher than in other cities.

Local Literature. Though they often tuck it away, hotel concierges usually have a gratis supply of *This Week in Rome,* with up-to-the-minute open hours of museums, opera and concert schedules and other current intelligence. The well-edited, locally published English-language *Daily American* is a visitor requisite. And don't let language difficulties keep you from perusal of such dailies as *La Stampa, Il Giornale d'Italia,* and *Il Messaggero,* not to mention the Vatican's *Osservatore Romano.*

Non-Catholic Places of Worship include the *American Episcopal Church* (Via Nazionale at Via Napoli), *Church of England* (Via del Babuino 153), *Church of Scotland* (Presbyterian) (Via XX Settembre 7), *Methodist* (Via Firenze), *Baptist* (Via del Teatro Valle); *Society of Friends* (Via Napoli), *Russian Orthodox* (Via Palestro 71); and *Jewish* (Great Synagogue, Lungotevere Cenci). Catholic churches operated by American and other English-speaking priests are recommended in earlier pages; these include *Santa Susanna* (Via XX Settembre), *San Clemente* (Piazza di San Clemente), and *San Silvestro in Capità* (Piazza San Silvestro in Capità).

Further Information. Commune of Rome Tourist Council, Piazza Campitelli 7; information offices of Ente Provinciale per il Turismo at Stazione Termini and Aeroporto Leonardo da Vinci at Fiumicino.

II

Florence

Florence: To Know

Florence rates an E for Effortless. In no other major Italian city is it as easy to achieve a satisfying holiday. If there is a city without a touristic enemy, it has to be Florence. Even Italians from other cities —who do not easily enthuse about towns not their own—become misty-eyed about Florence. The French have not forgotten that Catherine de Médicis took chefs with her when she went to become Henry II's bride, thereby laying the groundwork for the estimable French cuisine. The English remember that Florence was Destination No. 1 on the eighteenth-century Grand Tour. (One reason was that its hotels were the cleanest.) Germans, who do more intensive holiday homework than all the rest of us combined, have every Pitti Palace painting committed to memory before they step off the train. Scandinavians, pushovers for all things Italian, are at their most vulnerable in Florence. As for Americans, we have been enthusiasts, if not for as long as the English, with quite as much intensity.

Several factors contribute to the sense of well-being that one feels almost upon arrival. Size, first. Even though it's bigger in area than many of us allow ourselves to discover, it doesn't *seem* big. The scale is intimate. We feel that we can come to grips with this city without strain, rarely finding the need to get about other than on foot. Efficiency is another factor. Florentines are nothing if not well educated and organized, and at ease with foreigners. Things *work,* and without the confusion and near-hysteria that can be a part of the process when one heads south. Then we get to the final factor: content. And all of the romance and beauty of the past come into full play.

A jumble of names evoke the splendor of Florence: Medici dukes and even Medici popes, historic figures like Savonarola and Machiavelli, bankers like the Strozzi and Ricardi families, artists like Giotto, Fra Angelico, Leonardo, Michelangelo, Raphael, Lippi, Botticelli; sculptors like Donatello and Cellini; writers like Dante and Boccaccio; architects like Brunelleschi and Michelozzo.

But Florence had a quite respectable history even before it gave birth to the Renaissance. We need only travel up to the still beautiful village of Fiesole, high on a mini-mountain overlooking the city and the Arno, to appreciate how easy it is to visualize what had gone before.

It was in Fiesole that Florence had its beginnings. Early-bird Etruscans had established a settlement there, and eventually, as the years passed, some of their number descended the hill to the shore of the river and settled in. When the Romans headed north in the course of consolidating their empire, it was at the Etruscan settlement that they camped. Ere long the Arno village had become a town (their Forum was today's Piazza della Repubblica) with a name: *Florentia:* "destined to flourish."

And so it did. Christianity was widespread by the fifth century. (Its earliest missionary was the same San Miniato for whom a splendid Florence church is named.) Progress was interspersed with war and with invasion. Florence was to know Goths and Byzantines and Lombards before, in the twelfth century, it became a sovereign state, or commune, ripe for thirteenth-century emergence into the alliterative albeit confusing era of Guelphs and Ghibellines—antagonists who fought for control of the city. Which was which? The Guelphs (with the shorter name) were papists and the more democratic of the two groups, while the Ghibellines (with the longer name) were on the side of the longer-titled Holy Roman Emperor. Matters became more complex when the victorious Guelphs split into Black and White factions (with the Blacks, among other things, expelling Dante because he was White). All this transpired while the merchants and bankers and manufacturers' guilds thrived, enriching the city with their skills and their sought-after tapestries and silks.

There were losses (more than half the populace died in the fourteenth-century Black Death) and gains (Florence warred with and won control of cities like Pisa and Arezzo). Eventually it took the form of a republic, in which a remarkable family called Medici achieved power. The time was the fifteenth century (the Century of the Medici, as it came to be known) and the first major Medici was Cosimo the Elder. He set clan precedent, and the best of the Medici succeeding him were, like himself, strong-willed, dictatorial, and at the same time dedicated and knowledgeable patrons of the arts. After Cosimo the Elder in importance came his grandson, Lorenzo the Magnificent. (Nothing in Florence illustrates better the role of the Medici in the history and culture of the city than the family tombs in the Michelangelo-designed Medici Chapel, a part of the San Lorenzo Church complex. The Medici were much painted, too; Bronzino painted Cosimo the Elder, on view in the Medici-Riccardi Palace; Lorenzo the Magnificent appears both in a Bronzino portrait and as a youth in a fresco by Benozzo Gozzoli, in the same palace.)

The Renaissance, after its emergence under Lorenzo, continued for two brilliant Florentine centuries. Which did not preclude political turbulence. Lorenzo put down a plot hatched by Pope Sixtus IV and the family was expelled during the rule of his son Piero, to be succeeded for four years by Savonarola, the fanatic priest who got himself into such trouble with his anticorruption, antiworldliness campaign that he was hanged as a heretic.

The Medici made a comeback, first as dukes of Florence, later as grand dukes of all Tuscany, until the last of the line died in the early eighteenth century. The House of Lorraine-Hapsburg took over (the Napoleonic era excepted) until Florence became not only an intrinsic part of the new United Kingdom of Italy in 1860, but, in 1865, its capital. Today's visitors may see the throne room in the State Apartments of the Pitti Palace, seat of the royal family until 1871, when it moved to Quirinale Palace—from which the popes were displaced—in Rome.

Florence: To See

LAY OF THE LAND

No major Italian city is easier to get about, and, more often than not, by foot. Good maps are easy to come by. Even restaurants frequently give them away, as a convenience for customers. Best is that issued by Azienda Autonoma di Turismo, not only because it is clear and easy to read, but because it has an Index to Streets, so that when you're looking for an unfamiliar street, you can locate it on the map by first noting its situation from the Index.

Major landmark is the Arno River. But, unlike many cities which are nearly bisected by the river flowing through them, the great bulk of Florence is on a single bank—the north (or "right") side of the Arno. Eight bridges span the river, from *Ponte della Vittoria,* at Piazza Vittorio Veneto on the west, to *Ponte da Verrazzano* at Via Francesco di Sanctis on the east. Of these, ancient *Ponte Vecchio* is at once the most picturesque, easiest to distinguish, most central and most tourist-traversed, although its neighbor to the west, *Ponte Santa Trinità,* is worth knowing about too.

The heart of town has three principal squares. *Piazza Duomo* is easily remembered, with the dome of the cathedral, the slim silhouette of its campanile, and the octagonal baptistry. One may walk south from it, along Via dei Calzaiuoli to Via Speziala, and then head west to *Piazza della Repubblica,* the principal commercial square, surrounded by caffès and shops and leading, by Via Strozzi, to *Via Tornabuoni,* the principal shopping street.

Returning by Piazza della Repubblica to Via dei Calzaiuoli, one may proceed south, a few blocks, to historic *Piazza della Signoria,* whose major landmark is venerable pinnacle-towered *Palazzo Vecchio,* and the detached structure known as *Loggia della Signoria,* with an open triple-arched façade leading to priceless sculptures within. Piazza della Signoria is the near northern neighbor of the horseshoe-shaped *Uffizi Gallery.* From Piazza della Signoria one may walk only a couple of blocks east on Via dell'Anguillara and be at *Piazza Santa Croce,* and the major church for which it is named.

Return to the Uffizi Gallery. From it one is almost upon shop-lined Ponte Vecchio, over the Arno. Cross the bridge, follow Via Guicciardini, and in a few moments you've arrived at *Pitti Palace,* housing several museums and State Apartments as well, and overlooking *Giardini di Boboli,* formal gardens that constitute Florence's finest park. To the east lies elevated *Piazzale Michelangelo,* affording fine views of the city; due south of the piazzale is the important *Church of San Miniato.* Other important left bank churches—to the west and close to the river—are *Santo Spirito* and *Carmine.*

Back on the right bank, it is perhaps worth pointing out that from the central area it is a pleasant walk to any number of other important destinations. Walk north on Via del Servi, from Piazza del Duomo, to reach *Piazza Annunziata* and the church it takes its name from, and nearby *Piazza San Marco,* with the *Church and Museum of San Marco* and neighboring *Galleria dell'Accademia.* Walk due west from Piazza del Duomo, on Via de' Pecor, Via d'Agli, and Via Trebbio (one leading into the other) and within a few minutes *Piazza Santa Maria Novella*—and the major church for which it is named—is reached, with *Piazza della Stazione,* and the railway terminal, *Stazione di Santa Maria Novella,* just behind the church, to the north.

The Arno is lined on both banks with streets whose first names are Lungarno, and whose second names change as one moves along. Take the right bank Lungarno west to Via Magenta—a pleasant fifteen-minute walk—and one has arrived at *Teatro Comunale,* Florence's opera house.

THE ESSENTIAL FLORENCE

The Duomo Complex is not without surprises. It is at once medieval Florence (work began on the Duomo, or cathedral, near the end of the thirteenth century) and, if one might use the term in Italy, Victorian; the façade is third-quarter nineteenth century, undertaken while Florence was the first capital of the united Kingdom of Italy, and finished just after it lost that honor to Rome. No less a luminary than the painter Giotto was one of the building's early designers. The intricately worked dark and light marble design is joyous and eye-catching, and the adjacent campanile, or bell tower, is quite as elegant as befits a Giotto work. But it is the dome, the overscaled 351-foot-high Brunelleschi-designed dome that is the Duomo's glory. Inside, the building is gloomily anticlimactic if one excepts most especially a Michelangelo *Pietà* infinitely more moving, to at least one appraiser, than his *Pietà* in Rome's St. Peter's. Move over, then, to the octagonal Baptistry—well over a millennium in age, and Florence's cathedral before its neighbor. It is not always easy when there are groups of observers, but try to tarry at the trio of bronze doors before entering. They constitute a major Florentine treasure, are fourteenth and fifteenth century, with the choicest the East, or Paradise, Door; its ten exquisite panels depict Old Testament stories and took their creator—a sculptor named Lorenzo Ghiberti, who also worked in gold—more than a quarter century to complete for his sponsors, the Florentine Arte dei Mercanti, a merchants' guild. But there's more: a brilliant mosaic Christ embellishing the dome within.

Palazzo Vecchio and Ponte Vecchio. The Duomo group constitutes ecclesiastical Florence of old. This pair of landmarks are the secular city much as it was in the Middle Ages. The silhouette of Palazzo Vecchio—a slender pinnacle of a tower jutting upward from a crenelated stone box—is in itself evocative. Within, this onetime Medici residence and seat of government embodies the lavishness of the Renaissance, with its Salone dei Cinquecento. Leonardo and Michelangelo were among its planners. It is not only the biggest room in town (72 by 174 feet) but, more important, it's the most ravishing, originally for citizens' meetings in Savonarola's time, later for balls, today for awestruck rubberneckers. Nearly twoscore ceiling frescoes—each framed in gold—depict Florence's history. So do the jumbo frescoes on the walls. And there is a startling Michelangelo sculpture called *Victory*. Ponte Vecchio is indeed an old bridge, originally eleventh century, and rebuilt a couple of hundred years later. Since the seventeenth century, the unusually designed shops that have always lined its lanes have been mostly those of dealers in gold, silver, and jewels. It is over the Vecchio that we still find a corridor connecting the Uffizi and Pitti palaces, dating back centuries, when it was devised as an escape route for palace occupants wanting to get from one palace to the other in an emergency.

Four Great Museums: Bargello, Uffizi, Pitti, San Marco. If *Museo Nazionale Bargello* (Via del Proconsolo) is not the most internationally reputed of Florence museums, it is the most evocative of the grandeur of the medieval city. That is why I lead off with it. Formidable from without, with a single corner tower and lovely Gothic windows, it is somberly grand within and, as would befit a long-time police chief's palace, with prisoners' cells. A vaulted downstairs hall opens into an arcaded courtyard whose uncovered stone stairwell leads to upper chambers. Exhibits are eye-popping, most especially the sculptures by Donatello (this is where one sees his bronze *David*), Michelangelo (a *David,* of his, too), a bronze *Mercury* by Giambologna, lovely Della Robbias, and among much else a frescoed chapel with its treasure the death mask of Florence-born Dante.

The river-front *Uffizi Gallery* (Piazzale degli Uffizi) takes its name from the building it occupies—a U-shaped stunner that went up in the sixteenth century at the behest of Cosimo I—the Medici grand duke of the moment, who sensibly decreed that all government offices, or *uffizi,* be combined into a single headquarters, and that there be space, as well, for his works of art. And so began what is one of the world's finest art museums—with samplings of the whole range of Italian painting, Middle Ages through Renaissance. There are moving medieval masterworks—innovative Cimabue, Giotto with his pioneering interpretations of perspective, and on along the line—Uccello, Filippo Lippi (who was Botticelli's teacher), Botticelli himself (his *The Birth of Venus* is possibly the most reproduced of Uffizi paintings), Leonardo, the earlier-mentioned Vasari portrait of Lorenzo the Magnificent, Michelangelo's noted *The Holy Family,* a Raphael interpretation of one of the two Medici popes—Leo X, with a pair of cardinals; Titian's exquisite *Venus of Urbino.* You will stay a solid half day and want to return.

The *Pitti Palace* (Palazzo Pitti) is for me the most beautiful in town. It is just across Ponte Vecchio from the Uffizi, straddling the formal Boboli Gardens, and it shelters three museums, as well as the former Royal Apartments. The pity of the Pitti, in recent seasons at least, has been a budget that precludes keeping all of its component parts open at all times. Hardest to see are the Modern Art and Silver museums, and the Royal Apartments. But the most important, the Palatine Gallery of paintings, usually remains open when the others must be shuttered. I don't know of any other museum where art is displayed in a more opulent environment; one knock-'em-dead Renaissance reception room after another displays a collection that dates back to an initial group provided by Grand Duke Cosimo II (grandson of the Uffizi's Cosimo I). There are foreign stars here—a Murillo *Madonna and Child,* a Van Dyck cardinal, Rubens' *Four Philosophers,* a Velásquez (Philip IV on horseback). But the collection is mostly Italian Renaissance—Lippi, Raphael, Fra Bartolomeo, Titian, Perugino, many Del Sartos. Hopefully, you will be able to see the gold and ivory State Dining Room, the crimson Throne Room, the chapel with its paintings, in the Royal Apartments. And stroll past sculpture (the chubby *Bacchino* is Florence's answer to Brussels' *Mannequin Pis*), and the amphitheater of Boboli Gardens.

Museo di San Marco (Piazza San Marco), the last selection of my quartet, is the most moving experience of the lot, a purely Florentine adventure at once leading into the realms of architecture, religion, politics, and art. It is the only one-man show in town. It is a onetime monastery commissioned by no less eminent a Medici than

Cosimo the Elder. The designer was the prolific Michelozzo. The order was the Dominican, and the interior designer turned out to be a resident monk originally called Vicchio di Mugello, whose work earned him the name—never sanctioned by the church—of Blessed, or Beato, Angelico, which comes through to us in English, more often than not, as Fra Angelico. Adjacent to a church of the same name (see below), San Marco is first seen through Michelozzo's graceful cloister. One ascends, then, to the upper floor, and in cell after convent cell, including those inhabited by the fanatic Savonarola and, in the course of prayer retreats, Cosimo the Elder, there are Angelico masterworks—extraordinarily beautiful people, with the oddly gentle quality peculiar to Angelico, against a background of his lovely, luminous colors. The founder of his order, St. Dominic, has surely never been better portrayed. But there are so many more: *Annunciation, Transfiguration, Coronation of the Virgin, Flight into Egypt, The Last Supper;* our favorite Christmas cards, every one.

A Trio of Churches: Santa Croce, Santa Maria Novella, The San Lorenzo Complex. If Florence has a single most beloved church it is *Santa Croce,* the Franciscans' showplace (and the largest of their churches—anywhere) that is at once a place of worship, an art museum both in its sanctuary and in a separate building, and a burial ground of distinguished Italians. Friars have been on the scene since 1212 and are fond of pointing out that their church has known such visitors over the centuries as St. Francis and St. Anthony, several popes, and, as a student, one Dante Alighieri. Santa Croce is complicated and warrants a bit of geographic orientation. There is the church proper, and there is the adjacent convent area (entered from the right) which embraces both First and Second Cloisters. Pazzi Chapel and the church's art museum are in the former; the latter is a Brunelleschi-designed masterwork, where the friars live as they have for seven centuries. The church itself has one of the great Gothic interiors. Architecturally it is monument enough. But there are nearly three hundred tombs and cenotaphs. Michelangelo's tomb was designed by Vasari in the late sixteenth century, and pays tribute to his paintings, sculpture, and architecture. Donatello's sculpted *Annunciation* is one of his finest works. There is not one but a pair of chapels—the Bardi and the Peruzzi—decorated with Giotto frescoes. Still another chapel, the Pazzi, was designed by Brunelleschi, and its interior is a veritable gallery of Della Robbia ceramics. The museum has treasures by Cimabue, Giotto, Donatello, and Bronzino. And there is a leather-goods shop, with wares made by students of the church's leather school, that is one of the best in town.

Santa Maria Novella (Piazza Santa Maria Novella) is the Dominican counterpart of the Franciscans' Santa Croce: a Gothic monument—massive and magnificent—that also is a repository of art treasures. Like its Franciscan counterpart, it dates to the thirteenth century. The Strozzi Chapel—named for an important Florentine family—is resplendent with frescoes by Filippino Lippi. Still another chapel has Ghirlandaio frescoes, and there are masterful wooden crucifixes by both Giotto and Brunelleschi. Then come the Cloisters, operated—please note—as a municipal museum with precise open hours and an admission charge. Principal reason for one's visit is the Spanish Chapel—so called because the town's Spanish colony once used it as a place of worship—and a series of sumptuous murals believed to be the work of Andrea di Buonaiuto, in which the history of the Dominican order—black-and-white-robed friars appear throughout—is celebrated in infinite detail that requires considerable study.

The San Lorenzo Complex is triple-threat. First comes the church, off the piazza bearing its name, with an unfinished façade, apparently still awaiting the execution of Michelangelo's design for it. It's a Renaissance work by Brunelleschi, with a Michelangelo loggia, pulpit and other work by Donatello, a Bronzino fresco, and a Filippo Lippi *Annunciation* in its Martelli Chapel. Brunelleschi's domed Sacristy—designated as Old to contrast it with a later one later described—is in connection. Church and Old Sacristy inspected, one exits to the piazza, walks to its left, through a handsome cloister to a stair well that leads to the second major aspect of the complex: the *Laurentian Library,* designed by Michelangelo, who was also the creator of the beautiful stairway leading to it; I urge you to study the steps before you mount them—no one seems ever to have copied them. The library they lead to is a great oblong of a room, fitted with Michelangelo-created furnishings, and containing illuminated manuscripts and miniatures, some of which are always on display; it is one of the most exquisite and elegant of Florentine destinations, but is only the second of the San Lorenzo trio. Next come the *Medici Chapels,* requiring an exit without, and entrance from Piazza Madonna degli Aldobrandini. No single Florence destination more strikingly conveys the Medici power and the Medici connection with the arts. The Princes' Chapel, first visited, is a marble mausoleum with the tombs of half a dozen Medici rulers. From it one moves along to the New Sacristy (so-called to distinguish it from Brunelleschi's sacristy, attached to the church). In contrast to the ornate, multicolored marbles of the Princes' Chapel, it is restrained, neoclassic Michelangelo, with an uncompleted tomb and two completed tombs—one of Lorenzo de' Medici, Duke of Urbino (and Lorenzo the Magnificent's nephew) and the other of Giuliano de' Medici, Duke of Nemours, and a son of the Magnificent Lorenzo, each with statues of the deceased and allegorical sculpture surrounding. Give them some study.

A Drive to Fiesole. Older than Florence, and superseded by it as long ago as the Roman occupation, Fiesole—atop a little mountain a few miles northeast of town—makes for a diverting excursion. It can be taken in fairly comfortably of a sunny morning or afternoon. What one first wants to do is ascend the hill leading from its main square to a rest stop named for a stone visitors' bench—*la banchina*. The pause is as much for the spectacular view of Florence, way below, as to catch one's breath, before continuing farther upward, beyond the little Church of San Alessandro (really ancient, dating to the fifth century) to the Church of San Francesco, early Gothic, art-filled, with a honey of a cloister, even a little museum whose theme is the Franciscans' missionary activity in the Orient. Descend, then, all the way to the town's principal square, Piazza Mino da Fiesole. What one wants to inspect in this quarter is the remarkable Romanesque duomo—dating all the way back to the eleventh century; a surprise of an amphitheater that is an intact souvenir of the Roman era and adjacent to a little museum of local Roman artifacts; and Museo Bardino, a small but worthy repository of assorted local treasures, none great perhaps, but all with the patina of age. Pause, then, at Piazza Mino da Fiesole, for coffee or lunch—preferably on the terrace-cum-Florence-view of Hotel Aurora.

BEHIND MUSEUM WALLS:
A SELECTION OF FAVORITES

Galleria dell'Accademia (Via Ricasoli) is where one beelines to see the original of Michelangelo's great *David;* it had remained exposed to the elements in Piazza della Signoria for three and a half centuries when, in 1873, it was finally brought indoors and replaced in the square by a good copy. The original dazzles but so do the other Michelangelo sculptures on view, including a marvelous *Pietà,* this one designated Palestrina. There are paintings, too—including work by Botticelli, Lorenzo Monaco, Bernardo Daddi, even Raphael. Location is just across the piazza from Museo San Marco (above), so that it makes sense to take these two museums in on a single visit.

Museo Archeologico (Piazza Annunziata) is often neglected, especially by visitors who have experienced antiquity in strong and recent Roman and/or Neapolitan doses. Perhaps it is worth recounting that Florence, too, had been successively Etruscan and Roman. This museum has been headquartered for nearly a century in Palazzo Crocetta, which dates back to the Renaissance. There are literally scores of galleries devoted to Etruscan art and artifacts (only Museo Villa Giulia in Rome so graphically portrays the Etruscans), with a bonus an exceptional collection of ancient Egyptian works.

Museo Bardini (Piazza de' Mozzi) is a treat, first because it is housed in a beautiful sixteenth-century palace, with some remarkable ceilings. Then there are its contents: the bequest of a nineteenth-century antique dealer. Nothing is labeled, but no matter. There are paintings and portraits, furniture and fragments, a Della Robbia cluster of angels, a polychrome Virgin in red and white garb, an Archangel Michael in combat with a ferocious dragon, a gilded medieval crucifix. And very few visitors.

Museo Horne (Via de' Benci 6) is still another private collection in still another stunner of a palace. Mr. Horne was a turn-of-century English collector who restored this elegant fifteenth-century house and filled it with fine things—furniture and furnishings as well as paintings which include a Giotto of San Stefano, and works by Masaccio, Daddi, Filippino Lippi—to name some of the choicest. It is seeing the lot in the Horne house that makes the experience extra special.

Museo dell'Opera del Duomo (Piazza del Duomo) houses the cathedral's treasures. A Donatello sculpture of a ravaged *La Maddalena* is surely the single most exciting piece. But there are Byzantine mosaics, medieval paintings, a stone choir carved by Luca

Della Robbia, and sculptured saints that once graced the Duomo's campanile.

Museo Stibbert (Via Frederick Stibbert 26) is considerably away from the center of town, by no means easy to find, and wonderfully, wildly, eccentrically eclectic. Mr. Stibbert was a Victorian Briton who collected compulsively, filling his mock-Moorish palace with a dozen-plus life-size horsemen in Renaissance armor—aboard Renaissance steeds; the clothes chosen by Napoleon for his coronation as King of Italy, regalia worn by the military and aristocrats of such lands as India, China, and Japan; roomfuls of European and oriental porcelain; Rococo and Renaissance furniture, and paintings by Titian, Tiepolo, and Longhi. Among much, much else. There are so few visitors that the guards welcome those who do come with enthusiasm, if with no foreign-language skills, as they personally tour them about. Mind-boggling.

FLORENTINE PALAZZI: A SAMPLER

Casa Buonarroti (Via Ghibellina 70). You will have recognized the name as that of Michelangelo's family. I don't know why this structure is termed a *casa*. It is quite as big as many palazzi. More to the point, it is the house that the master bought for his family, which bequeathed it to the municipality in the mid-nineteenth century. A long time before, a descendant of Michelangelo hired a crop of seventeenth-century artists to embellish the house as a memorial. It is today a museum, full of Michelangelonia and some of his work, including marble sculptures and—my favorite—a carved-wood *Crucifixion*.

Palazzo Medici-Riccardi (Via Cavour) is a typically sober and somber Florentine Renaissance palace, the model for countless American banks, and designed by Michelozzo for Cosimo the Elder in the fifteenth century. The Riccardi family succeeded the Medici. The prefect of Florence is in contemporary residence. But some rooms operate as a museum, full of Medici portraits (there is a superb *Lorenzo the Magnificent*), Medici documentation, and, most breathtaking of all, a monumental fresco in the chapel—*Il Viaggio dei Magi* —with various Medici luminaries in its cast of beautiful characters.

Palazzo Davanzati (Piazza Davanzati) is also known cumbersomely, albeit accurately, as Museo della Casa Fiorentina Antica. It's the Middle Ages and the early Renaissance in three dimensions, an absolutely enchanting fourteenth-century stone residence—severe in line, vivid with frescoed and stenciled stone walls, ceilings, and fireplaces. Three floors of splendidly furnished rooms (including the original lavatories) evoke upper-class town life of half a millennium ago. Magical.

Palazzo Strozzi (Piazza Strozzi) is one of the great fifteenth-century houses, named for the powerful merchant family that built it, with a memorable courtyard—look up at the double rows of balconies—and a little basement museum with models of the building's restoration.

TREASURES OF ART AND ARCHITECTURE: SELECTED CHURCHES

Annunziata (Piazza Annunziata) has an unusual arched Renaissance façade. Beneath the elaborately coffered ceiling of the elongated Baroque nave are art works by a number of masters, most especially Andrea del Sarto. The square is one of the handsomest in town, with another of its occupants, an art-rich hospital, later recommended.

Apostoli (Piazza del Limbo) is at once intimate in scale, charming of ambience, with a Romanesque stone front. Within, the art works include Della Robbia terra cottas.

Carmine (Piazza del Carmine) startles with the utter plainness of its unfinished façade. Walk in, though, and it is richly if not entirely Baroque. The frescoed ceiling of the nave is a joy. But the special treasures are the Masolino and Masaccio frescoes in the Brancacci Chapel—the former, of Adam and Eve, especially beautiful, with exquisite Filippino Lippi works as well, and a don't-miss cloister.

Ognissanti (Piazza Ognissanti) was where Amerigo Vespucci worshiped (it contains his family's tomb) and today, appropriately enough, is the site of English-language masses, traditionally said at ten on Sunday mornings. At any time, this art-rich church warrants inspection: at once Gothic and Renaissance, it has Ghirlandaio frescoes, a handsome sacristy and cloister, and its main altar under a graceful mini-dome.

Orsanmichele (Via dell'Arte della Lana) looks more like a medieval town house than a house of worship. The statues of saints in wall niches are its only giveaways, from without. The interior is compact and ornate, with a number of finely wrought tabernacles the highlights. While you are in the neighborhood, pop into little *San Carlo,* just opposite, and note the fine painting over its altar.

Santa Firenze (Piazza Santa Firenze) is striking Baroque, with a coffered ceiling that is among the handsomest in town and good paintings along either wall of the nave.

San Marco (Piazza San Marco) is so often overlooked because visitors concentrate on the Fra Angelico frescoes in its monastery-museum (see The Essential Florence, above) that I make mention of it here. The façade is Baroque, and the church embodies refurbishings extending over several centuries. Look for the School of Giotto wooden crucifix, and Byzantine mosaics.

San Miniato al Monte (Piazzale Michelangelo) is awesomely handsome Romanesque, high on a hill overlooking the city. Its situation alone makes it visit-worthy. But then there are the green and white marble façade, a peculiar two-story altar, and—among many art works —Paolo Uccello frescoes in the cloister, and a mosaic-decorated apse. The friendly Benedictines of Mount Olivetto run an interesting shop in conjunction.

Santo Spirito (Piazza Santo Spirito) has a stucco façade, Baroque and pleasing. Within, it is somber Renaissance—elegant Corinthian columns flanking a central nave. There are precious art works including a Lippi *Madonna and Saints,* and a similarly titled Lorenzo Credi, among many others.

A FLORENTINE MISCELLANY

Cenacolo di Santa Apollonia (Via XXVII Aprile): There are a number of representations of *The Last Supper* in Florence. This one, a beauty by Andrea del Castagno, occupies an entire end wall of what had been the refectory of a convent. It is a fine and detailed mid-fifteenth-century work, an interesting contrast from the best known of all in this category—that of Leonardo, in still another onetime refectory in Milan.

Wine Estates: A number of vineyard operators in the vicinity of Florence open their houses and wineries to visitors, on tours run by Cimitato per la Visita alle Fattorie dei Dintorni di Firenze, through the city's Autonoma di Turismo. The season is autumn.

Forte Belvedere is a near neighbor of earlier recommended Church of San Miniato al Monte and below-recommended Piazzale Michel-angelo; all three can be taken in on a single journey. The Belvedere is a sixteenth-century military complex, dramatically sited, architec-turally strong, and with a gallery of detached frescoes by such lumi-naries as Botticelli and Paolo Uccello.

Galleria delle Spedale degli Innocenti (Piazza Annunziata) is a neighbor of earlier-recommended Annunziata Church. There are two visitor lures in this venerable hospital. First is a series of glazed terra-cotta decorations by Andrea della Robbia decorating the exterior. Second is an art gallery. Lining walls on two floors are exquisite paintings by such artists as Piero di Cosimo, Botticelli, and Ghirlandaio. Open hours are irregular. Try, though.

Piazzale Michelangelo is the No. 1 Panorama Spot, on a hill across the Arno from the main part of town, with views of the river, bridges, and skyline from a broad terrace; earlier-recommended Forte Belvedere and the Church of San Miniato al Monte are near neighbors.

Sinagoga (Via Farini) is elegant, opulent, and Byzantine, with an interior rich in mosaics and frescoes. Topped by a green copper dome, it dates back about a century.

Villas: The Medici and other rich Renaissance families were very big on country homes as a change of pace from their town palaces. Indeed, they were European innovators in this respect. A number of these beautiful—and beautifully-situated—villas are just outside of town, and visitable, but with limited open hours in recent seasons. (Double check before you go.) One—a few miles north of the city—is

Villa della Petraia, with very grand reception rooms, exceptional Flemish and French tapestries, an immense terraced garden, and fine views of the city from it. Its near neighbor is *Villa di Castello,* whose first landlord was Lorenzo the Magnificent. One wants to see both the rich interiors and the fountain-embellished gardens. Gardens of still other houses can be taken in on conducted springtime bus tours run by Comitato per la Visita al Giardini delle Più Belle Ville Fiorentine, in conjunction with the city's Azienda Autonoma di Turismo.

Florence: To Watch

Teatro Comunale (Corso Italia) is Florence's opera house-concert hall, and the principal seat of its world-renowned spring music festival, *Maggio Musicale.* The Comunale is home to the Orchestra del Maggio Musicale Fiorentino, as well as chorus and opera companies. The main—or winter—opera season is repeated in July—much to the delight of summer visitors—with both early spring and autumn concert seasons, and Maggio Musicale taking place each May. The theater, unlike traditional-style opera houses in other Italian cities, is essentially modern, more functional than beautiful, with ersatz stars illuminating it from the ceiling—rather than crystal chandeliers. Besides the orchestra, there are two immense balconies and two smaller levels higher up. Bronze plaques on either side of the hall at the level of the first balcony mark the point reached by the waters of the disastrous 1966 flooding of the Arno. There are good refreshment facilities. And—rarity of Italian opera houses—air-conditioning. Tickets are not as difficult to obtain as, say, those for Milan's La Scala, but they're tight at Festival time and when the town is tourist-packed; hotel concierges are often wizards at obtaining them.

Teatro della Pergola (Via della Pergola 12) is the scene of autumn-through-spring concerts on Saturday afternoons.

Teatro Verdi (Via Ghibellina 99) presents musical revues.

Other Festivals include the *International Festival* every September with concerts in various palaces and museums; *Pitti Palace Concerts* in the spring, and in late summer as well.

Florence: To Stay

This city, so well organized to receive tourists in every way, rarely disappoints when it comes to hotels. Choice is wide and, by and large, good. Again, given the Florentine personality—quick-witted, agile, agreeable—generally commendable service should come as no surprise. What follows is a personal selection of hotels and pensiones in which I have lived, eaten, drunk, or at the very least thoroughly inspected. They are presented alphabetically, with my categorization of each—*luxury, first class, moderate*—appended.

Hotel Adriatico (Via Maso Finiguerra 9) is a neat-as-a-pin, essentially modern house (eighteenth-century Venetian furniture is scattered about for contrast) with 110 pleasant rooms, all with bath or shower; restaurant and bar. Between the railway station and the Arno. *First class.*

Aerhotel Baglioni (Piazza Unità Italiana 6) deceives with the "Aerhotel" part of its name. It has nothing to do with airport or air terminal, but is rather an in-town old-school hotel of considerable elegance; 215 smart-looking rooms, handsome restaurant (that moves to the roof in summer), cozy bar-lounge. Near the station. *Luxury.*

Hotel Anglo Americano (Via Garibaldi 9) is an old-timer beloved of Anglos and Americans. There are 130 lovely rooms with bath, gracious lobby-cum-bar, a honey of a crystal chandelier-illuminated restaurant, and a nice situation. *First class.*

Hotel Astoria (Via del Giglio) occupies a capacious sixteenth-century palazzo (you must insist on seeing the party room with a Luca Giordano ceiling fresco, and the lavishly Baroque Salone dei Seicento) and has 90 bath-equipped rooms (some with super views of the Duomo), restaurant, cocktail lounge, with the Medici Chapel its near neighbor. Atmospheric. *First class.*

Hotel Augustus (Piazzetta dell'Oro 5) is tucked into the heart of town near Ponte Vecchio and has been recently refurbished. There's a winning lobby-lounge—Italian Modern at its best, with 65 pleasant rooms, original framed drawings on their walls. Breakfast only. *Moderate.*

Hotel Berchielli (Lungarno Acciaioli) is central, old-fashioned in the best sense, beloved of Americans over an extended period, and with 35 of its 78 rooms with bath or shower. Congenial lobby-bar, breakfast only. Charming. *Moderate.*

Hotel Bonciani (Via Panzani 17) is a venerable albeit updated palazzo, still with some original painted ceilings, and with antique furniture scattered about. More than half of the 70 rooms have baths (the bath of Room 214 is a former chapel with a painted ceiling!) and they vary in degree of comfort. Restaurant, bar. Near the station. *Moderate.*

Hotel Continental (Lungarno Acciaioli 2) is a step from Ponte Vecchio. Don't let the tiny lobby throw you off. There's a bar-lounge-breakfast room a flight up, and 67 of the rooms have baths, with many of them handsome, most especially a duplex tower suite. No restaurant, but a rooftop terrace. *Moderate.*

Hotel Croce di Malta (Via della Scala 7, just off Piazza Santa Maria Novella) is a seventeenth-century convent turned, relatively recently, into a hotel, with 120 stylish bedrooms and duplex suites, an arched-ceiling restaurant that is one of Florence's best looking (and most delicious), casual bar-lounge, dilly of an outdoor pool-cum-terrace. The lot is a modish meld of the antique with the mod. Very nice indeed. Officially first class but to my mind: *Luxury.*

Hotel De la Ville (Piazza Antinori, near Via Tornabuoni) is at once central, spacious, traditional-look, with nearly 80 attractive rooms, restaurant, cocktail lounge. Officially first class but to my mind: *Luxury.*

Hotel Excelsior Italie (Piazza Ognissanti 3) is elaborate Renaissance-style, river front, with 207 fully equipped rooms and suites, restaurant, bar-lounge. A CIGA hotel. *Luxury.*

Hotel Jolly (Piazza Vittorio Veneto 40), away from the center of town, is ultramodern—not unlike so many of the Jolly hotels in the

Italy-wide chain, with a cavernous lobby, a trio of restaurants, including one on the roof, big cocktail lounge, and 150 fully equipped rooms—44 of which have *two* baths. *First class.*

Hotel Kraft (Via Solferino 2) is uncentral (near Teatro Comunale) but very attractive; 70 rooms with excellent baths, a restaurant that goes outdoors in summer, cocktail lounge, rooftop pool, and nice touches like fresh flowers in the corridors. *First class.*

Hotel Londra (Via Jacopo da Diacceto 16) is restrained-modern in look, with 100-plus rooms with bath or shower, pleasant restaurant, bar-lounge. Near the station. *Moderate.*

Hotel Lungarno (Borgo San Jacopo 14) is left bank, near Ponte Vecchio and Pitti Palace, with its rear rooms directly on the water, affording super views of the skyline. There are 71 inviting rooms with bath, and occasionally—if one is lucky—with terrace. Attractive lobby and cocktail lounge. Breakfast only. *Moderate.*

Hotel Mediterraneo (Lungarno del Tempio 42) is a biggie—334 rooms with bath. The twins tend to be smallish but they're comfortable; so are the singles. Look throughout is ultramod if not distinguished, with a sprawling lobby and restaurant; away from the center. Groups a specialty. *Moderate.*

Hotel Michelangelo (Viale Fratelli Rosselli 2) is good Italian Modern, embracing some 140 handsome rooms (beds are a little narrow), smart public spaces including restaurant and bar-lounge. Near the station. *First class.*

Hotel Minerva (Piazza Santa Maria Novella) has an inspired setting as next-door neighbor to the Church of Santa Maria Novella (see The Essential Florence, above). It occupies a venerable though smartly updated palazzo. There are 110 comfortable rooms with bath, lobby-lounge that looks out on a patio-garden, good restaurant, rooftop pool that's a joy in summer, and astute management. Very comfortable indeed. *First class.*

Pensione Pendini (Via Strozzi) is enviably central, with 17 rooms with bath, comfortable public spaces (with green plants at every turn), and a warm ambience. Restaurant and bar-lounge. Groups are welcome. *Moderate.*

Hotel Porta Rossa (Via Porta Rossa 19) is the genuine old-fashioned article, attractive, heart-of-town, and with baths or showers in about a third of its 60 quite simple rooms; congenial bar. Breakfast only. *Moderate.*

Hotel Principe (Lungarno Amerigo Vespucci 34) is a beauty of an eighteenth-century palazzo, river front, near Teatro Comunale. All 21 rooms and suites have bath; intimate bar-lounge, tiny restaurant with its original painted ceiling, pretty garden. Charm with a capital C. *First class.*

Pensione La Residenza (Via Tornabuoni 8) is agreeable, with cozy bar-lounge, pleasant rooms (14 of the 23 have bath), small restaurant, roof garden. Most guests stay on demi- or full pension plan. Location is Florence's smartest shopping street. *Moderate.*

Hotel Ritz (Lungarno della Zecca Vecchia 24) is up to the minute; all 33 of its neat rooms have bath, and the front ones are river view. There's a lobby-cum-cocktail lounge. Breakfast but no restaurant. *Moderate.*

Hotel Savoy (Piazza della Repubblica 7) is enviably well located on the main downtown square. This is an attractive traditional-style house with nearly 100 smartly furnished rooms, capacious lobby, bar-lounge, grill-restaurant. *Luxury.*

Hotel della Signoria (Via delle Terme 1) is near the downtown piazza from which it takes its name. There are 32 cheery rooms, all with bath, and a nice traditional feeling. Bar and breakfast, no restaurant. *Moderate.*

Pensione Tornabuoni-Beacci (Via Tornabuoni 3) is almost too elegant to be true—as a pensione, that is. Antiques-accented lounge, restaurant, roof terrace, 35 rooms with bath, management by the same family for some 60 years, and a location on the principal shopping street. *Moderate.*

Hotel Villa Medici (Via il Prato 42) is what luxury-hotel living is all
about. Behind an original seventeenth-century façade is a beauty of
a 100-room and suite hotel, with a swimming pool in its ample garden,
lobby in traditional style with an adjacent cocktail lounge, a fine
restaurant that moves poolside in summer. The rooms are lovely and
oversized with tile murals in the baths. And a number have terraces.
There are sumptuous suites, overlooking the garden. Ambience is
intimate, service quite in keeping. Between the station and Teatro
Comunale. *Luxury*.

Florence: To Eat and Drink

Florence is the gastronomic as well as the political and cultural
capital of Tuscany. And as any traveler in Italy learns, every city has
its Tuscan restaurant; the food of this region, along with that of
Bologna, is perhaps the most popular country-wide. There is an admirable penchant for simply grilled meats that endears North Americans to the Tuscan cooking. And although it is safe to say that the
beef used for American beefsteaks is at least as good as Tuscany's,
there is no gainsaying that this region's beef is the best in Italy, and
that the Tuscan way with a steak can be winning. (Which is not to say
one can't get stung upon occasion.) Broiled chicken is popular too;
when well seasoned with garlic, sage, salt, and pepper, it emerges as
pollo alla diavola. Fritto misto—invariably made of seafood elsewhere in Italy—is a meat and vegetable mixture in Florence, the lot
deep-fried and delicious. Beans are deliciously prepared—as a basis
for a soup—*zuppa di fagioli,* as a vegetable, or in casseroles. Although
rice is not as popular as is the case in Milan and Venice, it has many
fans, when made into a local-style *risotto*—slowly simmered with
chicken giblets. Pasta is a pleasure—*pappardelle,* noodles with hare
sauce; a variation on the ravioli theme called *agnollotti;* Tuscan-
style *cannelloni,* with chicken livers included in the filling; and with
beans—as *pasta e fagioli.* Tuscan game dishes—hare and various
birds—are notable, too. Only in the area of bread does Florence
disappoint; it falls behind much of the rest of Italy.

Chianti, Tuscany's own much-exported wine, is favored locally,
not only the ordinary Chiantis—which run a broad gamut in taste—
but the premium-price, premium-quality (and presumably more
delicate) Chianti Classico, which, if it is the genuine article, will have

a black rooster on the label. The area's Vino Santo, a sweet wine, is interesting to sample. Restaurants invariably have Chianti as their house wine, but there is always a good choice of others, for the minority (of which I am a part) that is not unreservedly enthusiastic over Chianti—even Chianti Classico.

Here is a sampling of Florentine restaurants that I know and mostly like, presented alphabetically, with my own categorization—*expensive, moderate, inexpensive*—appended in each case. For the restaurants, as distinct from the caffès, advance reservations are recommended.

Alemagna (Piazza del Duomo) is the Florentine outpost of the nationwide chain that produces its own packaged baked goods, and other edibles, and operates caffès like this one, with ice cream, sandwiches, pastries, pizza, and other hot dishes; a proper bar, too. Go whenever you are hungry or thirsty. *Inexpensive.*

Buca Lapi (Via del Trebbio 1) is, to at least one sampler, Florence's most vastly overrated restaurant. Setting is a travel-poster-papered cellar, the food can be substandard and cold when it should be hot, waiters can be tricky-nasty, exposed-to-view chefs can be wearing soiled uniforms, and the queues of tourists go on and on, as if there were no place else to eat. *Moderate.*

Cammillo (Borgo San Jacopo 57) is at once attractive, buzzy, filled with a nice mix of affluent locals and visitors alike, with aged chandeliers illuminating a pair of stucco-walled chambers, and good contemporary art as embellishment. Food is delicious; try the *frito di zucchini* as an unusual starter, or a *tortino di carciofi*—an artichoke omelet, if you please. The rice dishes and pastas are commendable. So is the chicken, in a variety of styles. Super service. *Moderate.*

Caffè Cesarini (Piazza Ognissanti) is a worth-knowing-about spot for coffee, snacks, or drinks in this interesting shopping area, near the river, west of the central area. *Inexpensive.*

Dino (Via Ghibellina) is undistinguished but reliable with favored stand-bys like minestrone or *stracciatella* as soup choices, mixed grill or grilled chicken as entrees, and grainy hunks of Parmesan cheese with coarse bread for dessert. The setting is a series of clean and antiseptic rooms. *Inexpensive.*

Doney (Via Tornabuoni 56) is at once a restaurant (good choices are the broiled steak and fried chicken), but it's more fun as a caffè for morning coffee or afternoon tea, with the very good pastries. Cakes, candies, crackers, and pastries to go, too. *Moderate to inexpensive.*

Caffè Enrico Rivoire (Piazza della Signora) is venerable, atmospheric, and strategically situated for agreeable pauses in the course of one's explorations in the core of town. Good pastries, snacks, drinks, coffee. *Inexpensive.*

Il Fagiano (Via dei Neri 57) invites, with arched ceilings, antique fragments scattered about, and an open fireplace where delicious things are cooked, most especially skewered meats, over charcoal, and pheasant (for which the place is named) deliciously roasted. Pasta—especially the *canolli*—is good and chicken breasts are tastily prepared. *Moderate.*

Giacosa (Via Tornabuoni at Via della Vigna Nuova) is a good refreshment spot for shoppers; stop for tea, sandwiches, or drinks. *Inexpensive.*

Giannino (Via Borgo San Lorenzo 31) embraces a self-service section, with pizza among the specialties; and a sit-down restaurant with a standard menu. As I have tried both, it's the self-service section I'm recommending as quick, tasty, and *inexpensive.*

Al Girarrosto (Piazza Santa Maria Novella 10) is a charmer of the old school, with Tuscan specialties, a setting embracing a pair of high-ceiling rooms, with both old and mod art on the walls, and delightful service. Try the *pappardelle*—noodles with hare sauce. Hare, hunter's style—*cacciatora*—is delicious too. Or *Risotto alla fiorentina.* Desserts are among the more elaborate in town. *Moderate.*

Harry's Bar (Lungarno Vespucci 22) is river front, a short walk from the core of downtown. There is a popular cocktail lounge (go only for a drink if you like) and a dining room smartly understated in look, with generally swift service, and lovely things to eat, most especially the chef's own scampi and chicken breast with a rice pilaf. You can't go wrong with any of the pasta. Or sweets. Unusually good wine list. *Expensive.*

Mamma Gina (Borgo San Jacopo 37, on the left bank of the Arno, not far from Ponte Vecchio) used to be a hole-in-the-wall trattoria, with Mamma hopping about, slip showing, and the food delicious. Mamma's slip no longer shows, the place is vastly expanded in size, and it's considerably more attractive. But the food remains delicious. The minestrone is unbeatable. So are any of the pastas and grills. Always busy. *Moderate.*

Marchetti (Via dei Calzaiuoli at Via de Tosinghi) is a worth-knowing-about, well-located source of self-service lunches and snacks. *Inexpensive.*

Moka-Harrar is a pair of ice-cream parlors, one opposite the other on Via Ceratani in the shopping district. Try the sundae with four kinds of ice cream topped with fresh strawberries, blackberries, *and* raspberries. Or countless variations on this theme, to your command. Wickedly delicious. *Inexpensive.*

Motta (Piazza del Duomo) is a branch of a nationwide purveyor of good things to eat and snack on. There is a proper restaurant with *prix-fixe* meals, upstairs, and main-floor counters for sandwiches, and pastries. *Inexpensive.*

Otello (Via Orti Oricellari 19) goes on, room after room after room. It is beloved of locals as well, for some reason or other, of French tourists. The decibel count is high, the waiters good-natured, and the food variable. Skip the touted steaks, but the pastas—including *agnellotti* and *pappardelle*—are commendable. Mixed grill is a good bet; you select all you want from a trolley brought to the table. The salads are as good to eat as they are gorgeous to behold. Desserts are wheeled to you, and irresistible. *Moderate.*

Paskowski (Piazza della Repubblica) is a not very Italian-sounding caffè on this principal downtown square, notable principally because it has live concerts during the afternoon, so that you can listen to music while you sip tea or a drink. *Inexpensive.*

Sabatini (Via Panzani) is big and handsome but disappointing for so reputed—and so costly—a restaurant. There are interesting things on the menu—pasta such as *vermicelli espresso al pomodoro basilico* and *tagliatelle al doppio burro; al ragù di carne*—half a roast pheasant; or a novel turkey cutlet embellished with cheese, truffles, and peas. Desserts are elaborate. The wine list is long if hardly faultless. But the service can be oddly casual, disjointed, and unprofessional, which is unforgivable in such a top-rank place, especially when the food, once arrived, is only so-so. *Expensive.*

Sostana (Via dei Porcellana 26) is a plain-as-an-old-shoe trattoria with an illegible menu, no-nonsense waiters, and an invariably happy clientele, both local and imported. And why not, with such good food? The steak is the biggest and most succulent I know of in Florence. The vegetable soup is hearty and served in quantity. And wonders are worked with chicken breasts. Fun. *Moderate.*

13 Gobbi (Via dei Porcellana 9) is winning, very winning. Nice to look upon for starters, with picture-crammed walls, fresh flowers on the tables, smiling staff. Then there is the food: the house's own *tortellini* and *pappardelle* among the pastas; veal scaloppine and sausage with beans, peasant-style among the entrees, a special menu of Hungarian specialties as a surprise, splendid cheeses (nowhere have I had better Gorgonzola or Peccarino), good wines as expected, but Löwenbrau beer, from Germany, for a change. *Moderate.*

Walter (Borgo SS. Apostoli 66, at Piazza Santa Trinità, and also known as La Nandina) occupies a pair of agreeably decorated rooms, the first with a bar. Start with a plate of Tuscan salami or *spaghetti carbonara* and go on to the broiled veal chop, veal *piccata,* a beefsteak, or the mixed grill. The house's own cakes are indicated for dessert. *Moderate.*

Zi Rosa (Via dei Fossi 12): The vibes are good from the moment of arrival; the fare is fine—a beautiful antipasto or the egg-drop soup called *stracciatella* for starters, *osso bucco;* or tripe Florentine style, or a ham steak. Scampi, prepared half a dozen ways, are a specialty. So is hare stew. This place is smart and substantial. *Moderate.*

Florence: To Buy

All of the Florentine mercantile centuries—the tradition of the Medici, Riccardi, Strozzi, and all of the great families that traded and aided throughout Europe—come into play when one shops in Florence. No medium-sized European city—Florence's population hovers around half a million—surpasses this one. Milan and Rome come close in certain areas; indeed they surpass Florence when it comes to clothes. But in other respects, this is where quality, selection, courtesy, and linguistic skills reign supreme. (The merchant who is not trilingual—fluent in three languages—if not quadrilingual, is rare.)

Another bonus is the relative compactness of the central area. One walks all about on shopping expeditions, and with pleasure. Via Tornabuoni is the most celebrated of the shopping streets, but by no means alone. Via Por Santa Maria, Via Calzaiuoli, Via Parione, Via Roma, Borgo San Jacopo—all are areas where one finds clothes, shoes, gloves, leather, luggage, pottery. Via Por Santa Maria and the Ponte Vecchio are for silver and jewelry. One finds antiques on Via dei Fossi and Via degli Strozzi. Price ranges run the usual gamut. Generally, merchandise is price-fixed, but bargaining can be the rule in antiques shops and markets. Established merchants are generally experienced and reliable in overseas shipping. Nowhere that I know of are retailers more polite or more appreciative of their clients' patronage.

Here is an evaluation of personally inspected sources in categories of most interest to visitors. The presentation is alphabetical by category, and within each category.

ANTIQUES

Besides Via dei Fossi and Via degli Strozzi, mentioned above, one finds antiques on Borgognissanti and across the Arno on the left bank on Via Maggio and Borgo San Jacopo. Although Venice has superb quality antiques, Florence matches it in that respect and surpasses it in quantity. Indeed, it is a European leader in this category; way ahead, incidentally, of Rome. Probably more than 90 per cent of the old pieces in the shops are Italian in origin, and include late medieval (sculpture, wood-polychrome, gesso), Renaissance, and Baroque, with the subject matter embracing furniture, paintings, ceramics, and doodads. For example:

Alberto Bruschi (Via dei Fossi 40) specializes in seventeenth-century furniture and paintings, with some later objects, too. Beautiful quality.

Berti (Via dei Fossi 29) is for eighteenth- and nineteenth-century pieces, from the Orient as well as Italy.

Bruzzichelli (Borgognissanti 33) is mainly for good early-nineteenth-century furniture.

Cose del Passato (Via dei Fossi 27) offers a delightful mix of small things—mirrors, pottery, fragments, some paintings.

Fioretto (Borgognissanti 41) is a superior source of antique carpets, seventeenth- and eighteenth-century furniture, old wrought iron.

Gada P. Rafanelli (Borgognissanti 33) has small objects—ceramics, mirrors, some paintings—and eighteenth- and nineteenth-century walnut furniture, too.

Gentilini (Via Tornabuoni 10) vends exceptional quality furniture and furnishings of the seventeenth and eighteenth centuries; paintings, too.

Griffo (Via dei Fossi 17) generally has larger stocks than one finds in many places, of seventeenth- and eighteenth-century furniture; much of it is of moderate quality.

Le Due Dame (Borgognissanti 36) is indeed a partnership of two charming—and knowledgeable—ladies who mostly sell fine seventeenth-century furniture and objects.

Palloni (Borgognissanti 21) is for eighteenth-century painted furniture as well as pieces from the preceding and succeeding centuries, and hard-to-find things like overdoors and panels. Paintings, too.

Pier Ferruccio Cremasco (Via A. Canova 72) has smallish but choice selections of Renaissance furniture and objects; invariably in superb taste.

Scarselli (Borgo San Jacopo 33) has a pleasing range of good furniture covering several centuries.

Pasco Ughi (Via Tornabuoni 34) stocks elegant eighteenth-century furniture, accessories, and paintings.

Ventura (Borgognissanti 8) is for furniture and objects from the Italian provinces, mostly seventeenth and eighteenth century; decorative fragments, too.

Venturi Spadia (Borgognissanti 15) deals in gesso, plain wood, and granite sculptures; seventeenth-century (walnut) and eighteenth-century (painted) furniture; not to mention objects in silver and bronze, and paintings.

ANTIQUE PAINTINGS

Although many antiques shops sell paintings with other objects (see above), some tend to tip the scale in the other direction. Such as:

Enrico Frascione (Via dei Fossi 61) sells old paintings, many from the seventeenth and eighteenth centuries.

Franco Codognato (Via dei Fossi 49) has art works from the seventeenth through nineteenth centuries.

Giuliano Freschi (Via della Vigna Nuova 85) goes back mostly to the seventeenth century for paintings, many of them museum caliber.

Sabatini Daninos (Borgognissanti 48) has a mix of paintings, etchings, prints, tapestries, sculpture in polychrome, even hand-painted tile plaques.

BOOKS

Caldini (Via Tornabuoni 90) tempts with art books, antique books, and books published in the English language.

Libreria Salinnbeni (Via M. Palmieri 14) specializes in art books.

CHILDREN'S CLOTHES

Anicini (Via Parione 59) has likable togs for the kids.

DEPARTMENT STORE

UPIM (Piazza della Repubblica) is at once very big, very central, and with mostly moderate-range merchandise.

FABRICS

Antico Setificio Fiorentino (Via della Vigna Nuova 97) has both old and new decorative fabrics of considerable style and quality; all hand-loomed.

G. Lisio (Via dei Fossi 45) has a wide and beautiful range.

Lorenzo Rubbelli & Figlio (Via Tornabuoni 1): silks, cottons, brocades—and high style.

Zinelli & Perizzi (Via Tornabuoni 2) runs the gamut, with cut velvets a specialty.

FOOD

Alemagna (Piazza del Duomo): packaged cookies, crackers, candies, and other delicious comestibles to accompany drinks in your hotel rooms or for train rides; a restaurant-caffè, too (see Florence: To Eat and Drink).

Motta (Piazza del Duomo): a variation on the Alemagna theme, see above. Both are branches of national chains.

GLOVES

Chris (Via Por Santa Maria 42) has a good selection, moderate prices.

Gants (Via Porta Rossa 78) makes their own; the quality is excellent.

Martelli (Via Por Santa Maria 18) is a good place to lay in gifts; they're inexpensive.

Ugolini (Via Tornabuoni 20) is long established, with good style, for which a good price is paid.

JEWELRY, SILVER, GOLD

Biagini & Cappelli (Ponte Vecchio) has a wide range, with a big stock from turn of the century.

Bijoux Cascio (Via Tornabuoni 32) is moderately priced, with the emphasis on gold; they design their own.

Del Bono (Ponte Vecchio) is for silverware, especially pieces like platters, pitchers, and candlesticks.

Legnazzi (Lungarno degli Acciaiuoli 6) has perfectly beautiful jewelry in gold and coral, too.

Mario Buccellati (Via Tornabuoni 69), known also for his shops in Rome and New York; traditional Florentine designs in both fine jewelry and table silver. Expensive.

Melli (Ponte Vecchio) is a handsome shop with handsome antique jewelry, ivory, silver, clocks; other objects, too.

Peruzzi (Borgo San Jacopo 4) is for silver, much of it in the traditional style for which Buccellati (above) is known.

Tozzi (Ponte Vecchio) has contemporarily designed jewelry and silver, and reproductions of traditional styles.

Volterra (Ponte Vecchio) is a long-time source of watches, jewels, and antique silver.

LEATHER

Beltrani (Piazza dell Olio 1) runs a wide gamut—from women's handbags to men's suede jackets, with lots of luggage in between. Good design and quality. Expensive.

Fizzoni (Via Por Santa Maria 62): a wide range of sizes in handbags and totes.

Gazzarrini (Via Porta Rossa 71): considerable variety, good prices; gifts for your dog.

Gherardini (Via della Vigna Nuova 57) has outlets also in Rome and Milan, offers high-style leather and luggage, not to mention equally modish men's and women's clothes and accessories. Expensive.

Gucci (Via Tornabuoni 73): The Mother House of the phenomenally successful, much-imitated brass-bit designs. Two floors invariably mobbed with clamoring Americans and Japanese visitors who cannot seem to buy enough. The range includes luggage, women's handbags, wallets, and billfolds, men's and women's shoes, and non-leather accessories like silk scarves and perfume. Cheaper than in the U.S. but hardly cheap.

Perseo (Borgo San Jacopo 10) designs and makes its own luggage; they'll do it just as you want it if you specify. Smart and well priced.

Pescarolo (Via degli Strozzi 23) is known for its high-style luggage. Costly.

Santa Croce Church (Piazza Santa Croce) operates its own leather school and a retail shop that has one of the biggest and best selections in town of the traditional Florentine designs in boxes (pill to cigar, in size), wallets, bags. Top quality.

Scarabeo (Via Por Santa Maria) makes a specialty of well-priced, soft tote bags.

Uffizi Gallery Arcades: Don't let the open-air aspect of this group of leather merchants keep you away, on the assumption that they're fly-by-nights because they're alfresco. On the contrary, they are generally long-established merchants, even taking international credit cards, as do indoors competitors. Luggage, totes, small objects.

Straw Market (Loggia del Mercato Nuovo) is a downtown Renaissance landmark that, despite its name, is a source also of Florentine leather specialties—wallets, boxes, bags—not necessarily of the best quality, but moderately priced and good for minor gift-giving.

LINENS

Emilia Bellini (Via Tornabuoni) is a first-rank source of beautifully designed and hand-worked table and other linens, scarves, blouses. With a Rome branch.

Pratesi (Borgognissanti 3) is an outlet of a high-style chain's contemporary-design linens, towels, and related objects. Expensive. Elsewhere in Italy, and New York, too.

Taf (Via Por Santa Maria 22) has elegant linens, towels, and lingerie. Moderately priced.

The Linen Shop (Piazza Mino da Fiesole, Fiesole) has tastefully hand-embroidered linens.

MEN'S CLOTHING

Many shops have women's as well as men's clothing, and other types of merchandise as well. Gherardini and Gucci, above under Leather, are examples, with men's and women's clothing and accessories as well as leather. Others follow, under Women's Clothing.

Max (Via Porta Rossa 64) is for smart suits, jackets, raincoats, as well as accessories including shirts and ties. Moderately tabbed.

Ugolini (Via Calzaione 65) is at once high style and costly. The suits are super.

POTTERY AND CHINA

A. Menegatti (Via Tornabuoni 77) is long established, and for traditional-design majolica, with the hand-painted pottery-dinner-ware made by the noted Deruta and other factories in abundance. They're reliable shippers but it may take a long, *long* time.

S.E.I.A.N. (Via Porta Rossa 107) has enormous selections of pottery from every region of Italy.

U. del Guerra (Via Parione 53) specializes in antique pottery and ceramics of the seventeenth century.

MEN'S AND WOMEN'S SHOES

Ferragamo (Via Tornabuoni 16) is celebrated, stylish, and expensive; women's shoes and handbags.

Pollini (Via Calimala 12) is long on the scene, with modish men's and women's shoes; leather jackets, too. Expensive.

Raspini (Via Por Santa Maria 70 and other locations) makes a point of being expensively elegant, and succeeds. Both men's and women's shoes, suede and leather jackets and coats, too.

Romano (Piazza della Repubblica at Via degli Speziali) is moderately priced, and stylish; men's and women's.

Valentino (Via Tornabuoni 67): both men's and women's, high-styled and costly.

STRAW AND RAFFIA

Straw Market (Loggia del Mercato Nuovo) is the covered market—a Renaissance masterwork from the sixteenth century—whose much-photographed trademark is a sculptured wild boar in bronze (*Porcellino,* the locals call him), with the traditional Florentine straw and raffia work, as well as leather and other local products. Mild bargaining is not out of order.

WOMEN'S CLOTHES

Anna Giovannozzi (Borgognissanti 35): smart knitwear, ready to wear and to measure.

Frangi (Piazza della Repubblica): women's clothing and accessories, contemporary in style, moderate in price. Men's clothing, too.

Fusadoro (Via dei Brunelleschi at Via dei Tosinghi): good-looking, moderate through expensive. Men's wear, too.

Principe (Via degli Strozzi) is actually a small department store for clothing and shoes—men's and children's as well as women's. Style is good, prices are right, variety considerable.

Zanobetti (Borgorsanmichele 5 and Via Calimala 22) has been on the scene since the turn of the century; good style at fair prices is obviously the secret of its staying power. Men's as well as women's accessories and clothes.

Florence: To Note

Access. There is no transatlantic air service directly to Florence. However, there is domestic service to the nearest airport at Pisa via Alitalia and the domestic carrier, Aero Trasporti Italiani (ATI). Bus service from Pisa Airport to Florence takes about an hour and a half. Crack trains service Florence's Stazione di Santa Maria Novella, in the west end of the city, a moderate taxi ride from most hotels. Upon departure via train, the traveler is urged to book a *specific train seat* in advance or risk standing, even in first class; hotel concierges can be helpful in this respect.

Getting About. With a good map in hand—the best is the earlier-recommended free one published by Azienda Autonoma di Turismo because it has a street index—one does well to walk all about central Florence; most visitors get about on foot most of the time. Taxis are available at any number of ranks, cruising on the streets, and through hotels; they are metered, and drivers expect a 15 per cent tip. There is an extensive public bus system whose routes are printed on a free map, *Firenze: Carta degli Autobus,* obtainable from Azienda Autonoma di Turismo. Lines 1 (serving the railroad station and the Duomo, among other points), 7 (connecting town with Fiesole), and 13-Black (connecting the core of town with Piazzale Michelangelo), are among the more popular routes with visitors.

Sightseeing Tours are operated by a number of agencies, both of the city (morning, afternoon, and after-dark variations), as well as to the environs of town, and to nearby points like Pisa, Siena, and San Gimignano. Travel agencies, both at home and in Florence, have details; so do hotel concierges.

Clothes. Dress according to the normal temperate zone four-season year; summer can be hot and humid, during which time dress is very casual. In cooler months (which can be damp) Florentines tend to be dressier at better restaurants and, say, at Teatro Comunale.

Local Literature. Hotel concierges usually have gratis copies available of *Firenze Oggi*—a what's-on publication—but they tend to hide them. Ask and you shall receive. Daily newspapers, *Avanti* and *Avvenire,* are valuable for schedules of cultural events, and the *Daily American,* though published in Rome, carries some Florence news. Azienda Autonoma di Turismo (see below) has excellent free documentation.

Further Information. Azienda Autonoma di Turismo (the municipal tourist office that is one of the best such in Europe) has its headquarters at Via Tornabuoni 15, with a skillfully staffed visitor-information office at Piazza de Ruccellai.

III

Milan

Milan: To Know

It is fair neither to the Milanese nor to their countrymen to remark upon the un-Italian qualities of this richest and most contemporary of Italian cities. Still, there is no denying that outwardly, at first glance, both Milan's look and its demeanor are oddly unlike what one encounters elsewhere in urban Italy. Which is not to be critical.

It is simply by way of explaining to the first-timer the underlying reasons for the orderly taxi queues at the railway station . . . the immediately apparent low-decibel count . . . the unchoked progression of vehicular traffic without benefit of blaring horns, outstretched fists, or expletives from drivers; the startling contrasts—especially with cities in the south—in the way ordinary transactions are effortlessly, quietly, calmly, and efficiently undertaken.

What it comes to is that if Milan is perhaps less exotic, even less adventuresome and less fun than, say, Rome or Naples, especially to an outlander from northern climes, it has its reasons. It is as culturally and ethnically hybrid as any single Italian city. Location has seen to that. If a case can be made for being too strategic, let Milan make it. Its Lombard Plain situation became a major intersection in Europe's transport and communications scheme. While it gained tremendously because of this, in the areas of commerce, finance, and manufacturing, it was to pay a price for easy accessibility—for many centuries, down to and including our own.

This respectably long history—it goes back to the early Etruscans and later to Celts conquered by Romans who dubbed it Mediolanum —is not as easy to perceive in Milan as it is in, say, Florence or

Venice, because the industrious citizenry, always impatient with the course of progress, obliterated much of the old in order to make the new possible.

The antique aspect of Milan must, therefore, be searched for with more diligence than often is the case in Europe. Still, a backward glance indicates that it wasn't always the locals who were to blame for the succession of new looks. Hostile invaders were frequently the culprits.

Early Milan was calm and orderly enough, as the norm went in those days. The Romans made it the seat of their Western Empire, and the early Christian centuries saw it hold its own with Rome to the point where a poet, Ausonio by name, dubbed it Roma Secunda. It was in Milan that Emperor Constantine decreed a then revolutionary doctrine of free worship, and from Milan, too, that a local bishop, the later-sainted Ambrose, promulgated the use of the Ambrosian Rite wherein—among other features—the congregation joined in the service by singing hymns for the first time. (The Ambrosian Rite still is observed in Milan Cathedral.)

Warlike Goths came to destroy, and later warlike Huns, with the same successful goals. By the sixth century the Lombards—whose name the region still bears—had conquered Milan, and succeeding centuries saw it evolve commercially and politically to become strong, the while fighting battles, external as well as internal (this was the era of the memorably named—and antagonistic—Guelphs and Ghibellines).

There was a century of independence—the twelfth—but then the first of two great ruling clans came upon the scene. It was the Viscontis first and the Sforzas—the best-known of which was Ludovic the Moor—who followed, as Dukes of Milan. The Renaissance saw the city a pawn in one battle or political intrigue after another, with such landlords as Spain, Austria, and France. Indeed, Napoleon made the city the capital of his Cisalpine Republic and later of his Kingdom of Italy.

The mid-nineteenth century saw Austrians in control once again, during a period when the various Italian states took to the collaboration called Risorgimento, which was to result in the modern united Italy. Milan still remembers with pride a five-day period—it was in 1848—when it rid itself of the Austrians. The period was brief but it was incentive enough for this city to lead in the peninsula-wide freedom struggle.

Finally, in 1861, Milan became an integral part of a unified Italy, able to divest itself of matters military and concentrate on industry. But it was earlier—in the eighteenth century—that a pattern of development had evolved, whereby the old—meaning historic structures—was to be sacrificed for the new. The post-Industrial Revolution era saw evolution in that respect, much as was the case in the eastern United States, which today has so few architectural souvenirs of a history that extends back four centuries. Even more of the old Milan was obliterated as a result of devastating World War II air raids, when virtually every important building was at least partially damaged. The decades since have seen remarkable restoration.

If today's Milan is hardly an Italian leader when it comes to ancient architecture, it compensates with distinction in other areas. Aside from proficiency at commerce and manufacturing—banking, cars, textiles, clothes, machinery, even airplanes—Milan is extraordinarily gifted in matters musical—who does not covet a seat at La Scala?—and as a conservator of the fine arts, with a cluster of museums and galleries that are among the most sadly underappreciated of any major European city. Remaining are grace, style and éclat. Milan, along with Rome, excels at all three.

Milan: To See

LAY OF THE LAND

Milan's modernity makes for a kind of uniformity in its façade. Once one leaves the central core, there is a dearth of the kind of distinctive-looking structures that present themselves in many cities as landmarks. Ideally, what one needs to get the hang of Milan is to fly over it, at a low altitude. Immediately, its unusual radial layout would be perceived. The sprawling central sector of town is ringed by an artery that goes by a number of names—Via Mullino delle Armi, Via Santa Sofia, Via Francesco Sforza, to name some. Then, like spokes of a wheel, other wide streets lead from the periphery into the center—Via Dante, Via Magenta, Via Correnti which becomes Via Torino, Corso Italia, Corso di Porta Romana, Corso Vittorio Emanuele II, and, most important, because it is a principal downtown street, Via Manzoni.

The core to which they lead is *Piazza del Duomo,* the square named for the cathedral that is at once Milan's monumental souvenir of the past, and its most easily discernible landmark. From the *Duomo,* one passes through still another landmark structure—the shop-filled *Galleria*—to *Piazza della Scala,* which takes its name from the opera house at its edge, and which leads into earlier-mentioned Via Manzoni and other principal downtown streets. One can continue along Via Manzoni to *Piazza Cavour,* crossing it to Via Manin, passing the park called *Giardini Pubblici,* to *Piazza della Repubblica,* a generous-sized square that is the site of a pair of leading hotels and is in the direction, northeast, of still another important point— *Stazione Centrale,* the principal railway station, colonnaded and cavernous, and with an important group of hotels surrounding it. *Castello Sforzesco,* another major historic landmark (and home to a splendid museum) is a bit northwest of Piazza del Duomo, with *Arco della Pace*—a Milanese variation on the theme of Paris's Arc de Triomphe or New York's Washington Arch—just beyond, and not far from an enormous stadium, *Arena Civica.* Another important railway station, *Stazione Nord,* is in this neighborhood, and so is the *Church of Santa Maria delle Grazie,* site of Leonardo's *The Last Supper*—a major visitor destination. Scattered all about are the skyscrapers that are of more interest to visitors from countries other than America, which is not without concentrations of this kind of architecture that render Milan's of relatively little consequence.

THE ESSENTIAL MILAN

The Essential Milan, to a frighteningly high proportion of visitors, is boiled down to the Duomo, Leonardo's *The Last Supper,* and, if it is possible—which often it isn't—a performance at La Scala. For shame: these are but starters. Here is an appraisal of what is basic to a minimally informed understanding of so important a city. And mind, this ignores the shopping—some of the smartest in Europe— and the eating—some of the most delicious in Europe.

The Duomo: One senses the importance of the Duomo to the Milanese by simply regarding its situation: smack in the center of the city on a piazza that has intentionally been kept broad, the better to afford perspective. All of the major spokes of the artery of avenues that encircle Milan lead to the Duomo. Milan life revolves around the Duomo. Cultural life as embodied in La Scala is a hop and a skip distant. Business, shops, hotels are in the area. So are a number of museums, restaurants and caffès: the Duomo is a center for the lot. No major European city regards its cathedral with more affection, or with more importance, in its general scheme of things. Fortunately, this exceptional Gothic building is worthy of the attention.

Allot time for it. Consider, first, the span taken for its completion: Work began in 1386 and went on, with interruptions of course, until as recently as 1965, when the five great bronze doors—started at the turn of our century—were finally completed. Consider the most vital of the building's statistics. It's enormous, to begin: the second longest of Europe's major cathedrals, just after St. Peter's in Rome. There are some 3,500 pieces of sculpture, not counting the 150 marvelous gargoyles. There are no less than 135 pinnacle-like spires, including a central one with an elegant gilded Madonna atop it. Within, the scale is one of splendor and great beauty: The long central nave is flanked by a pair of aisles on either side, the lot supported by more than half a hundred chunky columns, topped with splendidly embellished capitals. The stained glass in and of itself is a treat. And in this of all churches, one does well to ascend to the roof (there are elevators) for the lacy perspective of the flying buttresses, crowned with saintly statues. The Duomo has both a Treasury of very very old things and, as well, a Museum—in a detached building across the square, dealt with on a later page. A final plea with regard to outdoor viewing: The front façade is impressive enough. But nothing like the Duomo as seen from either side and from the rear; these angles make clear the distinction of its architecture and the complexity of its decoration.

Teatro alla Scala: Americans can easily remember the date of its building—1776. The name is that of a church that had been on the site, Santa Maria alla Scala. (And the church in its turn was named for its benefactress, Beatrice Regina della Scala, wife of one of the Visconti clan who ruled as Dukes of Milan.) Performances have been taking place since 1778. La Scala is on a square that takes its name. The façade is low key, elegant, a cream- and putty-colored building in neoclassic style that surprises one, after passing through its portico, with the opulence to be found within. I recommend La Scala at this point in this chapter because, unlike many opera houses, it is generally open to the public during the day as is its museum (dealt with on a later page). After the severity of the façade, the interior can numb one with its opulence and size. Little of the original remains. One must not expect an eighteenth-century gem like Venice's La Fenice, or even as antique a theater as Naples' San Carlo. La Scala was remodeled in 1867, updated again in 1921, and restored in 1946 after devastating World War II bombing; Toscanini conducted the reopening concert. A monster of a crystal chandelier dominates a gilt and ivory auditorium embracing half a dozen levels of boxes and balconies (two of the former, four of the latter) superimposed over a single-aisle orchestra; total capacity is 2,800. The onetime royal box is now embellished with the solitary five-point star of the Italian Republic's insignia, but the coat of arms of the old royal House of Savoy has been left over the proscenium. A daytime visit, with house, stage, and orchestra pit empty, is better than none at all. Ideally, though, one attends a performance of either an opera (the season—*stagione lirica*—is November–May) or a concert (the season—*stagione sinfonica*—is spring through fall, the nonopera months). Besides the opera company, season in and season out, one of the best in the world, there is a resident orchestra, l'Orchestra della Scala with some 120 instrumentalists; and a chorus, Il Coro della Scala, with more than 90 voices.

The first opera, back in 1778, was *Europa Riconoscuita,* by a rival of Mozart named Salieri. It was in La Scala that premiers of operas by any number of greats were sung—Bellini's *Norma,* Puccini's *Madama Butterfly* and *Turandot,* Verdi's *Falstaff* and *Otello* among them, with still other premiers of operas by such composers as Donizetti, Mascagni, and Rossini.

Acoustics are unsurpassed, the ambience is coldly elegant. La Scala ushers, in formal black with silver necklaces bearing a likeness of the theater's façade on medallions, are so striking that one almost forgives them their arrogance. *Carabinieri,* in resplendent uniforms of an earlier century, strut about in pairs, not unlike soldier-characters in an opera. The audience tends toward the dressy (there is no better observation post if one would appraise the chattery smart-looking Milanese), with the intermission bar-crush quite as integral a part of the Scala experience as the architecture and on-stage or in-pit performances.

The Great Museums: Traditionally, when visitors had stayed long enough in Milan to get to a museum, it was the venerable Brera Gallery, usually to the exclusion of the others, excepting of course the church refectory with Leonardo's *The Last Supper*. In recent years the Italian Government, which operates the Brera, has closed something like two thirds of its rooms and allowed the building itself to deteriorate to the point where a visit is a Gloomy Gus kind of experience. When the Brera's current restoration is completed, it should be moved back to top-rank museum category. Until then, I include it in my secondary group.

Ambrosiana Gallery (Piazza Pio IX) bears the name of the early bishop-saint who created the rite that bears his name and is still observed in the Duomo. The gallery goes back to the collection of a seventeenth-century cardinal, enlarged over the years, and housed in an early-nineteenth-century structure that is also home to the Ambrosiana Library, itself a treasure trove of illuminated manuscripts and other works, including Leonardo's *Codice Atlantis*. But it is the gallery—bombed in 1943 and since faithfully restored—that most visitors will find important. The fourteen rooms are about evenly divided between two floors. Downstairs one does well to make a point of taking in works of local—Lombard—painters of the Renaissance. But it is upstairs that most excites, not only with Italian art but a higher proportion of foreign masters than is often the case in Italian museums. Suffice it for me to skim the surface: Botticelli, Ghirlandaio, Lippi, Vivarini, a slew of exquisite Luinis, Leonardo and his school, Bronzino, Reni, Giordano, Bassano, Tiepolo, Titian. Not to mention sculpture out of the Middle Ages, gorgeous Flemish works. My favorites: Ghirlandaio's *Adoration of the Child,* and what has to be the most sublime of still-lifes—a leafy basket of fruit by Caravaggio.

Museo Poldi Pezzoli (Via Manzoni 12): As if its alliterative name were not enough to draw one, the Poldi Pezzoli adds another ingredient: charm. This is a lovely mock-Gothic mansion a century or so old, with the nucleus of its collection the property of the man whose name it takes. Not unlike New York's Mr. Frick, Boston's Mrs. Gardner, and Stockholm's Countess von Hallwyl, he left the house-cum-treasures to be operated as a museum. There have been newer acquisitions, the lot embracing one of the choicest of the smaller-museum collections in Europe. A smashing *Portrait of a Young Woman* by Pollauolo has become this museum's trademark. But the second floor is full of eye-openers—Tiepolo's *The Fortitude and the Wisdom,* a Cranach of Martin Luther (a subject rarely come upon in Italy); a Guardi of Venice, a Botticelli *Madonna,* a Bellini *Pietà,* to give you a rough idea. Downstairs is a quintet of sumptuous rooms brimming with bronzes, tapestries, china, furniture, rugs, clocks, and glass.

Museo d'Arte Antica al Castello Sforzesco (Piazza Castello): Talk about walled castles! The Sforzesco, bearing the name of the Renaissance family that gave Milan a line of governing dukes, is first of all the structure itself, with turreted walls, tower of an entrance gate, vast inner court, the lot going back to the fifteenth century. A long period of deterioration ensued before turn-of-century and post-World War II restorations took place. Today, the castle shelters a sleeper of a museum of both the fine and applied arts. The paintings alone make it worth a trip—local Lombards and other Italians like Bellini, Lippi, Lotto, Correggio, Tintoretto, and Mantegna. But then there is gallery after gallery of tapestries, ivories, glass, gold, silver, and most especially china and furniture, with pieces from three centuries, concluding with the eighteenth. It is possible that not all galleries will be open in the course of your visit; no matter, those that are will be full of beautiful things. And the setting can't be beat.

Galleria d'Arte Moderna (Via Pelestro 16) is about as misleading a museum name as one is likely to encounter. Modern art—and good modern art—is but a part of the picture. This collection is housed in a park-enclosed palace away from the center of town—Villa Reale—that went up in the neoclassic style of the late eighteenth century. And it is well that you know before you go to allot enough time to look over the eye-popping suite of state rooms, as well as the paintings. Modern art, in the case of this museum, means most of the nineteenth century, especially Italian, not all of which is everyone's cup of tea. Upstairs, though, is the Grassi Collection, which embraces Frenchies whom we always enjoy running across, like Corot, Manet, Cézanne, Renoir, Gauguin, Vuillard, Bonnard. A next-door pavilion has more recent works by, among others, such Italians as Manzù, Marini, and Modigliani.

Leonardo's The Last Supper (Church of Santa Maria delle Grazie, Piazza Santa Maria delle Grazie), known locally simply as *La Cenacolo,* occupies an entire wall of what had been the refectory, or dining hall, of the convent attached to this church. Leonardo painted it in the late fifteenth century, at the request of the most famous of the Sforza dukes, Ludovic the Moor. And it was the subject of any number of subsequent restorations, many of them poor. The most recent came about as a result of World War II damage, and proved to be the best, for the painting was cleaned and early restorers' additions removed. What one sees today is a delicately colored dining-table scene, its reds and blues a foil for the brownish background, with the diners on either side intent on the Christ figure. The refectory is operated as a museum by the Italian Government, and well lighted, so that one is able to study the faces and expressions of diners at this most decisive of historic dinner parties. On the opposite wall is a fine fresco of the Crucifixion by Montorfano. The church itself—fifteenth-century—is unexceptional except for its massive and marvelous dome, and a charmer of a cloister (gained by a walk through the church interior)—both of them by Bramante.

Galleria Vittorio Emanuele II is but one of a number of these earliest-of-all shopping centers in Milan. To Milanese, it is simply *the* Galleria. Visitors come to know it straight off as it connects Piazza del Duomo with Piazza della Scala. It goes back a century, is cross-shaped, with an immense glass dome, and an elaborate mosaic floor. Lures within are fine shops, restaurants, caffès (some later specifically recommended) and most fun of all, the ambulatory Milanese.

A Lake Como Excursion: The enticements of Lake Como are two-fold. First is accessibility to the city. Zoom! A fast train or a good highway, and you're at your hotel in something like an hour and a half. Second is the species of astonishing beauty that results when staggering peaks—snowy atop, emerald-green lower down—descend to a shoreline, in this case a Y-shaped lake fringed by settlements in profusion enough to make selection difficult. *Como town* is a surprise because it's a substantial city—silk manufacturing is a major area enterprise—with only its lake-shore and adjacent Old Town areas of visitor interest. (The rest of town is unlovely.) A stay of a couple of nights can be agreeable—*Hotel Metropole Suisse au Lac,* overlooking the lake at Piazza Cavour, is old-school, with cheery service, capacious bath-equipped rooms, restaurant, bar-lounge, and some nice lake-view rooms. Amble about for an inspection tour embracing the rambling, elaborate Renaissance-style Duomo; Basilica di San Fidele—another multi-era structure partially twelfth century and of especial beauty; and Museo Civico—a catch-all with objects dating from Roman times to the Risorgimento, including what is believed to be the oldest extant portrait of Christopher Columbus. Stop in, while wandering—the pastries are superlative—for refreshments at Pasticceria Belli (Via Vittorio Emanuele 7). Pop into Templo Voltiano, a neoclassic confection housing instruments and manuscripts of scientist Alessandro Volta. The lakeside palazzo that is such a standout is called Villa Olmo, dating back to the eighteenth century; it's now a convention hall. You're ready now for the cable-car ascent to the peak of Mount Brunate. Then come the lake itself and its communities. If you've but a single lake day, settle for an excursion via Navigazione Lago di Como. Its boats depart regularly from Piazza Cavour and make stops at every lakeside village of any significance. One that you might want to headquarter at is *Villa d'Este,* with its ex-palace of a hotel by that name (an occupant was England's Queen Caroline of Brunswick, the consort of George IV, who treated her so badly that she spent considerable time on the Continent). Villa d'Este today is one of Italy's premier resort hotels, equipped with facilities ranging from swimming pool to eighteen-hole golf course. Still another recommended stop is *Bellagio,* a perfectly beautiful hilly village that straddles the peninsula at the point forming the center of the lake's Y-formation. *Hotel Villa Serbelloni,* lake-front and old-school, is my choice as the top hotel; others—all on the lake—albeit less grand, in declining order, include *Metropole, Grand Bretagna, Excelsior, Splendide, Du Lac,* and *Roma.* There are browsable lake-front shops (the area's silk, turned into ties, bathrobes, scarves, blouses, is a specialty), a variety of restaurants, and good caffès— including Rossi—with delicious snacks. A few minutes' boat ride from Bellagio is the region's handsomest historic house. It's called Villa Carlotta, dates to the eighteenth century, and its azalea-filled gardens vie with its evocative interiors. But I have only scratched the Como surface. Just to give you an idea: the boat from Como town to Bellagio stops, according to my en-route notes, no less than eighteen times. Which means eighteen lovely lakeside choices: Cernobbio, Colonno, Moltrasio, Nesso, Tremezzo, to name but a handful in addition to earlier-recommended Villa d'Este and Bellagio. At that, I've mentioned only possibilities on the *left* arm of the Y-shaped lake. There remain additional destinations to the north, and on the lake's right arm, subtitled Lago di Lecco, with the city of Lecco its counterpart of Como town.

BEHIND MUSEUM WALLS:
A SELECTION OF FAVORITES

Pinacoteca di Brera (Via Brera 28): One has the feeling that even in its heyday the Renaissance palazzo housing the Brera Gallery was not a happy place, despite the formidable scale of its stadium-size courtyard. What appears to have happened is that lack of funds has forced the Italian Government, the Brera's landlords, to let it deteriorate. At the moment this structure—housing since 1809 what had been one of Italy's ranking art museums—comes close to being as grim a kind of experience as I've encountered in considerable museum-going. Which would not be all that much of a detriment if the gallery's bosses had not—on my last visit, at least—chosen to close twenty-eight of the thirty-eight treasure-filled galleries. When the public is deprived of seeing that big a chunk of a museum's collection, even a prestigious repository loses status. And so with the Brera. There still are great works to be seen—Bellini, Titian, Tintoretto, Canaletto, Giordano, Guardi, Longhi, Tiepolo, and foreigners, too, including Rembrandt; a sampling, at least, of a superlative, mostly locked-away collection.

Museo Archeologico (Corso Magenta) is tucked into the onetime monastery adjacent to the later-recommended Church of San Maurizio. The setting alone makes a visit enjoyable. There are a number of choice relics of the classical past—capitals, sarcophagi, handsome busts, a striking sculptured likeness of Hercules, and some dazzling mosaics, the lot impressing upon the visitor the very great age of Milan.

Civico Museo di Milano and Civico Museo di Storia Contemporanea (Via San Andrea 6) share quarters in a gracious eighteenth-century house. You come upon the latter—its period is from World War I to World War II—first, when you should come upon it last, but no matter. It brings to mind, sometimes with ferocious honesty, that not always felicitous period, which included the fascistic Mussolini era. The Museo di Milano is mostly seventeenth through nineteenth centuries in scope. There are furnished rooms from the house's original period, and gallery after gallery of objects, including many delightful paintings.

Civico Museo del Risorgimento Nazionale (Via Borgonuovo 23) zeroes in on Milan's important role in the historical events—late-eighteenth through mid-nineteenth centuries—that led to Italy's unification. There are paintings, prints, documents, even including souvenirs of the 1805 ceremony at which Napoleon was crowned King of Italy in the Duomo. Later exhibits concentrate on the Big Three Heroes, whom we remember from school: Mazzini, Garibaldi, and Cavour.

Museo Teatrale alla Scala (Teatro alla Scala) has its own side entrance and is indicated for opera buffs, with its documentation—paintings, prints, programs—relating to composers, singers, performances, Scala firsts, and Scala history. There are two rooms devoted to Verdi alone, and still other exhibits relating to ballet and nonmusical theater, including Italy's commedia dell'arte.

Museo del Duomo (Palazzo Reale) occupies part of a fine old palace just across the way from the Duomo. Here are bits and pieces—and beautiful ones at that—from the six-century-long history of the cathedral—stone gargoyles, sculptured saints, jewel-encrusted crucifixes, rich tapestries, ancient stained-glass, even architects' drawings from various eras.

Tecnica Leonardo da Vinci (Via San Vittore 21) is technologically advanced Milan putting its best foot forward, in a onetime monastery, with a monk's cell and a monstery pharmacy the only remnants of the building's former function. Technical matters—metallurgy, engineering, oil research, modern vehicles—fill the basement and overflow upstairs. For us nonspecialists, the lure is on the second floor: a socko presentation of the achievements of the genius for whom the museum is named.

AFTER THE DUOMO: SELECTED CHURCHES

If Milan's churches are anticlimactic after the Duomo, they still are not to be ignored. At least not some of the best of them, to wit:

Sant' Ambrogio (Piazza Sant' Ambrogio) is a Romanesque beauty named for the sainted early-Christian bishop who gave the Catholic church the Ambrosian Rite. Indeed, St. Ambrose consecrated the original church in A.D. 387. One enters its successor through its cloister. Within there is a Bramante-designed portico and memorable mosaics. After the Duomo: tops in town.

Sant' Eustorgio (Piazza Sant' Eustorgio) is something like a millennium old—a Romanesque souvenir of importance. To note within are the chapels, especially the one dedicated to the Three Kings, and another, behind the apse, with superb frescoes.

San Lorenzo Maggiore (Corso di Porta Ticinese) has a smashing situation, just opposite a cluster of sixteen gorgeous Corinthian columns—all that remains of an early Roman temple. The domed church is the Renaissance successor to an ancient original; its chapels are embellished with also-ancient mosaics.

San Maurizio (Corso Magenta 15) is earlier mentioned in connection with the Archaeological Museum, which occupies its monastery. The church is sixteenth century, and odd in that a wall separates one part of its nave (where resident Benedictine monks worshiped) from the other (where the public prayed). The walls are the lure, for they are painted with important frescoes by Bernardino Luini.

San Satiro (Via Torino) is a Renaissance replacement for an earlier church. Designer of the present building was the master Bramante, and we may thank him for its splendid proportions and a lovely baptistry. There are fine frescoes.

Excursions might be considered to **Certosa di Pavia,** a long-time Carthusian monastery that goes back to the fifteenth century, which is oddly and excessively ornamented but is nonetheless architecturally impressive. It's interesting in that its monks were under a rule so strict that each lived, ate, prayed, and worked in his own little stone house, a series of which surrounded the larger of the two cloisters. Only on feast days did the monks get together for communal—albeit spartan—meals, and prayers in the chapel. The Carthusians departed in 1947 and a band of white-robed Cistercians are their successors. The drive south from Milan takes about an hour, each way, on ugly, traffic-clogged roads. . . . Another excursion destination is **Abbazia di Chiaravalle,** only four miles southeast of town and architecturally more felicitous; there is a towering campanile, a Renaissance church with a frescoed dome, and a fine cloister.

A MILANESE MISCELLANY

Antico Ospedale Maggiore (Via Francesco Sforza 29) is the onetime Main Hospital—for long known also as Ca' Grande—which is now headquarters for the Università degli Studi, with an extensive collection of old paintings (Quadreria dell'Ospedale Maggiore) traditionally shown from March 25 through April 25 each year, and of masterful, mostly Renaissance architecture that makes it worthy of inspection at any time. The façade is elegant, especially that section with a series of exquisite arched, mullioned windows. So is the serene and cloister-like courtyard.

Arco della Pace (Piazza Sempione) was planned in 1807 to commemorate Napoleonic victories. History changed that. The end result, some decades later, was a monument to Austrian-led battles. If the arch seems too narrow for its height, there is no denying the grandeur of the bronze chariot and horses up on top.

Bramante Cloisters (Piazza Sant' Ambrogio): Location is Università Cattolica del Sacro Cuore, Milan's Catholic university. To see is a distinguished pair of cloisters—one of Doric columns, the other Corinthian—created by Bramante in the fifteenth century.

Cimitero Monumentale (Porta Volta): One frequently finds much made of cemeteries in Latin lands. Not everyone enjoys visiting them, but Milan is so proud of this one—with its sculpture extending over the past century—that I make mention of it.

Giardini Pubblici is the garden-like park in the core of town, which makes for nice walks, bench rests, and, if one is interested, diversion at a small but interestingly populated zoo.

Palazzo Clerici (Via Clerici 5) is a fine eighteenth-century town house now given over to governmental functions but still open on a limited basis for painting buffs who would like the opportunity to see an eighty-foot-long ballroom with a whole vast ceiling fresco by Tiepolo. The Venetian master painted it in 1740; it has to do with Mercury and his Sun Chariot—and it's a honey.

Stadio San Siro is modern Milan at its most striking; a near-triangular-shaped structure that seats 100,000 soccer fans; at its best when filled.

Milan: To Watch

La Scala: One's objective is a performance. It is not generally, to understate the case, an easy matter. (There are only 2,800 seats for both Milanese and visitors per performance.) But first things first. The splendid theater itself is earlier recommended in some detail (and with some historical background) as a requisite Milan attraction. It is open daily for sightseeing (as is the museum attached to it, also earlier recommended) so that you can count on seeing the place, in any event, even if you don't snag a performance ticket. As for the opera season—and here La Scala is globally pre-eminent—it is limited to the period between early December (December 7—the Feast of Milan's own St. Ambrose is the traditional opening date) and spring, when for the remaining months—spring through autumn—a concert season replaces it. (And make no mistake, a chance to see La Scala's symphony, frequently led by international guest conductors, is not to be taken lightly.) Printed schedules for the coming months' performances are available at travel agencies in Milan, not to mention hotel concierges in the city and the bigger travel agencies elsewhere in Italy. Certain of the better travel agencies abroad, including the United States, try to keep up on La Scala performances and help their clients to see an opera or hear a concert. In town, the theater's box office is usually open daily, without a lunch break. There is always the possibility of customers wanting to sell an unneeded ticket just before the performance. (I shall never forget that I was able to buy my first Scala ticket this way.) So don't hesitate to stand outside an hour or so before curtain and plead to buy an unneeded ticket from anyone who looks a likely seller. (If you miss dinner in the process, you may obtain nourishment from the refreshment bar at intermission.)

Piccola Scala (Via Filodrammatici) is an alternative to the mother company, or a supplement. It is 1950s-modern, with performances of both traditional and contemporary works. The artistic level is high, and the likelihood is that more of the audience will be Milanese than at the internationally attended Scala.

Piccolo Teatro (Via Rovello) is a municipally operated theater; one might call it a Milanese counterpart of the New York City Center; the idea is culture for the masses at popular prices. Investigate, especially if you're a theater buff undaunted by language barriers.

The Triennale is a once-every-three-years exhibition of the decorative arts. Interior designers, architects, furniture and applied-arts manufacturers, and others in associated fields, converge upon Milan from the world over, with invariably high U.S. attendance. Setting is *Palazzo dell'Arte al Parco* (Via Alemagna).

Milan International Fair is an annual trade show held every April—usually the fifteenth through the twenty-fifth. Some ninety nations are generally represented with exhibitions and programs of interest to the international business community.

Discos, Dancing, Movies: Nightlife, as might be expected in a rich, business-oriented city with a substantial visitor population of affluent gents, is fraught with possibilities. Hotel concierges and the newspapers are good sources of what's happening where, this very evening.

Milan: To Stay

As befits a modern, efficient city, Milan's hotels are plentiful, in a variety of categories, and by and large excellent. They tend to be located in three broad areas: core of downtown; in the area between downtown and Piazza della Repubblica; and beyond, in and around the area of Stazione Centrale. Here are my selections—places in which I've lived, eaten, drunk, or at least thoroughly inspected, presented alphabetically; I've designated each luxury, first class, or moderate.

Hotel Anderson (Piazza Luigi di Savoia 20) is a chromy-modern house adjacent to Stazione Centrale, with an inviting lobby, restaurant, cocktail lounge, and nice-looking, fully equipped rooms. *First class.*

Aerhotel Executive (Viale Don Luigi Sturzo 45) is capacious (420 rooms and suites), contemporary, with good-looking, fully equipped rooms, several cocktail lounges, restaurant, and extensive meeting facilities. It's adjacent to the in-town Air Terminal, near Stazione Centrale but not downtown. *First class.*

Aerhotel Fieramilano (Viale Boezio 20) is popular with exhibitors and visitors to the annual Milan International Fair; it's just across from the entrance. Like its sister hotel (see above) it's ultramod, with sweeping lobby and full facilities—bar, restaurant, conference rooms—but fewer rooms (238), all of them attractive and convenience-packed. *First class.*

Hotel Ambasciatori (Galleria del Corso 3) is a neighbor of Stazione Centrale with 103 so-so rooms (the beds are not for large people), most, but not all, with bath; nice restaurant, bar, and breakfast terrace. *Moderate.*

Hotel Ascot (Via Lentasio 3–5) is recent, with comfortable enough rooms, all bath-equipped, agreeable lobby, bar; breakfast only. *Moderate.*

Hotel Berna (Via Napo Torriani 18) has some 75 bath-equipped rooms; they shine. Welcoming lobby-lounge. Breakfast only. Near Stazione Centrale. *Moderate.*

Hotel Bristol (Via Scarlatti 32) is functional-modern, with 71 pleasant rooms with bath or, in the case of singles, showers. Congenial bar-lounge. Breakfast only. *Moderate.*

Hotel Canova (Via N. Toriani 15) is a quiet, 59-room house, very modern, with comfortable rooms, all bath-equipped; agreeable lobby and bar-lounge. Breakfast only. Stazione Centrale is nearby. *Moderate.*

Carlton Hotel Senato (Via Senato 5) is on a quiet street near Stazione Centrale with some 70 exceptionally pleasant rooms, all of whose beds are equipped with insert-a-coin massage machines; the baths are big. Handsome restaurant, cocktail lounge. *First class.*

Hotel Cavour (Via Fabebenefratelli 21) is a conveniently located downtown house, modern and with a chandelier-lit lobby, rather grand restaurant and bar-lounge, and about a hundred well-equipped rooms-cum-bath. *First class.*

Hotel de la Ville (Via Hoepli 6) is inviting, contemporary, with an impressive lobby, 105 rooms with bath, good restaurant, cocktail lounge, and a super downtown location. *First class.*

Excelsior Hotel Gallia (Piazza Duca d'Aosta 9) is a Milan institution, beautifully run, with 200-plus handsome rooms and suites, in a variety of décor motifs, but each elegant and fully equipped. There is a spacious lobby, one of the city's most popular cocktail lounges, and a restaurant (of which more later). Location is Stazione Centrale. *Luxury.*

Grand Hotel et de Milan (Via Manzoni 29) is an old-timer, nicely updated and with an enviable downtown location. There are a hundred cheery rooms (all but ten with bath), popular cocktail lounge that serves snacks, and breakfast service, but no restaurant. Very pleasant. *First class.*

Jolly Hotel President (Largo Augusto 10) has a good near-Duomo location, and the sprightly mod look common to the well-run, Italy-wide Jolly chain. There are 200 snappy rooms, all fully equipped, restaurant, cocktail lounge, nice big lobby. *First class.*

Hotel Lloyd (Corso di Porta Romana 48) is smallish (under 60 rooms and suites) and with a downtown situation near the Duomo.

The severe façade puts one off but the interior is handsome: comfortable lobby-cocktail lounge and fine rooms, with massage machines for the beds and, if you please, second phones in the bathrooms. *First class*.

Hotel Marino alla Scala (Piazza della Scala 5) is lovely old-school, with 80 charming rooms-cum-bath, attractive reception area and bar-lounge. Breakfast only. And the location: you practically fall out of bed onto the stage of La Scala. *First class*.

Hotel Michelangelo (Via Scarlatti 33) is big, bustling, sleek Milan Modern, opposite Stazione Centrale, with 400 compact but well-equipped rooms with bath (some suites, too), handsome basement restaurant, busy bar-lounge, convention-meeting facilities. *First class*.

Milano Hilton (Via Galvani 12) is a compact modern house—one must not expect, say, Rome's capacious Cavalieri Hilton—with 200-plus fully equipped rooms and suites, main-floor cocktail lounge with an attractive English club-like look, rooftop disco, second-floor restaurant. Location is near Stazione Centrale. *Luxury*.

New York Hotel (Via Pirelli 5), hardly evocative of Manhattan, is a tranquil 72-room house, modern and agreeable, near Stazione Centrale. All rooms have bath. Bar-lounge and breakfast but no restaurant. *Moderate*.

Palace Hotel (Piazza della Repubblica 20) is a long-time Milan leader that a season or two back went Mod from stem to stern. The look, from lobby upwards, is severe ultracontemporary in the 200 fully equipped rooms and suites, and in the buzzy cocktail lounge and adjacent Casanova Grill, of which more on a later page. The Palace is a favorite with the rising and middle-level executive—British, Continental European, North American—not to mention pleasure visitors who like its snappy atmosphere and the skilled service. A CIGA hotel. *Luxury*.

Plaza Hotel (Piazza Diaz 3) is heart-of-town downtown, and with 120 agreeable rooms with bath, welcoming atmosphere, amusing bar. Breakfast only. *First class*.

Hotel Principe e Savoia and Annex (Piazza della Repubblica 17) is the across-the-square neighbor of the Palace Hotel (see above) and a fellow affiliate of the CIGA chain. Each has its own personality. The Principe e Savoia is traditional style in the very best sense. You like the vibes from the moment you step into the handsome lobby. There are 300 absolutely posh rooms and suites, no two exactly alike, every one superluxurious; those in the newer section have terraces. The cocktail lounge is a major Milan congregating place—smart and talky. So is the Grill (of which more on a later page). And breakfast is served alfresco, facing the broad piazza, in summer. The adjacent Annex has its own entrance, bar-lounge, and breakfast facilities; accommodation is in smart modern-design apartments that can be rented by week or month. Service throughout the Principe is at once professional—I would even say impeccable—and smiling. This is one of Italy's best hotels. *Luxury.*

Hotel Rosa (Via Pattari 5), a traditional-style 125-room house to the rear (the most beautiful part) of the Duomo, downtown. Almost all rooms have private baths. Bar and breakfast, but no restaurant. Pleasant. *Moderate.*

Hotel Select (Via Barracchini 12) is a modern 140-room house not far from the Duomo. Bedrooms are at once cozy and functional. There's a welcoming bar-lounge. *First class.*

Milan: To Eat and Drink

It should not be surprising that so rich a city—culturally as well as financially—eats as well as Milan does. There are restaurants with the food of the various Italian regions. But the Milanese cooking in and of itself is hardly to be despised. The supreme specialty is *risotto alla milanese*—northern-grown rice that is slowly simmered in butter, chicken broth and white wine, flavored with saffron and freshly grated Parmesan cheese. *Osso bucco*—stewed shin of veal—is another Milanese dish. Veal chops with a white-wine sauce are popular. Locals claim that fish is nowhere fresher than in Milan markets. The typically northern emphasis on rice by no means obliterates pasta's popularity. As in every area, locals tend to drink regional wines by the carafe in restaurants. Lombardy—Milan's province—produces both reds and whites, with Sassella and Grumello the best-known reds, and Frecciarossa emerging as red, rosé, and white, with white preferred. Like Frecciarossa, Clastidio is produced in red, rosé, and white types, with the white delightful. Wines from the nearby lakes area are popular—Bellagio's red, for example, and Como's whites. So are wines from neighboring Piedmont—the red Barolo and Grignolino; along with whites like Soave from the also-neighboring Veneto region.

Of the major Italian cities, Milan—as the richest—gives the impression of employing more novelty, variety, and imagination than the others, when it comes to the décor and design of restaurants. As in every case it's the food that counts, but Milan rates high marks for ambience. Here is a select group of restaurants in varying price ranges that I like. They are presented alphabetically, with my category—*expensive, moderate, inexpensive*—indicated in every case.

Alemagna is Italy-wide, but it's Milan-headquartered. This is a firm that manufactures its own chocolates and bakes its cookies, all of which it distributes to retail outlets throughout Italy and abroad. Additionally, it operates a chain of multifunction eateries, with so many good things one doesn't know where to begin—pastries, cakes, little sandwiches, pizza, hot dishes, soda fountains vending ice-cream concoctions and drinks, proper bars, too, with retail sections in conjunction. In Milan, important Alemagna locations for the visitor are Piazza del Duomo (which has a cafeteria); Via Monte Napoleone at the corner of Via Manzoni (with red velvet chairs and banquettes in one room, tapestried walls decorating another, and the china teapots in elegant silver serving frames); and Via Croce Rosa at Via Manzoni. Go for morning coffee, lunch, afternoon tea, snacks. *Inexpensive.*

Antico Ristorante Boeucc (Piazza Belgioioso 2) is heart-of-town near the Duomo, and very smart—with paneled walls and a dressy clientele to match. Which is not to disparage the food: try *risotto salta* for starters, and go on to a grilled fish—the *spada* (swordfish) is delicious. So are the roasts. *Moderate to Expensive.*

Bagutta (Via Bagutta 14) is a beloved old-timer. There seems to be no end to its continuing series of high-ceilinged rooms. And at mealtime they are all jammed and noisy. There's a help-yourself buffet at lunch (you pay for what you pick up, dish by dish). But for both lunch and dinner there's a printed menu as well. The antipasti are gorgeous to look upon and to taste. *Rigatoni alla Bagutta* is the pasta specialty—and super. Then go on to a vast range of meat and fish dishes, and have a salad if you can manage it. *Moderate*.

Biffi (Galleria Vittorio Emanuele II): This mod-look place has both cafeteria and waiter service areas; it's ideal for a nonsplurge but excellent meal after the opera or a concert at nearby La Scala. Go also for lunch, or a snack while shopping. *Moderate*.

Brasera Meneghina (Via Circo 10) is no-nonsense comfortable, with stick-to-the-ribs food—*sopa di verdura* (vegetable soup) or *osso bucco,* veal stewed in white wine, for example. Kindly, proficient service. *Moderate*.

Casanova Grill (Palace Hotel, Piazza della Repubblica) is Modish Mod, all blacks and browns, with a menu at once Italian and international, and a clientele likewise; mostly upward-mobile business types and especially amusing at lunch. *Moderate to Expensive*.

Caffè Cova (Via Monte Napoleone at Via San Andrea): Just the spot when you've shopper's feet in midafternoon. Stop for a cuppa and some pastry. Or a drink. *Inexpensive*.

Excelsior Hotel Gallia Restaurant (Piazzale Duca d'Aosta 9): A nice old-fashioned hotel dining room, with panache, and a well-heeled clientele. The set menus are popular—*risotto* is usually included among the first courses. Go on to the big lounge for coffee. *Moderate* if you order the good-value *prix-fixe; Expensive* à la carte.

Giannino (Via A. Sciesa 8) is all that a luxury restaurant should be: capacious and handsome, warm and smiling, with absolutely delicious food and a splendid wine list, which has representation from every major Italian wine-producing region, not to mention wine countries like France and Germany. The look, one gaily decorated room after another, is of a massive winter garden. There are plants and flowers everywhere, and you may peep into the glass-walled kitchen as you move along to your table. Pasta is superlative; ask for a plate embracing two or three specialties—whatever the captain counsels. Unless, of course, you are unable to resist the *risotto* prepared with seafood—another specialty. *Fritto misto*—a maze of deep-fried fish and seafood—is sublime. So are veal *piccata* and *tournedos Rossini*. Desserts are the most elaborate in town; why not splurge on *omelette confiture flambée?* Coffee? Espresso of course. But look carefully at the menu and you'll find *Chase e Sanborn* listed. This is one of Italy's very best restaurants. *Expensive.*

Gran Sasso (Piazzale Principessa Clotilde 10—which just has to be the grandest-sounding address in town) is anything but grand. It's a noisy, crowded, imaginatively overdecorated taverna, where the waiters—in costumes from the Abruzzi region—are so overworked that you expect them at any moment to snarl. Instead they carry tray after tray of a traditional fourteen-course meal that has not varied for as long as anyone can remember. Go for dinner when you've plenty of time. Along with an enormous pitcher of house wine and huge hunks of delicious coarse bread, you are served, in this order: skewered mixed grill, eggplant and peppers, *frittata* (a kind of omelet), beans in oil with parsley, black olives, salami and prosciutto, *pastini in brodo* (a soup), spaghetti with tomato sauce, a chicken casserole, roast lamb, a cheese platter, the day's cake, a monstrous basket of unshelled nuts, ice cream, coffee, and an assortment of liqueurs. More wine? Fill your pitcher from the nearby barrel. Withal: *Moderate.*

Motta (Piazza del Duomo extending into Galleria Vittorio Emanuele II) is a competitor to Alemagna (see above) and similar to it in almost every respect. I think Alemagna has the edge, ever so slightly, but that is a personal opinion. At any rate, this chain is to be found all over town (there's another big outlet on Corso Buenos Aires) but the big Duomo-Galleria Motta has everything, including an upstairs cafeteria. *Inexpensive.*

Le Nôs (Via Amedei 2) occupies a turn-of-century town house and is appropriately turn-of-century within—very grand indeed, to a point where the pretentiousness shows through. Still, it's agreeable, with a multilingual expense-account clientele. The menu, in bothersome-to-foreigners Milanese dialect, is in the shape of a folding fan and difficult to negotiate. Stick to classic dishes like *risotto* (which is very tasty), *gnocchi* (likewise), *osso bucco,* roasts, and grills. I recall a refreshing lemon sherbet for dessert. *Expensive.*

Hotel Principe e Savoia Grill (Piazza della Repubblica 17): What you should know first is that this restaurant is in two parts—one with music, if that is your mood; the other without, for conversationalists. Take a look at the salad, antipasto, and cheese tables as you enter. And at the chickens roasting on an open spit. The menu is at once the best of Italy and of the Continent. In the former category, consider a quartet of variations on the theme of *risotto;* of delectable antipasti, of the Grill's own *fettuccine,* and *scampi.* I heartily counsel the *cotoletta di vitello Pierrot.* There are top quality grills—lamb chops, steaks, veal *paillard.* And the *zabaglione al rhum* has to be your dessert choice. The staff are pros. *Expensive.*

A Riccione (Via Terramelli 70) is for seafood—fresh, delicious, and professionally served. One must excuse the eccentric décor. Consider instead the good things to eat—such as fresh shrimp with a homemade mayonnaise dressing, grilled fish of the day, pasta with fresh clam or seafood sauces, or the enormous and delicious fried-seafood platter. *Expensive.*

La Rinascente (Piazza del Duomo): Hie yourself to the seventh floor of this department store for the super view from picture windows and a delicious lunch—antipasti, salads, pasta, or the *prix-fixe;* afternoon tea; or cocktails, for that matter. Attractive and *Inexpensive.*

Caffè Sant' Ambroeus (Corso Giacomo Matteotti near Via Monte Napoleone) is for a splurgy afternoon tea. The pastries are nowhere more delicious. If you are very rich, you might want to buy a box of this house's own chocolates, packed in a velvet-covered box embellished with semiprecious stones. The clientele is Milan at its most stylish and good-looking. As such places go: *Expensive.*

St. Andrews (Via Sant' Andrea 23) is the name of the street cleverly translated into English, the better to give this restaurant a slightly snob air about it. And why not? It is among the smarter-looking in Milan, with good food in a wide range to match, both at lunch and dinner, but also—worth knowing this—for latish suppers. *Expensive.*

Savini (Galleria Vittorio Emanuele II): If you are going to dine in style after a performance at La Scala—*dopo Scala* ("after Scala") is the expression—it's going to be at Savini, traditionally but also wisely. The look is crystal chandeliers and red-silk-lamp-shaded tables and captains who know their old-time customers' every whim but are equally solicitous of newcomers. *Risotto* is indicated for starters—saffron or *al salto* style. *Fritto misto* (a seafood mix) or *scampi Savini*, or veal cutlet Milan style—all are main-course specialties. *Cassatta* is but one of a number of masterful desserts. *Expensive.*

Da Serafino (Via Bramante 34) is for the specialties of the neighboring Piedmont region. It embraces a pair of oversized, blue-hued chambers, with gregarious waiters and top-notch food. The mixed antipasto—including mortadella sausage, salami, and pheasant pâté— is counseled, and the Piedmontese variation on the theme of Swiss *fondue*—called *fonduta*—is a main-course novelty. Pastas are delicious, and so are such meat dishes as rolled veal with prosciutto. *Moderate.*

Milan: To Buy

Make no mistake; Milan is rich. Milan has style. And Milan has business visitors with money in their pockets. It follows that shops should be among the best in Italy; they are.

The commercial center of the city, as I have earlier indicated, centers around the Duomo. Via Manzoni is the main street, and the streets leading from it are important too; Via Brera is full of art galleries. Corso Buenos Aires is a center for department and chain stores. And, perhaps most noteworthy, Via Monte Napoleone is Milan shopping at its most elegant.

Herewith, my personally scouted selections in categories of interest to visitors, arranged alphabetically.

ANTIQUES

Florence is Italy's pre-eminent antiques city, but Milan has sources too. It is wise to elicit as much information about merchandise as possible from shopkeepers and to ask—no matter how fancy the shop

—if the price asked is indeed the final price. (Sometimes it is *not*.) Italians remain brilliant craftsmen—the finest such in Europe—so that reproductions passing as antiques are not all that uncommon.

Arte Antica (Via Sant' Andrea): old things—many of them choice—including china, clocks, and furniture.

Bellini (Via Gesù): mostly seventeenth- and eighteenth-century Italian objects. Good quality.

Franzini (Via Sant' Andrea): seventeenth-century walnut furniture, both Italian and English; antique paintings.

Frecchini (Via Sant' Andrea): Range is fifteenth through nineteenth centuries—antiques and paintings.

Galleria del Morone (Via G. Morone): Italian seventeenth-century walnut furniture.

Gianetti (Via Gesù): Everything is lovely; sixteenth- and seventeenth-century furniture, china, paintings, all Italian; one of Milan's best sources.

Grassi Bernardi (Via Sant' Andrea): Italian and French objects, fifteenth to eighteenth centuries.

Old Silver (Via Gesù) also sells old prints and a variety of smallish objects that make good gifts.

Tullio Silva (Via Sant' Andrea): seventeenth- and eighteenth-century Venetian mirrors and painted furniture; objects from other northern Italian areas, too.

BOOKS

Rizzoli (Galleria Vittorio Emanuele II): an enormous—and most attractive—outlet illuminated by crystal chandeliers and featuring foreign language art books. One of a national chain, with a New York store, too.

CHILDREN'S CLOTHES

Mancadori (Via Monte Napoleone 10): stylish tots' togs—mostly knitwear.

CHINA AND GLASS

Bernasioni (Galleria Vittorio Emanuele II): a good range of silver, china, glass, giftware, in an easy-to-find location.

Dom (Corso Giacomo Matteotti): quality glass and china in apparently infinite variety.

Forme Nuove (Corso Buenos Aires): glass, glass, glass. Big selections.

CONTEMPORARY FURNITURE

Milan is the Italian center for modern furniture, as for so much else of contemporary creation.

Elam (Via San Pietro all'Orto at Corso Giacomo Matteotti): high-style and inventive.

Borsani (Via Monte Napoleone): various Italian firms' modern furniture.

DEPARTMENT STORES

The concept of the department store, still not fully developed in the south, is at its most sophisticated in Milan.

Coin (Piazza Loretta at Corso Buenos Aires) is multistoried, with attractive merchandise, especially so in the clothing departments; one of the best men's shops in town.

J. C. Penney (Via San Pietro all'Orto just off Corso Giacomo Matteotti): a transplanted Penney's, in concept at least. Budget-quality merchandise is Italian; so is the staff, and, for that matter, the language of transaction.

La Rinascente (Piazza del Duomo) is a nationwide chain, at its best in this Milan store, especially for men's, women's, and children's clothing. The restaurant is worthy of recommendation on an earlier page.

Standar (Via Torino) is one of a low-price chain.

Union Militare (Via Monte Napoleone) may sound like an army and navy store, U.S. style, but is much smarter. Clothes for all the family.

UPIM (Corso Buenos Aires) is still another national cheapie-chain.

FABRICS

Galtrucco (Piazza del Duomo) is one of Milan's best sources of fabrics-by-the-meter for men's and women's clothing.

Carlo Colombo (Via Monte Napoleone): decorative fabrics, of exceptional quality in a country where they are a specialty.

FOOD AND WINES

Alemagna (Piazza del Duomo; other locations): retail sections sell candies, cookies, cakes, crackers, other comestibles for train or motor excursions, cocktails in your hotel room, or whatever.

Fattorie (Via Manzoni at Via Monte Napoleone): salamis, other things to eat, wines by the bottle.

Motta (Piazza del Duomo; other locations): Retail sections vend groceries, cookies, wine, candy, cakes—the works, in a mini-super-market.

Salumaio (Via Monte Napoleone): prepared foods to go—smoked fish, pastas, pastries, cheeses, caviar, salamis, all tempting.

GLOVES

Guanti Berni (Via Sant' Andrea): a good selection, men's and women's. If you haven't tried on gloves, on an Italian glove-trier-onner, this is the place!

JEWELRY

Caumont (Via Gesù): both women's and men's rings, watches, bracelets; amusing and camp.

David Columbo (Via Monte Napoleone): fine jewels and expensive costume jewelry.

Mario Buccellati (Via Monte Napoleone): Florentine jewelry from a Florentine firm—heavy and chunky silver, too; with a New York branch.

Martignetti (Via Monte Napoleone): The emphasis is on jade and gold. Smart.

LEATHER AND LUGGAGE

Coppola & Toppo (Via Manzoni at Via Monte Napoleone): The specialty is women's handbags of good quality and design.

Eve (Via San Pietro al'Oro): a good selection of luggage, men's and women's, in both leather and canvas; women's handbags, too.

Fratelli Prada (Galleria Vittorio Emanuele II): luggage, leather accessories, women's handbags.

Gucci (Via Monte Napoleone): not as jammed with Americans and Japanese as their stores in Florence and Rome, if only because there are fewer in Milan; Italian customers compensate. Beautiful leather, men's and women's shoes, accessories.

LINENS

Emilia Bellini (Via Sant' Andrea): perfectly beautiful hand-worked linens in traditional designs; a Florentine firm.

Pratesi (Via Monte Napoleone): an outlet of the firm that has branches elsewhere in Italy and in New York; very high-style, Mod-design bed linens, comforters, blankets.

MEN'S CLOTHES

Alle Dolomiti (Via Monte Napoleone): casual and sports clothes, suede jackets; boys' wear, too.

Caesar (Via Monte Napoleone): smart togs in a smart-looking toggery, and that includes suits, sport jackets, suede jackets, shirts, and ties.

Carrano (Via Sant' Andrea): suits, shirts, ties, sweaters, shoes—all high-style.

Ken Scott (Via Monte Napoleone at Via Sant' Andrea—arcade): a smallish retail outlet for modish ties and shirts designed by the American Mr. Scott. The ties look better than they tie; they're much too skimpy.

Larus (Galleria Vittorio Emanuele II): a conveniently located source of conservative haberdashery.

Pointshop (Via Monte Napoleone): Mod-look casual clothes—shirts, ties, belts, bags, suede jackets.

Raphael-Rossetti (Via Monte Napoleone at Corso Giacomo Matteotti): some of the most beautiful men's wear in Milan—from ties to shoes.

Red & Blue (Via Monte Napoleone): elegant accessories—with especially catchy sport shirts and bathrobes.

MUSIC

Messagerie Musicali (Corso Vittorio Emanuele II): sheet music, records, music, instruments, books.

Riccordi (Via Monte Napoleone) is a noted and venerable publisher and vendor of sheet music.

MEN'S AND WOMEN'S SHOES

Anglisano (Piazza Meda): high-style women's shoes, made to measure.

Comolli (Corso Giacomo Matteotti): conservative shoes for women; high quality.

Fragiacomo (Via Manzoni at Via Monte Napoleone): one of a chain; moderate tabs, men's and women's.

Magli (Corso Vittorio Emanuele II): men's and women's shoes in a chain outlet; medium-priced.

Tino Ferrario (Via della Spiga): attractively designed women's shoes; men's and women's luggage.

WOMEN'S CLOTHES

Cadette (Via Manzoni at Via Monte Napoleone): in a word—chic.

Carrano (Via Sant' Andrea): quite as elegant for ladies as for men (see above).

Ferragamo (Via Monte Napoleone): celebrated, high-style, expensive.

Fiorucci (Corso Vittorio Emanuele II): moderate-priced albeit smart; men's clothes, too.

Elena Giusti (Via della Spiga): a wide range of women's wear, some dressy, some casual; inventive.

Luisa Spagnoli (Galleria Vittorio Emanuele II): The ubiquitous Luisa is everywhere, Milan included. Always reliable, middle range.

Max Mara (Corso Vittorio Emanuele II): well-priced casuals.

Pintu (Corso Giacomo Matteotti): ultramodern designs, ultragood-looking.

Pirovano (Via Monte Napoleone): The thrust is accessories, including costume jewelry.

Milan: To Note

Access. There are two airports. *Malpensa Airport,* a long drive—much of it interesting—north of town in the very shadow of the snowy mountains, is used for intercontinental flights, including transatlantic ones. Approach is via the Autostrada dei Laghi. Alitalia links the U.S. with Milan on nonstop flights from New York and Boston. TWA flies nonstop New York–Milan. From Canada, there is Alitalia service from Toronto and Montreal to Milan, and CP Air flies from Montreal.

Much closer to town, and used for flights within Italy and Europe, is *Linate Airport.* Most economical means of access to and from both airports is the modern, well-equipped, in-town *Air Terminal* (Via Galvani 12); it's not far from Stazione Centrale. Arrival and departure by train generally mean use of *Stazione Centrale* (Piazza Duca d'Aosta)—a formidable specimen of Mussolini Modern equipped with lots of everything except waiting taxis. Arriving passengers queuing for cabs must surely set some sort of European record, and it's no fun having to drag your baggage with you as you inch along. (One must, at least, be grateful for orderly queues; in the south, they would be the exception to the rule, as indeed they still are in much of the United States.) Guests booked at better hotels might inquire if the hotel has mini-bus pickup for arrivals at Stazione Centrale; this has traditionally been one of the most appreciated services of the Palace and Principe e Savoia hotels. There are no less than eleven other railway stations, for domestic, mostly regional runs; ascertain which you will be using. For all train trips, ask your hotel concierge or a travel agent—or do it yourself—to book a specific seat for you, or risk standing all the way, even in first class.

Getting About. *Taxis* are metered, with the usual maze of *supplementi* tacked on for a variety of reasons—luggage, dogs, skis, nights, holidays, whatever. As in all large cities, they are scarce during rush hours. Tips of approximately 15 per cent are expected, and are generally accepted graciously. To telephone a cab: dial 117. There are extensive and modern *bus* routes. Last, there is the subway, or *Metropolitana*. Its stations are designated by the bold "MM" logo. There are two lines (in contrast to the single line on Rome's subway). The so-called red line (M-1) embraces about a score of stations between Sesto Marelli to Piazzale Lotto. The green line (M-2) is newer and joins Stazione Centrale with Stazione Lambrate—another rail terminal. Generally, trains run from early morning to about midnight. Inquire about special tourist tickets on public transport.

Sightseeing Tours. Bus-tour firms run both local and regional sightseeing excursions, including *Europabus* and *Autostradale,* whose more popular offerings include day-long inspections to Lake Como, some even extending over the border to lovely Lugano, in Italian-speaking Switzerland.

Clothing. Along with Rome, relatively dressy with lots of visiting jacket-and-tie businessmen in evidence. Casual during the day, for sightseeing, with a change indicated after dark, for La Scala and the better restaurants.

Local Literature. Hotel concierges usually have copies of the gratis giveaway what's-on publications *Ciao Milano* and *Milano Mese,* but you must specifically request them or they remain hidden under the concierges' counters. Check the newspapers, too; don't be afraid of them just because your Italian may be limited. Most noted—indeed it is the most famous of all Italian papers—is *Corriere della Sera. Il Sole-24 Ore* is still another.

Further Information. Ente Provinciale per il Turismo, Palazzo del Turismo, Via Marconi 1; Stazione Centrale; Linate Airport.

IV

Naples and the Bay

Naples: To Know

Let me preface what follows by making clear that Naples is well
worth the considerable effort that must be expended to appreciate
it. But it is not easy to come to love. It is hard work. Visitors are
willing to do their share on holiday, but with as relatively little effort
as possible, and why not, on vacation of all occupations? Naples is
special. From the very moment of arrival at the train platform there
is a hassle to find a baggage porter, a hassle claiming the baggage
from him (by then, his associates have joined in the inevitable
screaming session for more money, no matter how much he is being
handed), a hassle finding even the most broken-down of taxis (which
most appear to be) to get to one's hotel, a hassle with the driver,
upon arrival, over the amount of the fare, the added amount for *sup-
plemento,* and—regardless of its generosity—the amount of the tip.
And so it goes.

It has always been so. Certainly in the couple of decades I have
known Naples. And not only with foreigners. Neapolitans can be
quite as disagreeable with Italians from other regions. (Outlanders
are immediately discernible by their accents.) One has only to listen
to harrowing Naples tales from Venetians, Milanese, Florentines, or
even the relatively southern Romans. It is a matter of conditioning,
a point of view toward strangers often embracing suspicion, distrust,
and hostility, that has evolved over the centuries, more so in the case
of the less well educated, than with more sophisticated Neapolitans.
But I repeat, traffic-clogged streets notwithstanding: make the effort.

No city with the checkerboard past of this one could be other than rewarding.

Glancing backwards, one is astounded at the complexity of the Naples story. Virtually every power that could justifiably call itself a power—from the Spaniards to the popes—wanted, and in many cases had, Naples. To see what I mean, one has only to take a look at the façade of the Royal Palace. There, in niches, one after the other, are larger-than-life statues of kings representing eight different countries that have ruled. And by no means always wisely or well.

The beginnings were uncomplicated enough. Greek colonists drifted westwards and established a couple of settlements—Paleopolis (Old City) and later Neapolis (New City). (The third ancient name —still come upon today—was Partenope; it evolved from a Greek legend.) It was only a question of time before others would be as enchanted as the Greeks with the situation of Naples—flanking a magnificent natural gulf, on the slopes of a range of hills, the tallest of which is actually a volcanic peak, Vesuvius. Romans came south in the fourth century before Christ and fought with success for control of the area.

With good reason, they adored the mild climate, the pretty bay, the dramatic silhouette of Vesuvius; and they took to the Greek culture as ducks to water. Indeed, it was in and about Naples that the first vacation villas came into common use. Royal Romans—like Emperors Nero and Claudius—lived there. Rich Romans built country houses there; Roman poets like Virgil worked there. Roman politicians absorbed the nearby and also-beautiful islands of Capri and Ischia into the Naples colonial government.

It did not last much longer than a century. The barbarians came, and later the Byzantines. There was an independent spell. But in the twelfth century, Normans took over—the first of a line of European powers. They were there one after another lasting some six centuries, until the mid-nineteenth.

I cannot believe that even Neapolitan school children, under threat of the local equivalent of F and expulsion from the school system, ever really master this chunk of their history. And I am not about to burden my vacationing reader with the specifics. Suffice it to say that the range of rulers embraced various French, Austrian, German, and Spanish houses, with Napoleon and his family of Bonapartes the last of the lot. There were good guys and bad guys, but the crowd that did the most lasting damage were the Spaniards. They were on hand for two centuries—the sixteenth and seventeenth, ruling what had long since become the Kingdom of Naples, embracing all of Italy south of the Papal States around Rome. The Spaniards looked upon the region primarily as an income producer. They overtaxed the people while neglecting matters like agriculture, health, and education. Still, as with every society during that era, the upper classes fostered art, music, and architecture. Great institutions like the still-thriving Teatro di San Carlo, National Archaeological Museum and Capodimonte Museum are among the appreciated souvenirs of the long era of foreign rule.

One of the foreigners, Murat—a brother-in-law of Napoleon who ruled for less than a decade in the early nineteenth century—is remembered for admirable reforms in government and for encouragement of the independence movement, which didn't gain strength until some decades later, when the Risorgimento achieved its goal of Italian unification. In 1860, Risorgimento leader Giuseppe Garibaldi led forces that conquered what had come to be called the Kingdom of the Two Sicilies, a part of which was the southern mainland area dominated by Naples. Neapolitans welcomed Garibaldi and the consequence of his victory: the modern united Kingdom of Italy, which, if it—and the post-World War II republic following—has not brought Naples and the south all that was expected, has at least seen the region make progress, ever hopeful that eventually it will catch up with the advanced north.

Political domination over the centuries notwithstanding, it is the Neapolitans who have been the winners in one major respect: not even the cumulative power of assorted foreigners reigning as kings was able to dissipate or dilute its culture. Indeed, it has been quite the reverse. Despite economic privations, no region of Italy is more sublimely Italian. In Naples one finds the art forms at which Italians excel—painting (there was a major Neapolitan school), music, both classical and folk, dance, architecture, cuisine. All the Austrians or Frenchmen or Spaniards or Germans on the throne do not seem to have made any less brilliant the folk dance called *tarantella,* voices like Naples-born Caruso's, or, for that matter, the savory pie called *pizza.*

Naples: To See

LAY OF THE LAND

Once one comes to grips with it, its people, and its infuriating traffic jams, Naples emerges as a one-of-a-kind city of astonishing drive, an ebullient street life, considerable architectural beauty, and many more artistic treasures than it is generally given credit for. This is principally because most visitors stay an average of a day and a night—sometimes not even that night—using the city as a stepping-stone to a resort in the bay, and are convinced, often without knowing, that it has little to offer except the silhouette of Vesuvius. What is needed is a stay of three or four days, which is three or four times as much as the current average—but enough time to acquire a fair acquaintance with aspects of the city more flattering to it than the taxi drivers and baggage porters who are its own worst enemies.

Study a map and you see that it is a relatively easy city in which to walk about. (And the more one walks, the fewer taxi encounters are necessary.) Remember that the bay is south; inland from it is north. Areas of town fronting the bay that most visitors need to know are *Santa Lucia,* near which a number of the better hotels are clustered, and the adjacent *Mergellina* area, to the west, with *Posillipo* the most western of the sea-front districts.

Back to Santa Lucia and, presumably, one's hotel. The group of restaurants on the waterfront, it must be remembered, are but one aspect of Neapolitan dining, just as the adjacent hotels do not typify the town. One must move inland. Take Via Santa Lucia to Via Cesario Conole until you reach the first of three main downtown squares. This is *Piazza Plebiscito,* and you know you're there because of the neoclassic, colonnaded *Church of San Francesco di Paola,* on the one side, and the Baroque façade of the *Palazzo Reale* (Royal Palace) on the other. Continue in a northerly direction and, poof, you're in Square No. 2—alliteratively named *Piazza Trento e Trieste.* Its landmark, on the right as you look north, is *Teatro di San Carlo,* the Baroque-era opera house. *Galleria Umberto I,* the high-ceilinged late-nineteenth-century shop- and caffè-studded arcade, is at this point, and due northeast is the No. 3 square—*Piazza Municipio,* whose landmark is the principal downtown skyscraper housing Hotel

Ambassador's Palace. Main shopping street is *Via Roma,* running
north-south a block west of Piazza Municipio (and also easily gained
from Piazza Trento e Trieste). Via Roma changes its name at Piazza
Dante, continues north under several other a.k.a.'s—including Via
Sante Teresa degli Scalzi, on which one finds the important *Museo
Nazionale;* beyond, when it becomes Corso Amedeo di Savoia, ter-
minating at the park dominated by *Palazzo Capodimonte* and, within
it, another major museum.

Return to Via Roma, the main shopping street, and take it to
Piazza di Gesù and the *Church of Gesù Nuovo;* turn right and you
find yourself on Via San Biagio ai Librai in *Spaccanapoli*—the heart
of Old Naples—a requisite area for walking.

THE ESSENTIAL NAPLES

A Pair of Museums: If one is so pressed as to have to make a choice
between the two, then let it be *Museo Nazionale* (Via Foria 27).
The kicker here is Pompeii, a dazzling collection of its art treasures,
removed from the nearby ruined city that thrived some two millenniums ago, only to be buried—and astonishingly well preserved—by
an eruption of Vesuvius in the first Christian century. The building
itself is a grim albeit ancient palazzo with a respectable four-century
history of its own. But before you ascend to Pompeii on the second
floor, tarry on the main. Less celebrated than the upstairs exhibits
are this floor's galleries of classical sculpture that will take your
breath away. Greeting you are a tough-looking but striking pair of
Tyrant Killers, copied by Romans some two thousand years ago, from
a Greek original half a millennium older. You go on from there to
likenesses of Athena, Apollo, Orpheus, Diomedes, a drunken Silenus,
and an also inebriated Hercules, a reposing Hermes, a pair of
wrestlers, a sleeping satyr. Up a high flight, then, to Pompeian mosaics and frescoes of Alexander in battle, a still-life of fish and other
edibles from the sea that you've seen reproduced on cookbook covers,
portraits of beautiful Pompeian ladies, fresco after fresco with
Pompeian red backgrounds, scenes of daily life. It is a show manifest-
ing skill, style, and technique that would honor late-twentieth-century artists; when one considers its antiquity, the beauty is almost
incomprehensible. *Museo Capodimonte:* There are two royal palaces
in town; one heart-of-downtown (see below), the other on the northern fringe, in its own park. Capodimonte is unusual in that it was

built for the purpose it still serves. Its builder was Charles III, most enlightened of the Spanish Bourbon kings who, not incidentally, sided with the Yanks in our Revolution and won back Florida for Spain (temporarily at least) as a consequence. The Baroque façade is painted a lovely muted Pompeian red. You want first to head for the third floor and the paintings. Their range is extraordinary, and the quantity is equally so. One needs a good half day to cover the forty-odd galleries with even minimal thoroughness, for Capodimonte is a survey course in Italian painting and its schools, both regional and chronological, with selected foreign works from medieval primitives through to some choice early-nineteenth-century Goyas. One finds Lippi, Botticelli and Raphael, Del Sarto and Il Sodoma, roomfuls of Lombardians (Luini, for example), Venetians (a beautiful Bellini *Transfiguration* and a number of the very best Titians (*Pope Paul III with His Nephews,* for example); Neapolitans, century by century, including many Luca Giordanos, whose works are to be seen in a number of the city's churches. Down a flight—and, sad to report, not always open these days—are the State Apartments, full of fine eighteenth-century furnishings, not to mention remarkable collections of china (including the local Capodimonte) and tapestries.

Palazzo Reale (Piazza del Plebiscito), the in-town royal palace of the Kings of Naples, greets one with an earlier-mentioned statuary group of eight sovereigns, representing as many reigning royal houses. Best feature of the interior is a very grand grand staircase that is of near-skyscraper dimensions. The building has seventeenth-century roots, but is mostly eighteenth century with nineteenth-century restoration. What one gains from a tour of the immense and immensely elaborate dozen and a half state rooms is a picture of how much less subtle were the design skills of the southern Italian decorators than, say, French and northern Italians during the Rococo period.

Teatro di San Carlo: Along with the Fenice in Venice—than which no Italian opera house has more outrageous charm—San Carlo stands out because it goes back to the eighteenth century—1737—when it was built. There were early-nineteenth-century additions—especially the loggia above the entrance. But unlike Milan's La Scala, Rome's Teatro dell'Opera and Florence's Teatro Comunale, San Carlo is essentially the genuine Rococo article, happily open regularly during the day for nonperformance inspections, and with winter opera and fall–spring concert seasons. There are seven levels—a vast orchestra and half a dozen balconies, in a red and gold auditorium, with the onetime royal box framed by a gilded plaster canopy in the shape of a monster crown, adoring royalist angels guarding either side.

A Trio of Beautiful Churches: If Naples' museums are underappreciated, its churches are virtually unknown to the outer world. The visitor with any feeling for art and architecture misses a sampling at his own peril, leaving the relatively unattractive Duomo, or cathedral, for inclusion in the only-if-time category. If I had time for but a single church, it would be *San Gregorio Armeno* (Via San Gregorio Armeno), a Renaissance-Baroque meld in which there is not an unembellished square inch, with the decoration—just slightly crumbly with a mellow patina—as beautiful as it is profuse. Frescoes covering the walls are by the Neapolitan master Luca Giordano. There is a pair of exquisite Baroque organs, a delicate dome over the altar, a finely coffered ceiling over the nave, a rear grille behind which cloistered nuns attend mass. Around the corner is the convent of the Sisters of the Crucifixion of San Gregorio Armeno. Ask for one of the nuns if you would like a quick peep at the convent's beautiful cloister; postcards of the interior of the church are locked up in a drawer in the convent lobby and, I have the feeling, are so lacking of customers that some still may be available on your visit; the cost is whatever contribution you may want to make. *Santa Chiara* (Via Trinità Maggiore) is Naples' most elegant church—a masterful post-World War II restoration of a tragically bombed complex. The Gothic arches of the now severely simple nave are striking. The choir, with no less than two hundred Baroque stalls, is an achievement in itself. But the real treat is the cloister, whose pillars and benches are of gaily painted majolica tiles, accented by leafy arbors and tubs of plants. *Sant' Anna dei Lombardi* (Via Monteoliveto) has as its most remarkable treasure an unusual *Pietà,* in a chapel to the right as one enters, taking the form of a group of eight life-size figures sculptured of terra cotta in the very same year that Columbus discovered our shores. But there is so much else—an exuberantly-designed Rococo organ, works of art fashioned of inlaid wood, an intricately carved choir, one gorgeous art-filled chapel after another, and a knockout black-and-white tile floor.

Spaccanapoli: A Stroll on Via San Biagio ai Librai: Shopping streets like Via Roma, ocean-front Via Partenope: these attract visitors without special counsel. What one wants not to miss, though, is an ambulatory glance at Spaccanapoli, or old Naples, best gained by a walk along Via San Biagio ai Librai—morning or postlunch, when things are open. What to see? Good heavens, what *not!* Street vendors, shops selling gold and jewelry, once great palazzi, elaborate churches, banks and pizza parlors, tall, tenementy old houses with wash on lines extending streetwards, *cambios* for money changing, and caffès. Most of all, the pedestrians—intent and attractive and in quantity—as authentic a cross-section of Neapolitans as one is going to find, with the admission charge absolutely gratis. Take half a day, if you've time, and wander onto side streets, popping into churches and shops, even continuing on to Via del Duomo, a major intersection, at which you may turn left for a walk of several blocks to the Duomo, for which the street is named.

The Ruins of Pompeii: I have not known it to fail. Take a look at the treasures from Pompeii in the National Museum (above) and of course you want to make the excursion to the ruined city. There are organized day tours by bus, or you may go by ordinary train from Stazione Centrale (Piazza Garibaldi)—*diretto* trains take about 45 minutes—to the Pompeii town station near the main entrance to the ruins, called Porta Marina. Note also that there are even quicker trains—as little as half an hour. They're electric and depart from a station near the main one, on Corso Garibaldi; it's called Circumvesuviana, and it takes you to still another station in Pompeii, closer to the entrance and called Porta di Nova. The drive by car is some fifteen ugly *autostrada* miles, in which case head for Porta Marina and count on an hour, all told. The ruins are operated by the Italian Government as a museum, with regular hours and an admission fee. Traditionally, in summer at least, there have been evening as well as daytime hours, with highlights illuminated. And in summer, traditionally, there have been dramatic presentations in the amphitheater. Pompeii itself is considerably larger in area than many visitors expect. A full day is just enough to take it in with any kind of thoroughness. But I would say a half day is a more typical stay and sufficient for a nonscholarly inspection. I counsel beginning in the on-site museum—rather quaintly called Antiquarium—with its most memorable, and rather ghoulish, exhibits those of people and their pets whose bodies were petrified, as a result of the eruption of Vesuvius that destroyed the town in A.D. 79—seventeen years after an earlier eruption that had been only minimally disastrous. You will already have learned of the advanced state of Pompeian civilization from your National Museum visit in Naples. What you want to concentrate on, at the site, is the physical picture of the city. As absolute requisites I recommend that, after the Antiquarium, you visit the broad and expansive Forum, what remains of a temple dedicated to Apollo, Temples of Jove and Jupiter, well-designed baths; marble floors, frescoed walls, and other architectural details of House of the Faun; frescoes—in royal blue and Pompeian red—on the atrium walls of Vettii House; and the eye-popping décor of the Amorini Dorati and Orpheus houses. With the amphitheater as a finale. There is a relatively recent restaurant-cafeteria-bar-caffè (washrooms are upstairs) on the site, where you may have lunch. Or go into Pompeii town for a lunch break (*Zia Caterina,* Via Roma 18, is suggested), and inspect the murals of the Villa dei Misteri (House of Mysteries), detached from the main ruins and so called because its art is believed to depict the initiation of Pompeian brides into a rather spooky order.

The Amalfi Drive is the most celebrated of our planet's single-day motor excursions. What we are dealing with is a magnificently mountainous promontory whose steep slopes are dotted with venerable smallish towns—some at the top, some climbing from beach to plateau, some a combination. Go on a day-long bus tour, go to a single town—Positano, Amalfi, Sorrento—making it your headquarters for a matter of days, or a week or two. Abbreviate that week to a three- or four-day tour, with a night each in one of the resorts. Or, if a single day seems rushed, make it for two, with an overnight in Sorrento.

Leaving Naples after an early breakfast, head south along the coast, passing *Ercolano* (a kind of small-scale Pompeii that you know in English as Herculaneum and that is later recommended on its own), continuing to Castellammare, thence turning westward onto the elevated peninsular coastal highway that is actually the Amalfi Drive. You go in the direction of Sorrento, but just short of it, at the little town of Meta, turn inland and take a southerly road over the peninsula to its south coast, thence driving eastward to *Positano.*

This is an enchanting village which climbs the coastal hills, with as much charm per cubic meter and as many inviting hotels in proportion to its size as any resort in the area. Alight and walk about. There are caffès, boutiques (the international Positano visitor crowd is modish), and good restaurants. My suggestion is a lunch break here at *Chez Black* for seafood, beachfront.

Should you decide to tarry longer, consider any one of these hotels that I like: *Miramare* (20 beautiful rooms with bath, no two alike, with the furnishings—bar, lounge, rooms—antique, the restaurant top of the world); *San Pietro* (equally stylish, with an elevator to its beach just below); *Le Sirenuse* (50 antique-furnished rooms with bath, a super pool, ravishing views); and *Palazzo Murat* (an in-town eighteenth-century palace, very grand, with capacious public rooms, 28 perfectly beautiful no-two-alike bedrooms, charming patio-caffè, and of course The View).

From Positano, move along a few scenic miles east to *Amalfi*, the town that gave its name to the drive. What you want to see here is the Duomo, which is at once Romanesque and Gothic, with strong Moorish-Sicilian lines, and an exterior that surpasses what lies within, most especially the cloister—aptly called Chiostro del Paradiso. Surrounding Amalfi streets are at once hilly, narrow, shop-filled, and fun to explore. If I were going to stay overnight, or for a few days, first choice would be *Hotel Cappuccini Convento,* a one-time monastery that goes back to the twelfth century, on a plateau so high that it's reached by its own exterior elevator from the street and contains, in addition to nearly half a hundred rooms (32 with bath) that had been the monks' cells, a Gothic chapel (still sanctified and the site of weddings) and antique-furnished public rooms including restaurant and bar, as well as a covered terrace overlooking town and sea. Neighboring *Hotel Bussoli,* with a terrace for sunning on its roof, is a good moderate-category hotel.

From Amalfi, head directly inland just a few miles to an enchanter of a little town, *Ravello*. Its situation is easily the equal—as regards vistas—of the coastal communities. And there is so much of beauty that one easily understands why Richard Wagner settled there for a while in 1880 and wrote *Parsifal*. Little Ravello is no longer the see of a bishop, but had been for centuries after its cathedral first went up nearly a millennium ago. Take a look within and also visit neighboring Villa Rufolo, a curious Moorish-Gothic style palace that dates to the thirteenth century, with a splendid cloister and a

view of the Amalfi coast from the garden-terrace that Wagner ex-
claimed over (he turned it into the Garden of Klingsor in *Parsifal*),
and that is the site, traditionally in summer, of Wagnerian concerts.
Other Ravello delights: Villa Cimbrone, with its medieval garden-
cum-view and the cloister and the duomo of the next-door village of
San Lorenzo.

From Ravello return to Amalfi on the coast and drive west along
the sea; you will be backtracking as far as Positano, but from then on
the route will be new territory and will take you almost to the tip of
the peninsula for a curve north and east to *Sorrento,* biggest of the
towns on our excursion, in time for an overnight stay, preferably at
Hotel Excelsior Vittoria. The Vittoria has the patina that comes from
advanced age; restaurant, cocktail lounge, and many rooms with fine
views. There are English (leading) and German (in No. 2 spot)
tourists in abundance, a must-see church—Gothic San Francesco with
a memorable cloister; an antique villa—Correale—turned museum,
and quantities of hotels in every category.

Hotel Carlton, unhandsome but functional modern style, has the
advantage of a pool of its own and a downtown situation. *Hotel Villa
di Sorrento,* central and modern, is a moderate-level suggestion.
Ristorante La Favorita (confusingly also called Parrucchiano, at
Corso Italia 71, the main street) is agreeable and moderate-priced.
Likewise, *La Minervetta* (Via del Capo 25, and cum-view). Sorrento
is a convenient point of departure—one goes by boat and the distance
is much shorter than from Naples—to the island of Capri (see below).

BEHIND MUSEUM WALLS:
A SELECTION OF FAVORITES

Certosa di San Martino Museo Nazionale (Collina di Sant' Elmo al
Vomero): This hilltop *certosa,* or monks' charterhouse, is essentially Baroque, and beautiful Baroque, with an elegant cloister, and
chamber after handsome *certosa* chamber, now constituting Museo
Nazionale San Martino—a collection telling the story of Naples—
historically, culturally, and artistically, with varied documentation—
maps, prints, coins, medals, clothes, applied arts locally made like
china and glass, paintings by Neapolitans from the sixteenth through
nineteenth centuries, and, perhaps most charming, eighteenth-century
Christmas crèches—with hundreds upon hundreds of exquisitely detailed figures—that were a Neapolitan specialty. (New Yorkers will

note that one of these crèches surrounds the Christmas tree each year at the Metropolitan Museum of Art.)

Museo Civico Filangieri (Via del Duomo) occupies a formidable Renaissance palazzo—Cuomo by name—that, within, is at once intimate and treasure-filled. Collections, mostly all relating to Naples, are a mixed bag, filling galleries on two floors. There are two Luca Giordano paintings, another by Bernardino Luini, exceptional European eighteenth-century porcelain, other objects ranging from coins to armor. The galleried upstairs hall and a small, paneled library are treats.

Museo Nazionale Duca di Martina (Via Cimarosa al Vomero) makes its home in an early-nineteenth-century, park-surrounded palace. The subject matter is the applied arts—comprising porcelain, both local and otherwise, crystal, enamels, silver, majolica pottery, and some very good Ming Chinese. And there is the handsome house, and the views to be had from it.

Banco di Napoli Galleria di Arte (Via Roma 420): Bravo, Banco di Napoli! It was this civic-minded firm that helped finance the restoration of the church and cloister of Santa Chiara (above), and this same bank has one of its branches in an ancient palazzo with an exemplary chapel (see below). This gallery is devoted to choice Neapolitan works, sixteenth through nineteenth centuries, and as good a way as any to get to understand the painting movements that originated in Naples.

TREASURES OF ART AND ARCHITECTURE: SELECTED CHURCHES

Cappella, Banco di Napoli (Via San Biagio ai Librai): This branch of a major bank is located in a handsome antique of a palazzo. Walk through to the far side of the courtyard to the chapel, among whose treasures is a Luca Giordano fresco; even when it's closed, you can look in the windows.

Duomo (Via del Duomo) is among the least beautiful of Italian cathedrals. It has a Gothic façade with other eras represented within.

The coffered ceiling has some estimable frescoes. Cappella del Tresor di San Gennaro is behind an immense gate to the right, and is elaborate Baroque with a frescoed dome and with many silver objects. New Yorkers will recognize the saint—the patron saint of Naples —whose feast day is an annual Lower Manhattan institution.

Gesù Nuovo (Piazza del Gesù Nuovo) is distinguished by its massive gray façade and an elaborate Baroque dome. Within it is busy with frescoes and sculptures, the lot under a magnificent coffered ceiling.

Sant' Angelo a Nilo (Corpo di Napoli) is a little Baroque gem, with a guardian angel over its door and a well-proportioned interior.

Santa Brigida (Via Santa Brigida) could double as a gallery of Neapolitan Baroque paintings. You must go back to the sacristy for a look at the ceiling frescoes by Luca Giordano, but there are splendid works by other seventeenth-century locals, especially Giacomo Ferelli and Massimo Stanzione.

San Domenico Maggiore (Piazza San Domenico Maggiore) could be taken for a medieval castle, at least from without. Inside, there is a very long and narrow nave under a gilded ceiling, and a Baroque organ behind the altar. Glittering.

San Fernando di Palazzo (Piazza Trento e Trieste) is a near neighbor of the Royal Palace and is quite as richly embellished. Every inch of this superior Baroque specimen is decorated.

San Francesco di Paola (Piazza Plebiscito) is masterful neoclassic; strong and severe and monumental. Behind a long, curved colonnade and central portico is an immense cupola sheltering the interior, around whose walls stand 34 Corinthian columns.

San Lorenzo Maggiore (Piazza San Gaetano) is Baroque without, Gothic—well restored Gothic—within, at once cold and splendid, with Giordano paintings as a bonus.

Cappella di Sansevero (Via Francesco de Sanctis) is what is meant when one says big things come in small packages: an exquisite study in Baroque at its most exuberant, sculpted angels in an over-altar sunburst . . . on the altar platform . . . on walls and ceiling; a *Pietà,* too.

A NEAPOLITAN MISCELLANY

Aquarium (Via Caracciolo) is, appropriately enough, sea front, in the pretty Villa Comunale park. This is an old-timer, established more than a century back, and the contents are local. By that I mean every one of the 200-plus species of marine life is from this corner of the Mediterranean.

Castel Nuovo is the heart-of-town landmark that looks as though it could be an opera set: crenelated medieval towers wrapped around a somber stone façade, originally thirteenth century. Pass through the Renaissance entry arch, and you're in an open court leading to the castle's great hall with an oversized fireplace and a charming Gothic chapel whose claim to fame is that it once held frescoes—long since missing—by Giotto.

Catacombs (Al Tondo di Capodimonte): This two-story underground cemetery bears the name of San Januarius, the very same to whom the Duomo is dedicated; he is buried here, in one of a great maze of niches carved from rock and decorated with frescoes.

Parks: The handsome one fringing Palazzo Capodimonte has already been recommended; so has that fronting Villa Comunale and containing the Aquarium. Another, with fine views of the bay, is Parco Virgillano.

Vesuvius: It is 4,200 feet high, buried Pompeii in A.D. 79, and last erupted in 1944. Grand views of town and bay, lots of lava rock. Go by train to Herculaneum, then by bus to the mountain's funicular station.

Zoo (Via Domitiana): As nice a way as any to encounter Neapolitans of all ages and the usual run of animals.

CULTURAL COUNTRYSIDE:
A TRIO OF EXCURSIONS

Herculaneum, considerably smaller than Pompeii, was buried at the same time, as a result of the Vesuvius eruption of A.D. 79. Most of the excavation is within the last half century—much more recent than Pompeii's. The special excitement here is the remarkable art that remains—still-bright frescoes, lovely mosaics, capitals, columns. (Californians will recall that the J. Paul Getty Museum in Malibu is a reconstruction of a Herculaneum villa—one of a number of upper-class houses that are more elaborate than those of Pompeii and a prime reason for a visit to this smaller city, as well as Pompeii.) The area to head for, if one's visit is abbreviated, is the south, where houses—including Tramezzo and Cervi—are the most sumptuously decorated. There are still-lavish public baths and a theater, too. Access is via train (Circumvesuviana Railway), bus, and car. Distance from town is only five miles.

Paestum, so much less contemporarily celebrated than Pompeii and Herculaneum, deserves more attention. It is a onetime Greek colony, conquered by Romans in the third century before Christ, and still with structures in remarkable states of preservation, almost all in Doric, the simplest of the three classical styles. The Temple of Neptune is, in its way, quite as majestic as the Parthenon in Athens. The Temple of Ceres, though much more in ruins, remains impressive nonetheless. So do the basilica and forum. There is an on-site museum, too. Paestum is about 50 miles south of Naples, accessible by car or bus.

Caserta is the relatively unheralded site of a magnificent eighteenth-century royal palace bearing its name. Builder was King Charles III of Bourbon, and the idea, at least partially, was to make Louis XV sit up and take notice. Caserta is, then, an attempt to compete with Versailles. It lags aesthetically—not that its elaborate interiors are to be put down, and it is no slouch as regards size. Consider that it is built around a quartet of enormous courtyards, is six stories high with a score and a half of staircases, some 1,800 windows, and no less than 1,200 rooms. The visitor, have no fear, is not shown about in anything like detail. Just enough to get an idea of how the

Kings of Naples, and their families and courtiers, squeaked by. Usually shown are the principal royal apartments, with king's and queen's bedrooms, and the rooms in which they worked, ate, entertained, and relaxed. As in the Royal Palace in Naples, the southern Italian variations of Baroque furniture are less felicitously proportioned and less subtle than those of northern Italy, and of France and Germany. But quite beautiful. As are the paintings and frescoes, most especially those on the ceilings of the Hall of Alexander the Great and the Throne Room. The fountains of the surrounding park are a major Caserta treat. Distance is about 15 miles from Naples via train or bus.

THE RESORT ISLANDS: CAPRI AND ISCHIA

Capri: It would be hard to beat Capri's staying power. Roman emperors—Augustus first and later his stepson, Tiberius, were among its first holiday makers, a couple of millenniums back. (One may still see the ruins of the estate where they lived.) Capri fortunes, ever since, have more or less followed those of Naples. There are perfectly good reasons why Capri should never have made it. It is not, to begin, a beachy island. There are places to swim but they can be a bother to reach. It is more than hilly, it is mountainous, which means that getting about entails huffing and puffing. And by virtue of being surrounded by water, it is, like all islands, more difficult of access than mainland competitors.

But nobody has ever seemed to mind. In the quarter century that I have known it, Capri has, to its credit, changed less than any other major resort with which I am familiar. It remains small-scale, casual, charming, and in its own hard-to-define way, just zippy and modish enough to be fun. It would never, for example, go to the extremes of, say, St. Tropez. But, by the same token, one should not expect England's Bournemouth or New England's Rockport. There has always been a healthy, forthright live-and-let-live attitude toward a remarkable clientele—multinational, multilingual, young through elderly, gay through macho-straight, all having themselves a good time.

In order to be successful it seems ordained that a resort area should have a minimum of the kind of distractions—museums, galleries, churches, theater—that attract visitors to the big cities. Capri conforms in this respect. What it mostly offers are magnificent vistas of the gulf, neighboring Ischia and mainland points, and of the oddly shaped rock formations—the Faraglioni—that extend from its shore. The views, in other words, are sublime.

Geography is relatively simple on this smallish oblong of an island. The boats from Naples and Sorrento disgorge passengers at a north coast settlement called Marina Grande; they invariably proceed without delay to a little funicular railway that takes them to another settlement, elevated and mid-island, called, simply enough, Capri. And to restaurants, caffès, shops, after-dark activity, and, for proper sightseeing, a charterhouse, with a spectacular cloister and handsome chapel. Marina Piccola, on the south shore of the island, is the takeoff point for Canzone del Mare, established in the 1950s by the English actress-singer Gracie Fields, and nice for a pool swim and lunch-cum-drinks. The Blue Grotto—popular because of the phenomenon of the eerie light within, is on the northwest corner of the island, and is entered by sightseeing boats; it's not something one keeps returning to, but you want to go on your first Capri visit. San Michele is the name of a charming house built some decades back by a Swedish physician-writer named Axel Munthe, and imaginatively furnished with antiques emanating from Capri's classical era as well as pieces from more recent centuries; it now operates as a museum. Anacapri is the top-of-the-island town, with the most sublime views of all and some hotels. One gets about in Capri by foot, otherwise by little public buses and taxis, not to mention the earlier noted Capri town-Marina Grande funicular. Still, when all is said and done, the most popular diversion is taking coffee or drinks, the while checking on who is with whom and what the day's new arrivals look like, at the caffès on the Piazzetta, which no one ever calls by its proper name, Piazza Umberto I.

There are dozens of hotel possibilities. Starting with the luxury category and working downward, my favorites include Hotel-Residence *Punta Tragara*—a onetime private villa with 30 no-two-alike suites (there are only a few regular twins), antique-filled restaurant-bar-lounge, a pool and dining terrace-caffè affording exciting panoramas of the shore, and clublike ambience; *Hotel Quisisana*—traditional in-town luxury leader, with 130 rooms, summer garden-restaurant-caffè at the pool, restaurant-bar, middle of everything location; *Hotel Luna*—first class, modern, and splendidly sited, with striking views and inviting facilities, including restaurant-cum-terrace, bar-lounge-caffè, pretty pool; *Hotel La Palma*—first class, in town, with attractive tile-floored rooms, capacious terrace-caffè-pool area, handsome restaurant, bar-lounge, and lobby; *Hotel La Scalinatella* —intimate club-like first-class house with 30 distinctively decorated rooms (some with two baths), pool in the garden, sublime vistas, interesting clientele, about half Italian, the rest French-British-American; bar and breakfast, no restaurant; *Hotel Pazziella*—under same management as Scalinatella but with lower tabs and less luxury and, like its sister hotel, bar and breakfast but no restaurant; *Hotel Tiberio-Palace* (which I first knew as the Morgano-Tiberio) is first class, central, refurbished, with good restaurant bar-caffè, nice rooms; *La Pineta* is moderate category albeit appealing with terrace-attached rooms, restaurant, bar, and of course views. Among the pensions, *Pensione Villa Margherita* is a leader and so is *Pensione Esperia.* Way up in Anacapri, the traditional favorite is luxury-category *Caesar Augustus,* with incredibly beautiful views; it has modern competition of which I am not especially fond. But when it comes down to it, I don't see the advantage of living in detached Anacapri; a visit for the vistas has always seemed adequate to me. If Caprese restaurants are not as good as the crisp, slightly rough-around-the-edges but appealing white Caprese wine, they are not to be despised. Good bets—all in Capri town—include *La Capanna, La Pigna* and *Faraglioni; Grotta Verde,* in Marina Grande; and *Canzone del Mare* in Marina Piccola.

Ischia: Ischia is bigger in area, bigger in population, in its own way quite as beautiful as Capri, and with the kind of beaches that Capri simply does not have. Withal, it has never had quite the celebrity of the smaller island, and certainly not the international clientele. Contemporarily, the overwhelming majority of visitors are German. Which is not to say that other nationalities are not welcome, nor that their languages are not spoken.

Like Capri, sightseeing attractions take second place to a relaxing atmosphere that visitors coming for a week, a fortnight, or more are after. Boats from Naples land on the north shore of this roughly oblong island, usually at the Ischia Porto sector of Ischia town. (Although some boats dock at the marina in the nearby community of Casamicciola—a few miles west of Ischia Porto.) A day-long tour can be rewarding. Ideally, one would take in the tiny island connected to the mainland by the bridge at Ischia Ponte; its landmark is a story-book castle on the scene since medieval times.

The route would then be roughly clockwise: stop next at Barano, just inland from the south shore, with a view of the long strand of Maronti Beach below. Fontana, a pretty town even farther inland, is near Monte Epomeo, the vineyard region from where originates the good white wine that is the mainstay beverage of the Bay of Naples. At Serrara Fontana, there is a belvedere with tables, for a drinks stop, and the best of the south shore views. I would detour a tiny bit south then, to Sant' Angelo, a resort community on a mini-isle connected by causeway to the mainland, and fringing Maronti Beach. Access to Sant' Angelo's hotels is by foot, over elevated paths leading to a cluster of inns on a high perch with perfectly sublime views of my favorite corner of the island. Move along to the west coast and Forio, a picture-book settlement with a crenelated medieval tower (Torrione) and picture-book church (del Succorso)—glistening white in the sun—tucked onto the edge of a sea-straddling cliff, and surely the most photographed single structure on Ischia. Onward, then, to the same north shore where we landed, to Lacco Ameno, with its lures thermal waters, hotels in all categories, and the two churches (one built on Roman foundations a millennium ago) of Santa Restituta Sanctuary; Casamicciola, an older resort-thermal community is next door. Hotel choice is among the best in the Bay of Naples, with every category represented. Starting with luxury class, my favorites include *Hotel Excelsior*—a beauty in Ischia Porto, with 70 elegant rooms, handsome lobbies, bar-lounge, one of the island's best restaurants, garden-caffè-pool, pretty beach; *Hotel Regina Isabella*, luxury-class, sea front, with pool, thermal spa, very grand public spaces, including a terrace restaurant, and what is perhaps the most formal ambience of the island's hotels; *Hotel Punta Molino*, top-class with 88 rooms, smashing view of the earlier-mentioned Middle Ages castle at Ischia Ponte; restaurant, bar, pool, and beach; *Hotel San Michele Terme*, good-value moderate category, with half a hundred modern rooms with bath, inviting public spaces including restaurant, bar, terrace caffè, and pool—and a top-of-the-world setting at Sant' Angelo, over-looking nearby Maronti Beach; *Hotel delle Terme-Jolly*—a part of the Italy-wide Jolly chain, and modern, with 220 rooms, garden-pool area; and *Pensione Vallarosa*, attractive, with a convenient Ischia Porto locale and nice rooms. You can't beat the *Hotel Excelsior Restaurant;* other good ones include sea view *Zi Nannina a Mare*

(Ischia Porto), *O Padrone d'o Mare* (Lacco Ameno) and *Dal Pes-catore* (Sant' Angelo), with local seafood and the excellent Ischia white wine recommended at each.

Naples: To Watch

Teatro di San Carlo (Piazza Trento e Trieste): Earlier-recommended and described as a sightseer's requisite, this eighteenth-century beauty is Performing Arts Center No. 1, with its own exemplary opera, ballet, chorus, and symphony orchestra. The opera season, as else-where in Italy, is essentially winter through early spring, beginning in December. The rest of the year, however, is not to be dismissed lightly, as it embraces regularly scheduled, interestingly programmed symphonic concerts, with chorus and/or distinguished guest soloists, many from abroad. Tickets are nothing like as difficult to buy as at Milan's La Scala; still, if one's visit is short, it pays to book a San Carlo seat immediately upon arrival in Naples, either through hotel concierges or oneself, at the box office, which usually keeps weekday hours from 10 A.M. to 1 P.M. and 4:30 to 6:30 P.M., and which prints gratis seasonal schedules.

Teatro Mediterraneo (at the Mostra d'Oltremare, exhibition com-plex for trade shows and the like), is for stage plays and musicals.

Teatro Politeama (Via Monte di Dio): a setting for dramas and revues.

Agnano is the top race track, among Italy's best known, with a trio of covered grandstands, refreshment facilities, and a near-town location.

Stadio San Paolo holds some 80,000 soccer fans; as good a place as any to watch Italians watching their national game being played.

Naples: To Stay

For so large and important a city, Naples offers relatively few agreeable hotels, thanks, one supposes, to the relative difficulty it finds in attracting visitors to stay longer than overnight, if indeed that. Here are my hotel suggestions, alphabetically, and with my own categorical breakdown—*luxury, first class, moderate*. I have lived, eaten, drunk in, or at least thoroughly inspected each of them.

Ambassador's Palace Hotel (Via Medina 70) is the slim skyscraper of a Piazza Municipio landmark, overdecorated perhaps but modern, spotless, with an immense, much-marbled lobby, attractive albeit compact bedrooms, many with ravishing views thanks to the 30-story height, some fine suites, a rooftop restaurant with an unusually extensive—and authentic—menu, as hotel menus go; back of lobby bar-lounge, barbershop, beauty salon. *First class.*

Hotel Excelsior (Via Partenope 48) is Naples' longtime leader—a gracious, traditional-style house with few enough rooms and suites—162 all told—to retain a relatively intimate ambience. Accommodations are oversized (including wonderfully high ceilings), with elegant baths, modish furnishings, and, thanks to the curved-front façade, a splendid view of the bay from a high proportion of rooms, many of which have mini-balconies. Restaurant, bar. The location is Santa Lucia, with its sea-front restaurants across the way, and the heart of downtown a five- or six-minute walk in the other direction. No question: the very best in Naples. A CIGA hotel. *Luxury.*

Grand Hotel de Londres e Ambasciatori (Piazza Municipio 64) is nothing like as formidable as its six-word title implies. Withal, as its handsome façade promises, it is an agreeable period piece, and if not all of its rooms are of the same standard, the better ones—especially those with views of Piazza Municipio and Castel Nuovo—are recommendable. There's an unlikely but convenient Teutonic-accented *birreria*—Paulaner Thomasbrau by name—next door, with a passage to the lobby. *First class.*

Hotel Majestic (Largo Vasto a Chiaia) is at once downtown, modern, and pleasant, with an on-high restaurant, rooftop solarium, bar, and 130 compact but fully equipped tile-floored rooms. *First class.*

Hotel Mediterraneo (Piazza Municipio) greets one with a contemporary lobby of multihued marbles and an attached bar. There is a restaurant on the roof with a terrace for summer dining, affording panoramas of the bay; and there are 230 spotless, well-equipped rooms. *First class*.

Parker's Hotel (Corso Vittorio Emanuele 135) is an old-timer dating back a century—from the time when hotels with *Anglo* names attracted *Anglo* tourists. It is nicely mellow and with spectacular views of city and bay; restaurant, bar. The visitor must decide, though, whether this detached, away-from-the-center location is what he wants, given the impossibly slow traffic situation in contemporary Naples. *First class*.

Hotel Royal (Via Partenope 38) is a well-run, modern 316-room-and-suite house, with a big, buzzy, mural-decorated lobby, balconies attached to bay-view rooms, off-lobby cocktail lounge, striking rooftop restaurant, swimming pool. Location is convenient Santa Lucia. *First class*.

Hotel Santa Lucia (Via Partenope 46) is one of the Via Partenope quartet, along with the Excelsior, Vesuvio, and Royal—all of which are more elaborate. The elderly Santa Lucia has 132 rooms, all with bath, bar-lounge, and breakfast but no restaurant. *Moderate*.

Hotel Vesuvio (Via Partenope 45) is relatively modern, with gracious public rooms, bar-lounge, and a rooftop restaurant accorded special attention on a later page. Bedrooms—180—are comfortable but relatively plain. It's the restaurant that distinguishes this house. *First class*.

Naples: To Eat and Drink

It is possible to approach the cuisine of Naples and the Campania Province of which it's a part somewhat patronizingly. It's because we have, in the back of our minds, too many Italian-American restaurants where the touch is anything but light, the tomato sauce heavy, the scaloppine thickly breaded, the minestrone more pasta than soup. Naples food, at its best, is something else again. Tomato sauce—the famous *pommarola* of the region—tends to be light and delicate and fresh. Pasta is encountered in limitless variety—spaghetti, to be sure, but variations on the theme like *bucatini, vermicelli, ziti,*

and *cannelloni*. Pizza is Naples born and bred, and invariably better
—if less fun to eat—in restaurants than when bought in the street
stands of Spaccanapoli. (Not that one does not want a sampling; and
when pizza is folded in two, wallet-style, it's called *libretti*.) But when
all is said and done, the glory of Neapolitan cuisine is the seafood.
Fish and seafood. Fresh. Fresh. Fresh. In no other major world city,
anywhere, does seafood play so significant—or imaginative—a role in
the cuisine of the people. Order a fish from the catch of the day
simply grilled. It might be *spigola* (sea bass), *orate* (sea bream),
iniglie (red mullet), or *tonno* (tuna). Order pasta with any number
of superb seafood sauces—made with clams (*vongole*), mussels
(*cozze*), shrimp (*gamberi*), lobster (*aragosta*), squid (*calamari*),
eels (*anguille*), or oysters (*ostriche*). Look for *zuppa di pesce* (fish
soup), *cassuela di pesce* (fish casserole), *frittura di pesce mista*—an
assortment (usually featuring squid or octopus), deep fried and delicious.

There are other good things; the Neapolitan *minestrone alla na-
politana*—is special. So is the antipasto, because it so often includes
local seafood. Bread is coarse, chewy, and as good as to be found
in Italy. Most popular wines are the good dry whites of nearby Ischia
and to a lesser extent Capri, whose production is smaller; these are
available by the carafe in restaurants and are inexpensive. Little
Ravello, on the Amalfi coast, produces good reds; Lacrima Cristi
(white) comes from the ashy soil of Vesuvius, along with other, less
celebrated wines. There is no way of predicting what Neapolitan service will be like, except to say that it can range from snarling to effu-
sive, and to generalize about the group (dealt with below) that attracts tourists from the world over, in the Santa Lucia district; I
recommend one restaurant there where service can be agreeable, but
by and large one is advised to dine in more typically Neapolitan parts
of town, where the foreign visitor is not so much a target as a guest.
Here are my selective recommendations, presented alphabetically,
with the category of each appended—*expensive, moderate, inexpensive.*

Da Chico-Santa Lucia (Via Lucilio 8) is on a street just behind the
Santa Lucia-Via Partenope hotels, could not be simpler or more rustic, nor is there better seafood in any Naples restaurant that I know
of. *Fritto misto* is inspired, and so is *spaghetti alla vongole*. Service
can be slow (table capacity is limited), but in my experience it is
pleasant. *Inexpensive.*

Caffè Cristallo (Piazza dei Martini) is a pleasant place for a refreshment stop in a part of town with good shops. *Inexpensive.*

Dante e Beatrice (Piazza Dante 44) fronts a broad downtown square, is unpretentious, family-run, friendly, and with corking good food. The platter of five little grilled fish of the day is recommended; so are the pasta dishes with seafood sauces—any of them. Meals are served on the piazza in warm weather. Remember now, very simple. *Inexpensive.*

Caffè Gambrinus (Via Chiaia) is the perfect downtown observation point for Neapolitans on the go, with Palazzo Reale as a backdrop. Drinks, coffee, snacks. *Inexpensive.*

Da Luigi (Via Domenico Morelli 14) is a good spot to remember if you're quartered in one of the Santa Lucia hotels; it's on a street to their rear, is modest-looking but with fresh and tasty pastas and seafood, and happy customers. *Inexpensive.*

Luise (Via Roma) is a *tavola calda,* which means cafeteria, Italian-style; all kinds of meat, seafood, and pasta dishes are displayed on a vast buffet; you make your selections. *Inexpensive.*

Motta (Via Roma at Via Ponte di Trappia) is a branch of the nation-wide chain selling its own pastries, cookies, candies, ice cream—even potato chips. And, in addition, sandwiches, and a variety of other snacks, invariably delicious. Proper bar, too. *Inexpensive.*

Peppino (Via Palepoli 8) lines its walls with tile plaques, fills its tables with a lively clientele, specializes in seafoods. Near the Santa Lucia hotels. *Moderate.*

Rugantino (Via dei Fiorentini 45) is heart-of-downtown, modern, with gracious service, and a first-rate kitchen. *Contorni*—cooked, cooled vegetables—make a good first course here; the *paglia e fieno*—straw and hay—is tasty pasta (of two hues) for starters; the roast chicken is good, and so is the grilled fresh fish. Nice sweets. *Moderate.*

La Sacrestia (Via Orazio 116): Smart, stylish restaurants are not in oversupply in Naples; La Sacrestia is one such, high on a hill overlooking the city, with good portraits of priests and cardinals lining its walls, the better to do justice to its name. Service is professional and cheerful, food is exceptional. Why not begin with a platter of three species of pasta—*rigatoni, scarpiello,* and spinach-stuffed ravioli in a cheese sauce? Then order the jumbo shrimp—*spiedino di gamberoni*—grilled and delicious. Or *involtini alla papalina*—sautéed veal rolled in prosciutto and cheese, bathed in a delicate sauce. A good place for desserts. *Expensive.*

The Santa Lucia complex: There are five restaurants straddling the pier, and adjacent floats, at Santa Lucia, on the bay, with almost that many Via Partenope hotels to feed them foreign customers. One should not be surprised then, that service can be patronizing if not downright nasty. Cooking, with such a largely non-Italian clientele, can be mediocre, despite the freshness of ingredients. Of the quintet, I would never, ever, return to *Ciro,* so hostile did I find the service and so inadequate the fare. The others are *Starita, Transatlantico, Zi Teresa,* and *La Bersagliera;* I have enjoyed the food—nicely grilled fish, freshly sauced pasta, fairly priced Ischian white wine—at the last mentioned, La Bersagliera. *Moderate.*

Steak House (Via Partenope 12) is a put-on. That Anglo name, at least. This attractive, well-located spot is for snacks and short orders through the day and into the evening, both Italian and international. *Inexpensive.*

Umberto (Via Alabardieri 30) is good-looking and comfortable, with a wide-ranging menu. Pizza—light, puffy, with a sauce of fresh basil, tomato sauce, and garlic—is superb. *Spaghetti alla provenzale* —with capers and olives—is tasty. So is the *frittura di pesce*—mixed fried fish, and *saltimbocca alla romana*—the veal and cheese classic. Crispy green salads, too. The wine list is more extensive than in many other Neapolitan restaurants. As outstanding as the food is the traditionally kindly service; unsurpassed in Naples. *Moderate.*

Hotel Vesuvius Restaurant (Via Partenope): You may order international-hotel dishes here—tomato soup, *steak au poivre,* cold meat platters, lamb chops; no hotel can be without these staples. But you do well to concentrate on things Italian—antipasti from the trolley or the chef's own pizza with a profusion of toppings. The grilled fish, in considerable variety, and the *fritto misto di mare* are ideal selections. So are the veal specialties. Desserts are among the best in Naples, especially the *zabaglione*. Location is the roof; indoors in winter, out on a broad terrace with a super view in warm weather. Depending on what you order, *Moderate to Expensive.*

Naples: To Buy

If Naples is nothing like Rome, Milan, or Florence when it comes to shopping for the kind of merchandise that interests foreign visitors, it holds its own. And it has the advantage of a relatively compact, easily walkable central shopping district, with Via Roma the main thoroughfare. Via Costantinopoli and Via Domenico Morelli have antiques shops. Via Santa Brigida, off Via Roma, is lined with smart boutiques. Naples being Naples, many shops are without visible street numbers; when that is the case, none is listed. Streets tend to be relatively short in length, so there should be no location difficulties. What follows is my own personal selection alphabetized by category, and within each category.

ANTIQUES

Bowinkel (Via Santa Lucia 25) is a mine of old prints and etchings.

Brandi (Via Domenico Morelli) specializes in eighteenth-century Italian antique furniture and accessories.

British Trade (Via Domenico Morelli 32) sells mid- to late-nineteenth-century British objects, of which the Italians are fond.

Francesco Bugli (Via Costantinopoli 34) has smallish, elderly things, sometimes interesting.

De Angeli (Via Domenico Morelli 26) is a source of nineteenth-century antiques, mostly out of England.

G. V. Errico (Via Costantinopoli 43) has good eighteenth-century ceramics and tiles, among other things.

Florida (Via Domenico Morelli 13) has mostly eighteenth- and nineteenth-century Italian antiques.

G. Olga Fuscone (Via Costantinopoli 32) specializes in small objects, some of them charming.

BOOKS

Alinari (Via Calabritto) is for books and postcards.

CHILDREN'S CLOTHES

Monetti (Via Roma) has natty children's togs.

CHINA AND PORCELAIN

Richard Ginori (Piazza dei Martini) is an outlet of the distinguished Italy-wide porcelain firm. They manufacture their own quality line, with dinnerware a specialty.

DEPARTMENT STORE

Rinascente (Via Roma) is one of the nationwide chain. Men's and women's, children's, other departments.

CANDY AND FOODSTUFFS

Gay-Odin (Via Roma at two points, also Via Chiaia and Via dei Mille) is an old and distinguished firm that makes its own chocolates and other candies. You may buy little bags for sustenance while you shop, and fancy boxes for gifts. Everything is wickedly delicious.

Motta (Via Roma at Via Fonte de Trappia) is the Naples outlet of the nationwide candy-cooky house that runs retail outlets in many cities. Aside from eat-on-the-spot choices, (see Naples: To Eat) there is a big grocery department, with snacks for cocktails in your hotel room, train-ride nourishment, a picnic, or whatever.

Perugina (Via Roma at Piazza Carità and Piazza dei Martini) are a pair of Naples branches of the estimable Perugia-based candy firm, with outlets all over Italy and in New York, among other places. The chewy, chocolate-almond *bacci,* or kisses, are habit-forming. Fairly expensive.

JEWELRY

A. de Caro (Via Santa Lucia 171) has Italian coral fashioned into necklaces, brooches, bracelets, and rings. Other jewelry too. Very smart.

LEATHER

Giannotti (Via Roma) stocks a variety of leather products with style and quality both commendable.

LINENS

Brava (Via Santa Lucia 17) specializes in fancy linens, and—not that you're likely to be in the market—the most modish maids' uniforms you're going to come across.

MEN'S CLOTHING

As in every Italian city, there is no dearth of men's shops. Here is a selection; note, also, that some of the shops in the Women's Clothing category sell men's wear, too.

Carrano (Via Calabritto 1) has branches in Rome and Milan and is smartly high style; accessories as well as clothing.

Fusaro (Via Roma) has just about the handsomest shirts in town, as well as robes, sweaters, and ties of the same caliber.

Monetti (Via Roma 26) is for nicely styled accessories.

Palumbo (Via Chiaia 73) is a source of distinctive shirts.

Flli. Romano (Via Roma) makes a specialty of slacks in profusion and at moderate prices.

Sartoria di Pandi (Via Cesario Console) sells sport shirts and sweaters of considerable panache.

MEN'S AND WOMEN'S SHOES

Flli. Piccini (Via Roma) has a big selection, interesting designs.

Spattafora (Via Roma): The lure is the prices; they're moderate for both men's and women's shoes; a chain.

WOMEN'S CLOTHING

Jean-François Claude (Via Partenope 10a) is a boutique with stylish clothes; a men's department, too.

Ianotti (Via Chiaia 67) has accessories as well as dresses and separates. Trendy men's wear in addition.

Mario Valentino (Via Roma) has women's clothing with style; accessories, too.

Old England (Via Roma) has English-imported sportswear, men's as well as women's. Neapolitans go for it.

Portolano (Via Chiaia 11) is for casuals, including raincoats.

Qualteri (Via Chiaia 221) is Mod-look, with Mod-look clothes.

Naples: To Note

Access. There are crack express trains, and more ordinary trains, as well. In all instances, even in first class, be sure to reserve specific seats in advance, or risk standing. Naples' principal station, Stazione Centrale, is on Piazza Garibaldi, a fair-sized taxi ride from the main part of downtown and the Santa Lucia hotels on the bay. Baggage porters and taxi drivers are invariably disagreeable with outlanders; it is a kind of traditional welcome to Naples. Naples' Aeroporto di Capodichino has service via Alitalia and the domestic line Aero Trasporti Italiani (ATI), as well as foreign carriers, including British

Airways and Lufthansa; many other airlines have Naples reservation offices.

Getting About. Within Naples there is an extensive, fairly modern system of buses, smaller trolley-bus and trolley networks; conductors can be surprisingly helpful. The taxis are more often than not decrepit, and their drivers often take pleasure in being unpleasant and quoting fares which include *supplementi* that one never dreamed existed. There are nearly a dozen legal *supplementi*—enough so that one simply accepts the drivers' quotations or risks a high-pitched argument. Tips of 15 per cent are expected but are rarely considered adequate. The wise customer is on the street before the complaints are voiced, however, and ignores them. Avis and Hertz are among the rent-a-car agencies on the scene.

Sightseeing. Bus tours, by companies like Via—one of a number —offer excursions in and around the city and to such nearby places as Pompeii, the Amalfi Drive (including Positano and Sorrento), and Capri.

Clothes. Naples can stay surprisingly warm all the way into October, and by that I mean summery—hot and humid. Informality is the rule in dress during this period; cool winters, mild springs call for dressier clothes in better places and at the opera.

Local Literature. Ente Provinciale per il Turismo publishes a monthly multilingual what's-on booklet called *Napoli;* it is packed with current information, including transport schedules (plane, train, and boats to the islands), the open-hours of museums; and a lot else: ask your hotel concierge for a copy. Don't overlook local dailies including *Il Mattino, Corriere di Napoli,* and *Roma.*

Further Information. Ente Provinciale per il Turismo di Napoli (EPT): Via Partenope 10a, with information desks at Stazione Centrale and Aeroporto di Capodichino.

V

Venice

Venice: To Know

It is sinking. It is not sinking. The international argument goes on, while concerned citizens the world over—many of whom have never seen Venice—kick in funds to societies dedicated to its preservation. No other living city may make that statement.*

The consequence of a makeshift settlement built on Adriatic coastal swamps by refugees fleeing barbarian invaders, Venice went on to become a substantial power, in politics and war, as well as trade and commerce, the funnel through which East and West bartered their wealth. That eminence is past, but the meld of architecture and art that its canny citizens created on a canal-patterned maze of muddy islands still draws the curious as flies to sticky paper. Pore over locally written history and one finds that changes have been made here, destruction has taken place there; progress has reared its ungainly head at the cost of precious preservation. Of course these complaints make sense. Still, no other major city on the planet is as similar to look upon today as it was two or even three centuries ago.

There will be changes from the Carpaccio painting one might study at the National Gallery in Washington; the city is no longer quite what it was when that native son portrayed it in bold, precise

* There are both official and private Save Venice programs. The former is that of the Italian Government, originally budgeted at $475 million, ongoing, and described by UNESCO as "the biggest operation ever undertaken anywhere in the world to preserve, restore, and revitalize a historic town." The latter include the commendable and hard-working Venice Committee of the International Fund for Monuments; for information on its activities, write to it at 15 Gramercy Park South, New York, N.Y. 10003.

strokes in the fifteenth century. But if one pops into, say, the Boston Museum of Fine Arts to look at the way Guardi interpreted his city in the eighteenth century, or if the choice is a Canaletto at, say, New York's Metropolitan, well, then, Piazza San Marco, Palladio's island-church of San Giorgio Maggiore, the joyous Baroque conceit called Santa Maria della Salute, the same Rialto Bridge for which a design proposal by Michelangelo was rejected, the gondola-dotted Grand Canal—even the garb of the gondoliers: that Venice is about as recognizable as the snapshots we capture it with today. It is the easiest history lesson on the planet because it is there for us to see and touch and walk through in that rarity of situations, an urban environment without automobiles.

I think that's why we love it so. We seem to want to contemplate what happened in advance of our arrival. Mainland Venice had been part of a province of the Roman Empire. But when aggressive northerners took the offensive, Venetians began retreating to the marshy islands of a lagoon that had long been known principally to fishermen. They came to build houses on log piles, and then they began to dig canals where streams had been. Between the middle of the fifth century and the end of the seventh they organized as a proper ministate, naming their ruler *doge,* after the Latin *dux,* for leader.

It may well be that they had not realized how much they had going for them with a location that straddled Occident and Orient. They soon learned. Ere long they had organized maritime commerce, and they became strong politically and militarily. They became aggressors, controlling the Adriatic coast and expanding across its waters, to become lords of an eastern empire that brought riches at once commercial and cultural. One has only to consider St. Mark's Basilica and early painters like Paolo Veneziano to appreciate the strength of the Byzantine influence on medieval Venice.

All this while, expansion continued. Involvement in the Crusades won more territory. Envoys to foreign courts, both East and West, were the forerunners of the diplomatic corps that was to become a requisite of every sovereign state's foreign policy. Thirteenth-century accounts of the eastern travels of native son Marco Polo were to serve as the West's primary frame of reference on the Orient.

The originally representative Venetian Republic turned repressive and autocratic. Its much-feared Council of Ten was ruthless in wiping out suspected state enemies and gradually usurped many of the doge's powers. Withal Venice, as the Middle Ages turned into the Renaissance, prospered mightily as the maritime power that linked the commerce of East and West, as a colonial power dominating the Veneto mainland area surrounding it. And as a fountainhead of culture.

The Renaissance was later in coming to Venice than the rest of Italy, but it was worth waiting for. The Venetian school of painting that embraced the Bellini family—most especially Giovanni—but Gentile and Jacopo, as well; Giorgione, Carpaccio, Veronese, Titian, and Tintoretto, not to mention architects like Palladio and Sansovino, and later artists like Tiepolo with his vibrant Baroque frescoes; Canaletto and Guardi, with their evocative cityscapes; Longhi, with his charming insights into upper-class domestic life, the lot portraying in paint what the same era's playwright Carlo Goldoni interpreted in his dramas.

Venetian strength began to subside with the discovery of the New World and the somewhat earlier Turkish conquest of Constantinople; both tended, for different reasons, to lessen the power of Venice while strengthening that of nations directly involved in trade with and settlement in the Americas. By the time Canaletto and Guardi were painting in the eighteenth century, Venice had lost its Adriatic territories and, along with them, considerable of its riches and its prestige. The Serenissima—as the officially styled Serene Republic had been called—was subsiding in strength. The early nineteenth century saw it acquiesce as a territory of Napoleon's arbitrary Kingdom of Italy, with a later switch—at Napoleon's behest—to distinctly unwelcome control by Austria.

Early stirrings of the Risorgimento—the national Italian independence movement—came at just the right time for Venice. The years before the middle of the last century were a period of struggle and conflict and innovation throughout the peninsula, no less so in Venice. The revolutionary Daniele Manin organized fellow Venetians to resist Austrian domination, eventually resulting in the occupiers' expulsion at mid-century; Venice joined the new Kingdom of Italy not long thereafter, in 1866.

Through all of these centuries of triumph and defeat, the city has resisted physical change. There is some industry—traditional manufactures like glass, lace, jewelry, and ships, a modern port (Porto Marghera), and a modern city (Mestre) on the nearby mainland, good air and rail service. And a tourist industry wherein the centuries-old skill of the Venetians at dealing with strangers stands them in good stead. They know their city cannot survive without tourists, and most act accordingly. Nowhere that I know of is the visitor industry more sensibly organized. Generally, everything works well, and despite the unusual qualities of the Venetian terrain, the newcomer, thanks to his hosts—and these range from baggage porter to hotel concierge to the Venetian on the piazza—usually feels welcome from the moment of arrival. As why should he not, in what is, after all, a fantasy city come to life?

Venice: To See

LAY OF THE LAND

There are prefatory points to be made about Venetian exploration. Most important is that *Piazza San Marco* and its environs are only a small piece of the pie. An important piece, of course. But, I repeat, because I know how many well-intentioned visitors never leave the area: only a piece. Second point is that canals and frequent boat rides on them notwithstanding, Venetian sightseeing is synonymous with walking.

It is easy walking because it is flat, without hills, and because there are no motor vehicles or traffic lights. But the conscientious explorer must not be surprised if he finds himself walking eight or nine or ten or—if he is assiduous—twelve miles a day, even allowing for a generous midday lunch-siesta break. And not realizing it. (Venetians are the world's all-time champion urban walkers.)

Third point is geography. As soon as one realizes that this is a city of some 120 islands, spanned by some 400 bridges and intersected by some 150 canals, it is easy to become fainthearted. Instead, lay hands on a good map. Italian Government Travel Offices in the United States distribute excellent ones, gratis. So does Ente Provinciale per il Turismo, in Venice, and so do CIGA Hotels in what is, after all, their home town. Each of these maps is good, each has its own distinctive features. Note peculiar Venetian terminology not encountered elsewhere in Italy. Except for the major canals—like the Canal Grande and Canale della Giudecca, the word for canal is *rio*. Except for Piazza San Marco, its satellite Piazzetta San Marco, and Piazzale Roma, a square is a *campo*. There are other names for thoroughfares

—*largo, fondamenta, riva, ruga,* but most of the time a street is a *calle,* as in Spanish.

There is no point in attempting to memorize anything like each major *campo* and *rio* and *calle;* these come into place as one ambles about. What is important is a familiarity with the basics. Start at the beginning. Arrive by plane and you land at Venice's aptly named *Aeroporto Marco Polo* near the mainland town of *Mestre.* You may take a boat direct from Marco Polo to the in-town air terminal near Piazza San Marco. Or go by bus some five miles across the *Ponte della Libertà* to *Stazione Santa Lucia,* Venice's railway station on the west side of town at *Piazzale Roma*—precisely where you'll arrive if coming by train. There a porter will take your bags to one of the public canal ferries that operate much like city buses in more prosaic communities, to the stop nearest your hotel. Or, if you're willing to spend a fair sum, hire a private motor launch to take you directly to your hotel's own pier. (Most hotels are on a *rio* as well as on a *calle.*) If you are rich and romantic, you may hire an even costlier gondola all to yourself for the trip to your hotel.

Now then, the body of water on which you first travel is the Grand Canal (*Canal Grande*). It is in the shape of a backwards "S" and winds through the core of town, with gorgeous palazzi lining its banks, to the body of water called *Canale di San Marco,* which is actually a channel to the sea, and changes its name going west to *Canale della Giudecca.* At this point it divides Venice proper from *La Giudecca Island,* whose major landmark is *Redentore Church.* Continuing eastward, with a turn to the south, Canale di San Marco leads to the *Lido of Venice,* an oblong strip that is the region's major summer resort, with a series of beaches fringing its Adriatic side. The major visitor islands of the lagoon—*Burano, Murano,* and *Torcello*— lie a short distance beyond.

Back then to Venice proper. If Canale di San Marco is the water at the south end of Canal Grande, *Piazza San Marco* is the land at its southern extreme. Among the world's best-known squares, its landmarks are *Basilica di San Marco;* a tall neo-Renaissance campanile, or free-standing bell tower; the Gothic-era *Doges' Palace;* the series of arcaded pavilions (*Procuratie Vecchie,* its so-called Napoleonic Wing, and *Procuratie Nuove*) that bound three sides of the square. The area between the piazza and the water is *Piazzetta San Marco.* Follow it to the harbor, turn left, and the thoroughfare is historic *Riva degli Schiavoni,* named for the merchant Slavs (*Schia-*

voni) from across the Adriatic who traded there in earlier centuries. (It is still the takeoff point for passenger liners to Yugoslavia.)

Of the bridges spanning the Grand Canal, there are two important ones. *Ponte dell'Accademia,* closer to San Marco, is a relatively modern wood affair worth knowing about because it leads directly to the *Gallerie dell'Accademia,* most requisite of the museums. Farther north is the much-painted and photographed *Ponte di Rialto,* the Rialto Bridge that is the core of Venice's main market area. Now another major geographical hint: most direct route between San Marco and Rialto Bridge is via the principal shopping street; it's called *Mercerie.* Another point: No area of the city is without historic, architectural, cultural, or simply social interest, if only because of the vibrant street life. Venetians live in close-together, fairly sunless houses and enjoy being out of doors as much as possible. The old ghetto, for example, is in the north, around *Campo Ghetto Nuovo.* There are splendid churches, like Scalzi, near the railway station. Fondamenta delle Zattere, bordering Giudecca, is the site of such landmarks as the Gesuati and Spirito Santo churches. Little *Isola di San Giorgio Maggiore* is the site of a church designed by Palladio, the local architect who gave his name to a style of neoclassic architecture, and whose houses for the gentry in neighboring mainland communities inspired English greats like Inigo Jones and later William Kent and Robert Adam. The east end of town is the site of what has to be the world's most beautiful arsenal. The great Frari Church and Scuola di San Rocco are near neighbors in the landmark-filled area to the west of the Grand Canal. I make mention of this handful of landmarks only to underscore the importance I attach to getting *all* about the city. Every *calle* and *rio* and *campo* is well labeled. Locals are usually kind and helpful. And there are welcoming caffès on virtually every *campo* where one may relax over espresso, tea, or a drink, and seep in splashes of local color.

THE ESSENTIAL VENICE

Basilica di San Marco: It is a debatable premise, but not difficult to accept: I submit that there are four rarely confused landmark churches in Europe. Notre Dame in Paris, St. Peter's in Rome, Westminster Abbey in London, and St. Mark's in Venice. Of the four, St. Mark's is the oldest, most distinctive, smallest, and surely the most exotic. St. Mark's is Byzantium in Western Europe. It is the fortunes

of Venice for nearly a millennium. It is the epitome-destination of
the eighteenth-century Grand Tour—and of today's packages. Devout
Venetians stole the remains of their patron saint, Mark, from infidels
of Islamic Egypt in the early ninth century, when the doge of the
moment began plans for a church in the saint's honor. The first St.
Mark's was razed; the one we see today is No. 2. Even so, it dates
back nine hundred years, its Eastern architecture embellished over
the centuries by gifts of treasures representing a multitude of styles
and epochs and areas.

The interior—provided one goes, especially on a first visit, in the
sunlight, most especially not at dusk or in the evening—is as ravishing
as the façade. St. Mark's is at once a history book, art gallery, and,
as a cathedral, seat of the Patriarch—ancient local name for bishop—
of Venice. A relatively recent occupant of that post was the late Pope
John XXIII, beloved of Venetians as of admirers around the world,
as it is easy to perceive from the photographs of him in churches
around the city that he visited, either as Patriarch or Pontiff.

Cross-shaped, and with no less than five elegant domes, St. Mark's
deserves more study than many visitors afford it. Like so much else
of Venice, it is recognizable as the same St. Mark's that Gentile
Bellini and Carpaccio both painted in the fifteenth century, with its
five mosaic-embellished entrances, beneath as many similarly decorated arches. These last lie between the still-visitable *terrazza* (for
views of the square, and up-close inspection of the quartet of prancing
horses of gilded copper that Napoleon briefly spirited away to Paris)
and the jumble of domes above.

To enter is almost to be transported to, say, Istanbul. The domes
are lined with mosaics and frescoes. The rood screen, of the kind
popular in Eastern churches, separates altar from nave and is outlined
with statues of saints. The jewel-embellished golden altar piece (*pala
d'oro*) is studded with enamels of episodes from St. Mark's life. The
separately entered Museum and Treasury are repositories of art
works, not the least of which—to whet your appetite—is a Veneziano painting of St. Mark afloat, with the patterned sails of his ship
quite the loveliest ever painted.

The Doges' Palace, it should be understood from the outset—but often
is not—doubles as one of Europe's most remarkable art galleries. The
visitor is, understandably, caught up with the excitement of a trek
through the Gothic castle in which a long succession of doges lived

from the ninth century onward. And well he might be. The palace is a 3-D fairy tale, and would be even if its walls and ceiling were without their priceless frescoes. The courtyard alone is of a breathtaking grandeur, with its busy mix of styles and a grand stairway leading to a maze of opulent chambers within.

One requires time and a strong neck for the gilt-framed frescoes embedded in the ceilings, not to mention wall expanses covered with art. Indeed, the palace is almost too much of a good thing for a single viewing. Consider Bassano and Tintoretto in the Halls of Avogaria, Tintoretto and Veronese in the Square Hall, Tintoretto and Titian in the Four Doors' Hall, Veronese's celebrated *Rape of Europa* in the chamber known as Antecollege; more Veronese, joined by Tintoretto in the adjacent College Hall. In the immense, magnificently scaled Senate, a Tintoretto on the ceiling (*The Triumph of Venice*) and on walls as well; and in the Council Hall, behind the magistrates' bench, still another Tintoretto, this masterwork called, simply albeit accurately, *Paradise*.

I have not mentioned works by lesser-known painters, nor the golden staircase. I will, though, at this point recommend traversing the Bridge of Sighs (you will have observed this inappropriately beautiful work from outdoors), which links the palace to the also visitable, very grim jail. The idea behind the bridge's name was that prisoners, en route, looked out of the marble-framed windows of the bridge, en route to their cells, sighing at the loss of their freedom.

Gallerie dell'Accademia (Campo della Carità) is a *vaporetto* ride away from most visitors' hotels. It is justly honored by the boat station bearing its name, and the Grand Canal bridge in its vicinity is also named for it. As well they might be. This is a major European gallery, called after a society of eighteenth-century Venetian painters and occupying a onetime church-monastery-school complex that had originally been designed by Palladio but was later substantially rebuilt. The collection's nucleus is eighteenth century. It is a great collection and one must hope that the Italian Government, which operates the gallery, will, by the time of your arrival, not find it necessary to close down, without notice, on scheduled-open days; such in recent seasons has been the case. One begins with sadly lovely Venezianos of the Virgin and of saints. A sublime group of works by Giovanni Bellini—*Sacra Conversazione, Madonna degli Alberetti, Allegoria*

dell'Incostanza, among others—in themselves make a Venice visit
worthwhile. So, for that matter, does the earlier-mentioned Gentile
Bellini of a religious procession before St. Mark's. There are brilliant
Carpaccios—*Miracolo della Croce a Rialto*—and other works depict-
ing Renaissance Venice, Giorgione's *Tempest,* Lotto's *Gentleman,* a
Titian *Pietà,* Veronese's *Cena in Casa di Levi,* and Tiepolo, Canaletto, and Guardi, from the later eighteenth century.

A Pair of Art-filled Churches: *Santa Maria Gloriosa dei Frari*
(Campo dei Frari), along with San Giovanni e Paolo below, would
each, in a city without a St. Mark's Basilica, have achieved the celebrity of St. Mark's. But such are the disadvantages of competition
to churches such as this, that they go unseen by many Venice visitors.
The Frari, as Santa Maria Gloriosa dei Frari is known to locals, is
masterful as much for its architecture as for its art. It is called after
the Franciscan Friars (*i Frari*) who founded it. The present structure
with its somber, elongated Gothic façade, is the third Frari church
and early fifteenth century, with a massive vaulted nave. Newcomers'
eyes seem first to focus on the elaborately carved choir, then Titian's
Assumption at the altar. But one must take some time and walk
about; there are more Titians (not to mention the painter's tomb),
one of Bellini's exquisite Madonnas and works by Vivarini, Sansovino, Donatello, Veneziano, and Canova. *SS Giovanni e Paolo*
(Campo San Zanipolo) has a façade oddly similar to that of the
Frari, which is not surprising in that they are about the same age.
The Frari dates to 1420, Sts. John and Paul to 1430. While the
former is the principal Venice seat of the Franciscans, the latter is
the Dominicans' counterpart. (Both St. Francis and St. Dominic
are believed to have visited Venice.) Both churches are the burial
places of substantial numbers of doges. Sts. John and Paul's great
Gothic interior, architecturally masterful like that of the Frari, is also
studded with treasures. A Giovanni Bellini polyptych of St. Vincent
Ferrer is one such. Also on the scene are Vivarani, Bassano, Lotto,
and most especially Veronese.

Scuola Grande di San Rocco (Campo San Rocco) is the most spectacular of the peculiar group of so-called schools in Venice. These
were charitable organizations, religious-sponsored but lay-endowed,
to the point where they were able to build sumptuous headquarters,

the while carrying on their good works. San Rocco, in a handsome Renaissance building adjacent to a church of the same name, is an absolutely astonishing treasure-trove of Tintoretto. His many and diverse works in the earlier-recommended Doges' Palace are incredible enough. But on San Rocco's second-floor Great Hall there are more than half a hundred wall and ceiling frescoes by the master, who spent nearly two mid-sixteenth-century decades on the project. Themes are religious. There is a ceiling fresco of the church's name saint, Rocco; a moving *Crucifixion* and a *Last Supper,* not to mention a number of Old Testament subjects. Happily, there are benches on which one may sit to study the ceilings.

Ca' Rezzonico (Canal Grande at Santa Barbara) is an effortless step into the bright and gay and lilting Rococo grandeur of eighteenth-century Venice—an entire palazzo turned into a museum of that major Venetian artistic era. The single most splendid aspect is a ballroom to which you would like—without delay—to cable your friends to come at least for cocktails if not for dancing into the wee hours; it has opulent chandeliers and a frescoed ceiling. Two other rooms have ceilings covered with Giovanni Battista Tiepolo frescoes. Chamber after chamber is decorated in period, with the painted furniture peculiar to Venice. Another room is chockablock full of paintings by Longhi that show how the Venetian rich lived in the eighteenth century. China, books, clothes, other objects, too. And views of the Grand Canal, which the palace fronts.

The Island of Torcello is to me the most interesting of the major trio in Venice's lagoon. It was Torcello that the early Venetians first built up in their flight from invading barbarians some fifteen hundred years ago. The gem of the now-quiet island is an originally Byzantine cathedral that dates to the seventh century, with mosaics quite as exciting as those of St. Mark's Basilica in town. As if the cathedral were not enough, there is a fine Romanesque church—Santa Fosca—next door, with a brick-walled circular interior, the carved capitals of its pillars the principal decorations. Nearby is a little museum (*Museo dell'Estuario*), with a winning mixed bag of local historical lore exhibited in galleries on two floors of an ancient structure. Torcello is Venice's surprise package.

BEHIND MUSEUM WALLS:
A SELECTION OF FAVORITES

Galleria Internazionale d'Arte Moderna (Canal Grande at San Stae):
The art is hardly to be despised in this Museum of Modern Art. Still,
the setting is the prime reason for one's visit. Ca' Pesaro, the palace
in which the museum occupies two floors, is among the more splendid
in town, and larger than one would believe a Venetian palace could
be. Completed in the early eighteenth century, it has been a museum
since the end of the nineteenth. The decorations of the building, starting with the entrance on the street floor, are in themselves visit-
worthy, so is the very grand scale of the place, and so are the Grand
Canal vistas from the front windows. There is a good deal of nineteenth-century and some contemporary Italian work, mostly by artists
unfamiliar to most foreign visitors. There is a sampling of French—
Bonnard, Corot, Rouault, Chagall, and other luminaries like Ernst,
Nolde, Kandinsky, Klee, and some striking contemporary sculpture.
Withal, it's the house, hands down.

Galleria Giorgio Franchetti (Calle Ca' d'Oro) is the collection of a
turn-of-century baron who had money and taste. He bought fifteenth-
century Ca' d'Oro—long considered the finest palace in Venice—and
restored it to much of the grandeur that had been lost in various
refurbishings. Then he filled it with his own art and, not long after,
killed himself. His estate gave both house and collection to the Italian
Government, which later added some treasures from the Accademia
(see above). Many Italian masters are represented—Vivarini, Mantegna, Paris Bordone, native Venetians including Carpaccio and
Guardi. But there are distinguished foreigners whom you'll recognize,
a refreshing change in Venice museums.

Museo Correr (Procuratie Nuove, far end of Piazza San Marco, directly opposite the basilica) is at once the most conveniently located
of Venice's museums, and to at least one visitor, No. 2 after the Accademia. Actually, we are dealing with a trio of museums here, one
having to do with documentation relating to the Risorgimento—the
nineteenth-century pan-Italian independence movement; another devoted to derring-do Venetian history—with revelations about matters
local, from doges to gondolas. Most important, though, is the Quad-

reria, or painting-gallery, a score of rooms brimful of beautiful things
—a Bellini *Crucifixion,* bewigged Longhi gents, a blue-robed Lotto
Madonna and Child framed by scarlet-robed angels, a prim-lipped,
red-capped Baldassarre Estense youth-cum-pageboy haircut, an extraordinary *Pietà* by Antonello da Messina, and a pair of most un-
happy-looking Venetian ladies by Carpaccio—among much, much
else.

Museo di Icone dell'Istituto Ellenico (Scuoletta di San Nicolò, Ponte
dei Greci): There have been Greeks in Venice for half a millennium
or more. They built a church in the sixteenth century, which developed into a cultural complex embracing a first-rate collection of
icons; one will see none of better quality in the mother country. They
are brilliant of hue, with a scarlet-robed St. George killing a nasty
black dragon from his white steed, the most dramatic of the lot; along
with an equally fierce St. Minas, golden shield at the ready.

Collezione Peggy Guggenheim (Calle Gregorio) is the collection of
a long-resident American, on the ground floor, basement and little
garden of her eighteenth-century palace. Museum buffs have seen
more extensive and more interesting collections of nonrepresenta-
tional art than this, in far more congenial settings. A museum charg-
ing a no-nonsense admission fee might at least label its paintings so
that customers do not feel obliged to purchase the not inexpensive
catalogue.

Museo Storico Navale (Campo Angelo Elmo) occupies an ancient
building that was for long the Official Granary of the Serene Venetian Republic. It's an unembellished five-story stone box, with its
most engaging exhibits those having to do with Venice on the High
Seas, in the old days; most especially an elaborate model of the cere-
monial galley, an original of which still is used at regattas. Around
the corner is the exciting building that was for long the Venetian
Arsenal; be sure and pass by.

Pinacoteca della Fondazione Querini Stampalia (Campo Santa Maria
Formosa) is nothing if not a mouthful. But one must not let the ap-
pellation stand in the way of attendance. This is a treat far too rarely
taken advantage of by visitors. We may thank a nineteenth-century
count—Querini Stampalia by name—for leaving to the public his

eighteenth-century palace with its scholars' library, beautiful furniture, and painting collection. To have a look at the paintings and furniture, one passes through the ground-floor library to the upper story. There, an attendant—usually glad of visitors, of which there appear to be precious few—acts as tour escort. There is a score of rooms, a number with the Rococo painted furniture of Venice, all with paintings, by such masters as Bellini, Giovanni Battista Tiepolo, Pietro Longhi, and Giordano. Most charming of a charming lot is a chubby lady named Laura Priuli painted by Palma Il Vecchio.

Scuola di San Giorgio degli Schiavoni (Calle dei Furlani) is another of the so-called Venetian schools, church-founded, privately funded, of which San Rocco (above), with its Tintorettos, is the best known. This is a dazzler of a fifteenth-century Yugoslav-founded institution that to its everlasting credit commissioned Vittore Carpaccio to decorate it. The artist painted a series of vivid, color-splashed frescoes that ring the walls of the ground-floor chamber. No St. George has ever killed a dragon with more panache. The adventures of Sts. Jerome and Triphon are a bonus.

TREASURES OF ART AND ARCHITECTURE: SELECTED CHURCHES

They are at every turn. More often than not they are uncommonly beautiful, if only because of their architecture—Gothic, Renaissance, Baroque, sometimes a meld. Then there is the extraordinary art that decorates them. The point is that the curious visitor does well to pop into any church that appeals; in many, priests or sacristans on duty sell guide booklets, brochures, or postcards, and will point one in the direction of major treasures. Helpful, too, are the yellow-and-black plaques—giving relevant historic and artistic details—on the exteriors of many churches. Here is a score-plus of my favorites, presented alphabetically.

Carmini (Campo Santa Margherita) is a felicitous hodgepodge: Renaissance façade, a couple of dozen Romanesque columns dividing the naves within, paintings by Lotto, among others; pretty cloister.

Degli Scalzi (Fondego Scalzi) is quite the most dazzling Baroque church in Venice, well worth a trip to Piazzale Roma, even if you're not yet ready to leave town. (An idea: combine a visit with your departure.) The façade is elaborate, on the order of San Moisè and Santa Maria del Giglio. Within, a modern ceiling fresco successfully replaces one tragically destroyed in a World War I air raid. There are half a dozen exquisite chapels; the one dedicated to St. Teresa of Avila was restored by the Italian Government relatively recently, and has a fine Tiepolo on its ceiling.

Gesuati (Zatteri al Gesuati, facing Canale della Giudecca—not to be confused with the also-recommended Gesuiti, on Fondamente Nuove, Baroque and on the northern fringe of town) is neoclassic-handsome with its lures ceiling frescoes in both main church and presbytery by Tiepolo, as well as a Tintoretto.

Redentore (Isola La Giudecca) is the principal reason for a visit to La Giudecca Island. This is one of Palladio's two complete Venice churches (the other is San Giorgio Maggiore, below). It is beautiful neoclassic, as would be expected of Palladio. The severe interior's sumptuous Corinthian columns are the chief decorations. Ask one of the Franciscan priests on duty to show you the pride-and-joy paintings, one each by Vivarini, Bassano, and Tintoretto.

San Francesco della Vigna (Campo Confraternità) is the result of an unusual collaboration: classic-style Palladio without, but by Sansovino within, where the attractions include superlative art: works by Veronese, Vivarini, Giovanni Bellini—among others.

St. George's (Campo San Vio) is pure and beautiful Renaissance, the seat of Venice's Anglican congregation, and with its namesake saint, George, slaying his dragon right over the front door.

San Giorgio Maggiore (Isola di San Giorgio Maggiore) is a scenic little *vaporetto* ride from Piazzetta San Marco's pier. It's the church that along with Santa Maria della Salute is such an intrinsic part of the Venice skyline. Palladio designed it in his elegant neoclassic way. The façade has a handsome pediment supported by a quartet of the Corinthian columns he so liked. (See Redentore, his other Venice church, above.) The pale gray interior is sublime in its simplicity, the wood-carved choir stalls are as masterful as the choir's geometric-pattern black, tan, and white marble floor. Paintings? Carpaccio, Bassano, Tintoretto, if you please.

Santa Maria Formosa (Campo Santa Maria Formosa) was *re*built the year Columbus sailed west. Go for the lovely Vivarini triptych.

Santa Maria del Giglio (Campo del Giglio) is a Baroque confection that has never looked better, thanks to a relatively recent—and major —restoration by the Venice Committee of the New York-based International Fund for Monuments. The façade is one of the most brilliant in a town where such are commonplace. Within, there is a Rubens *Madonna and Child* in the tiny chapel to the right as you enter, a Tintoretto in the choir, and assorted other treats.

Santa Maria della Salute (Campo Salute) is the gracefully domed Baroque work that is a Venice landmark, thanks to its profile and an inspired situation at the extreme southern terminus of the Grand Canal, as it flows into the wider body of water with Piazzetta San Marco just beyond. Erected as an act of thanksgiving for the termination of a seventeenth-century plague, it is engagingly octagonal and art-filled with major Titians, a Tintoretto, and a pair of Giordanos.

San Martino (Campo San Martino) is relatively uncelebrated but a stunner with a fine brick façade, and pale pink and white frescoes gracing its square Baroque interior.

San Maurizio (Campo San Maurizio) is smallish, early-eighteenth-century neoclassic, with striking marble floors and some fine paintings, by the workshop of the Veronese school and that of Tiepolo.

San Moisè (Campo San Moisè) has an everything-but-the-kitchen-sink façade, by which I mean busy—with scrolls and busts, and full-length statues of saints, and garlands, and columns and a neoclassic pediment. It works. So does the cozy interior, whose considerable art includes a Tintoretto in the left chapel, as you enter.

San Nicolo dei Mendicoli (Campo di San Nicolo dei Mendicoli) goes back, in part at least, to the seventh century, is mostly Renaissance, and the lot, as you see when you enter, is very attractive.

San Pantalon (Campo San Pantalon) is among the more completely successful Baroque churches in town, in large measure because of a smashing eighteenth-century ceiling fresco by a relatively unheralded painter named Fumiani, for whose achievement three cheers.

San Sebastiano (Campo San Sebastiano) might better be called Veronese's Church. It has half a dozen—a brilliant half dozen—of this sixteenth-century master's works, even including the decoration of the doors of the organ, under which the painter is buried, along with his brother Benedetto. But look around also for a Titian, a Tintoretto, a Paris Bordone.

San Stefano (Campo San Stefano) is a Gothic beauty with paintings by Tintoretto, and, unusual for Venice, a decorated ceiling that is one of the loveliest in Italy.

San Zaccaria (Campo San Zaccaria) has a broad, expansive, six-level Renaissance façade—strong and handsome. Within, it does not disappoint, what with paintings by Giovanni Bellini, Tintoretto, and Vivarini, to name a few. And a rather special choir.

A VENETIAN MISCELLANY

Arsenal: The most visitor-neglected of the great Venice buildings. Understandable, because one can't enter. Have a walk-around in conjunction with a visit to the earlier recommended Museum of Naval History. This could be an old Errol Flynn movie set—moated, with a trio of ferocious albeit handsome lions guarding its elegant Renaissance arch, and a formidable crenellated wall.

Columns: The two free-standing columns on the Piazzetta San Marco that you pass by so often are worth a stop and an upward glance. They came from the East some eight centuries ago. The one on the right as you face the water is topped by a statue of St. Theodore, St. Mark's predecessor as Venice's patron saint. Its mate is a lovable bronze lion that, along with the copper horses over the entrance to St. Mark's Basilica, was taken to Paris by Napoleon's forces but later, like the horses, returned.

The Ghetto remains a remarkable entity, more so perhaps than that of any other important European city. It's in the northern part of town, in and about broad Campo Ghetto Nuovo. What one wants most to see is the interior of the sixteenth-century synagogue known as Scuola Grande Tedesca—elaborately furnished and with a graceful oval of a women's gallery. Italy gave the word *ghetto* to the other languages of the world. The centuries-old houses of its ghetto are the tallest in Venice. There are little shops selling souvenirs of the district.

Gondolas: They can be exorbitantly expensive to ride unless one is in on a group deal (see Venice: To Note), but one can watch them being made, just as they have been for centuries, at a little piazza called Squero San Trovaso, surrounded by low-slung tile-roofed houses of great age.

Islands: *Torcello,* most important of the trio of major lagoon islands, is honored by inclusion in The Essential Venice, above. One might also want to explore quiet little *Burano,* a pretty spot with fishermen's houses painted in primary colors, and lady lace-makers busy at their work, alfresco in the good weather, selling what they create, including linen handkerchiefs which they've decorated with their designs. Go in the morning and you can take in the action at the fish market, staying on for a seafood lunch, perhaps, at Da Ramano—inelegant but delicious. *Murano,* whose name has for so long been synonymous with glassmaking, attracts masses of curious visitors. It is possible to see glass hand blown as it has been for some seven centuries; there are also factories. If it is open (which is not always the case), take a look, too, at the Museo di Arte Vetraria—a onetime palazzo full of glass, with the old stuff the handsomest. Even if it is not open, inspect the exterior of eight-century-old San Donato—one of the most important structures in the lagoon. It has a severe front façade and, in contrast, a magnificent apse. The interior is arched Romanesque, with a long, high nave.

The Lido is Venice's rather kicky summer resort, an eye-filling fifteen-minute *vaporetto* ride from San Marco, with a wide white-sand beach extending for several uninterrupted miles, and very attractively populated. Major hotels—notably CIGA's Des Bains and Excelsior—have sections of the beach reserved for their guests, dotted with cabanas. (Stay at a CIGA hotel in town and one of its boats will transport you directly from your hotel to a CIGA cabana on the beach; boats cut through a Lido canal to arrive beach-front.) There is, as well, a municipal beach for day-trippers, where one may rent a locker or *camerino,* for changing. After-dark action centers in and about the Casino. In summer at least. In winter, the Lido shutters and the Casino (see Venice: To Watch) moves to a sumptuous Grand Canal palazzo.

Libreria Vecchia is too frequently passed by, what with all the architectural competition in the neighborhood. It fronts Piazzetta San Marco, to the right as you face the water—a Sansovino-designed sixteenth-century treasure, arcaded and arched and, within, up a flight, the site of a salon aptly called the Gilded Hall, with paintings by Titian, Tintoretto and Veronese, not to mention priceless aged books and manuscripts.

Palazzi, Assorted: As if the palaces turned museums, hotels, and what not else are not enough, there are others serving more prosaic purposes, a few of which I call to your attention. *Ca' Grande* is by the prolific Sansovino—a mid-sixteenth-century work of such substantial proportions that it is now seat of the Prefettura, or municipal government, of Venice. *Palazzo Contarini* is a Gothic-Renaissance mix with its ace-in-the-hole a breath-taking exterior spiral staircase. *Fondaco dei Tedeschi,* where German traders stored their wares during the Renaissance, is still seeing service. Function: Main Post Office. *Fondaco dei Turchi* was where the Turks did business, and there are touches of the East in its multiarched façade. The town's Natural History Museum—mostly frequented by students—is within.

Panoramas: Skyscraperless Venice surprises with the possibilities it offers for bird's-eye views. Uppermost, as regards elevation, is the *Campanile* of St. Mark's, the early-twentieth-century copy of an ancient bell tower that collapsed. Location is just in front of St. Mark's, and there is, blessedly, an elevator. *Torre dell'Orologio* is another Piazza San Marco landmark—a fifteenth-century fantasy, with the great bell on its visitable terrace surrounded by a pair of darkened copper gents who have been ringing in the hours these many centuries. Below, against a gay blue and gold background, a gilded lion of St. Mark looks onto the square, the while protecting other features of the same façade—a *Madonna and Child* and an ancient clock that tells seasons and movements of the sun rather than the time. Then there is the *terrazza of St. Mark's Basilica.* Ask inside how you may reach it. Once arrived, you're right up there with the copper horses, enjoying a smashing view of the piazza. Last, there is the perspective —lower down than the others but still exceptional—of the Grand Canal and surrounding territory, to be seen from *Rialto Bridge,* the sixteenth-century crossing that is the most important of the city's bridges, shop-lined as always and the core of a vibrant market quarter (see Venice: To Buy).

Venice: To Watch

Teatro La Fenice: The only way you're going to see the interior of this originally eighteenth-century opera house is to buy a ticket for a performance. That is, unless management decides to open up for daytime sightseeing, as do Milan's La Scala and Naples' San Carlo. La Fenice went up in 1792 but less than half a century later it was pretty much destroyed by fire. To their credit, a pair of brother-architects—pupils of the original architect, Giannantonio Selva—rebuilt, taking great care to reproduce the original. To look at the theater from its own little piazza, one would have no idea of what a large auditorium lies within. The façade is restrained, neoclassic, with a little four-column portico leading to the lobby. Under a sky-blue ceiling centered with a crystal chandelier, there are six levels of seats—a vast orchestra, three rows of boxes, with a pair of narrow balconies, 1,500 seats in all. The décor is pink, green, and gold, with a curtain following that scheme—green velvet embroidered with pink roses. Electrified antique sconces with pleated silk shades—hundreds of them affixed to the balconies—complement the ceiling chandelier. The lobby bar becomes animated during intermissions, vending drinks, coffee, and snacks. And some people go next door to Ristorante al Theatro for sustenance. Opera tradition is strong at La Fenice. Consider the world premieres of Verdi operas alone; they included *Rigoletto, La Traviata,* and *Simon Boccanegra.* And firsts continued into this century, with maiden performances of such works as Britten's *The Turn of the Screw,* Prokofiev's *The Flaming Angel,* Stravinsky's *The Rake's Progress.* The winter season, usually running from early December into May, sees something like a hundred performances of opera and not too many fewer concerts. There is an annual fall season—*Autonno Musicale Veneziano*—with La Fenice's own symphony, alternating with visiting chamber and other groups. Americans might be interested to note that notwithstanding the wealth of art in Italian museums, which must surely include likenesses of historic La Fenice, the illustration on the covers of La Fenice's programs and brochures, in recent seasons, has been a reproduction of a drawing of the theater by the Venetian painter Guardi, from New York's Metropolitan Museum of Art—with full credit given to the source. *Viva la Fenice!*

Casino Municipale: Venice's casino is the only one that I know of, anywhere, with separate winter and summer headquarters. Warm-weather months see the operation in a modern full-facility structure that becomes the core of after-dark activity at the Lido, with a theater in its Perla auditorium and floor shows in its night club. In winter (October to March) the locale changes to the Grand Canal and Ca' Vendramin Calergi, a fifteenth-century palazzo that is one of the more opulent in a city that does not skimp on interiors. It is one decorative extravaganza after another—a grand stairway, beautifully arched doorways, first-rate paintings, elaborate fire-places and salons—Fireplace Room, Gilt Leather Room, Royal Drawing Room, Yellow Room, Red Room—that even the staunchest of nongamblers will want to inspect. For those who do play: games include craps, vingt-et-un, trente-et-quarante, and roulette. Refresh-ment parlors, too.

Biennale: This is the internationally reputed every-other-year inter-national exhibition of contemporary art. Additionally, there are annual movie festivals in the Biennale Pavilion next to the Casino, at the Lido (usually late August into early September), a contempo-rary music festival in September, and a theater festival later each autumn.

Venice: To Stay

Today's Venetian hoteliers have inherited centuries-long compe-tence at dealing efficiently and compatibly with foreigners. They are among the best such in Europe. As for hotels, no European city has a higher proportion of beauties. When you say you have stayed at a Venetian hotel, what you are saying is that you have been living in a Venetian palace. The hotel plant is one vast collection of fine old palazzi ingeniously converted into modern hostelries, with all of the amenities, in atmospheres of old, usually with furnishings—or at least accents—of old. And more often than not, efficient service. Herewith, my selection of hotels—a compendium created as a result of having stayed in, eaten, drunk in, or at the very least thoroughly inspected. The presentation is alphabetical, with my own categorization—*luxury, first class, moderate*—appended in each case.

Hotel Ala (Campo Santa Maria del Giglio) is modish—65 stylish, recently decorated rooms, each with bath, corridors lined with black and white antique etchings, a beamed lobby and adjacent bar-lounge. Breakfast but no restaurant. *Moderate.*

Hotel Bauer-Grünwald (Campo San Moisè) is partly a Gothic palace on the Grand Canal, partly a modern building facing Campo San Moisè, opposite the church (see above) for which the square is named. There are 200 elaborate rooms, sumptuous suites, capacious public rooms including a bar-lounge and a restaurant that in summer moves to a canal-view terrace and is commented upon on a later page. *Luxury.*

Hotel Bel Sito (Campo Santa Maria del Giglio) is a small house whose chief attribute is a location at once scenic and central. About 20 of the 32 rooms have baths; bar and breakfast. *Moderate.*

Hotel Bisanzio (Calle della Pietà) is near the Arsenal, away from the center, and here included because a good proportion of its 35 rooms are singles; most all have baths. Breakfast but no restaurant. *Moderate.*

Hotel Bonvecchiati (Calle Goldoni) is a good-looking, good-sized (90 rooms, 81 with bath) house with a good restaurant (outdoors in summer) and a good location near San Marco. I like. *Moderate.*

Hotel Boston (Ponte dei Dai, just off Piazza San Marco) is an agreeable, recently refurbished 50-room-cum-bath house, centrally situated. Breakfast, bar. *Moderate.*

Hotel Cavaletto e Doge Orseolo (Calle Cavaletto, off Piazza San Marco) is at once attractive, central, and with 80 nice rooms all with bath or shower, as well as a pleasant lobby, restaurant, and bar-lounge. It shines. *First class.*

Hotel Cipriani (Giudecca 10) is one of a kind—a resort hotel in the city. Well, almost. A two-minute gratis shuttle-boat ride from St. Mark's to its own landing on Giudecca Island. A modern building built for the purpose it serves, it is furnished period style, with 107 rooms and suites, a pair of restaurants, disco, bar-lounge, enormous outdoor pool around which summer lunches and drinks are served; same management that operates Locanda Cipriani and Harry's Bar (see below). *Luxury.*

Hotel Concordia (Calle Larga San Marco) is central, nicely updated, with private baths in all of its 60 period-décor rooms; restaurant, bar-lounge. *First class.*

Hotel Danieli Royal Excelsior (Riva degli Schiavoni) was my first Venice home and remains my favorite Venice home. The setting—a Gothic palace wherein had lived a doge, and next door to *the* Doges' Palace—is at once historic, opulent, and convenient. The interiors of the original palace (there is a newer building as well) are part Gothic, part Renaissance, with just the proper contemporary touches. The nearly 250 bedrooms and suites are good-sized, handsome, and luxurious, with those on the Grand Canal affording extraordinary views. Even the corridors leading to them are aesthetic adventures. Rooftop restaurant moves to a covered terrace in summer but is at any time of year the most exciting eatery in town, and is later described. Big bar-lounge, too. A CIGA hotel with CIGA staffing and service at their best. *Luxury.*

Hotel Des Bains (Lungomare Marconi, Lido) is long, low-slung, glistening white, beach front: a picture-book summer-holiday home. There are 255 handsome rooms, one of the best-looking dining rooms in the area, swimming pool-cum-snack bar and disco, underground passage to the hotel's beach, 18-hole golf course in connection. Cheaper than the sister-hotel, CIGA's Excelsior, but still decidedly *Luxury.*

Hotel Pensione Dinesen (Fondamenta Bragadir at Campo San Via) has baths in about half of its 29 rooms, is in a quiet quarter near Santa Maria della Salute. Restaurant, bar. *Moderate.*

Hotel Europa (Via XXII Marzo, at the Grand Canal) is an atmospheric palazzo converted with panache into one of Venice's most agreeable hotels. There is a fine lobby and adjacent lounges, leading to a bar and a restaurant, with a canal-side terrace for warm-weather meals—and views of Santa Maria della Salute. Bedrooms and suites have been beautifully refurbished in recent seasons. Bravo, CIGA! (That chain's first-class Hotel Regina, recommended below, is next door.) *Luxury.*

Hotel Excelsior Palace (Lungomare Marconi, Lido) is the more posh companion to CIGA's other beach-front hotel, above-recommended Des Bains. The Excelsior is an exuberantly detailed Moorish fortress from without, and an ever-so-tony contemporary playpen within. CIGA's interior designers have done it all up Ultra Mod—and amusingly, with the exception of the traditional-style dining room. There are also places to eat, snack, and drink on the hotel's beach, dancing under the stars, and private motorboat service between the Excelsior and CIGA's in-town Danieli, Europa, Regina, and Gritti Palace hotels. On-site tennis and 18-hole golf course in connection. *Luxury.*

Hotel Gabrielli-Sandwirth (Riva degli Schiavoni) is a dilly of a waterfront house, with a substantial history (the fourth generation of the owning family is now running the place), 120 rooms with bath (mind you don't get one of the smaller ones), a contemporary marble lobby, bar-lounge, and restaurant—all framed by a Gothic exterior. Bonuses: a roof for drinks, sun, and vistas, and a patio-garden for dining in summer. *First class.*

Hotel Gritti Palace (Campo Santa Maria del Giglio) is named for a Renaissance doge who built it half a millennium ago. There are 91 rooms and suites; the better rooms—especially the corner ones—are among the most elaborate in Venice, and the suites are sumptuous; a number have views across the Grand Canal to Santa Maria della Salute. Bar, restaurant (which moves to a canal-side terrace in fine weather, has one of the best kitchens in Venice and is dealt with on a later page), and traditionally superlative concierges. Withal, the ordinary traveler should know that the Gritti puts its best foot forward for prominent personalities; it can be very hoity-toity. Lacking a high-priority V.I.P. introduction, the visitor wanting to stay in a luxury hotel might be happier in the more beautiful and more conveniently located Danieli, or the Europa, Cipriani, or Bauer-Grünwald. A CIGA hotel. *Luxury.*

Hotel Locanda Cipriani (Island of Torcello) is for a get-away-from-it-all vacation in rustic elegance, on the most interesting of the lagoon islands (see The Essential Venice, above). This is a rambling country house set in a garden. Meals (among the better in the Venice area) and drinks are served on a vast terrace. Each of the half-dozen rooms is a rambling suite, with its own sitting room, as well as bedroom and bath. Official classification is First Class Pensione, but when I tell you that fairly recent guests were Queen Elizabeth II and Prince Philip, I think you'll have a more accurate idea of what the Locanda is all about. *Luxury.*

Hotel Londra (Riva degli Schiavoni) is superbly situated with a welcoming lobby, adjacent restaurant and bar-lounge, and nearly 70 recently refurbished rooms and suites. The restaurant is special and recommended on a later page. *First class.*

Hotel Luna (Calle dell'Ascensione off Piazza San Marco) has a nice hum to it—big lobby, attractive restaurant and cocktail lounge, 127 snappy, up-to-the-minute bedrooms and suites in a onetime monastery that has fifteenth-century origins. (Ask to see the Baroque-era ballroom.) *First class.*

Hotel Metropole (Riva degli Schiavoni) is smallish (64 rooms and suites, and smart, and by that I mean lobby, restaurant, cozy cocktail lounge, and bedrooms—the lot in period style. Good location, too. *First class.*

Hotel Monaco e Grand Canal (Calle Vallaresso, off Piazza San Marco, and just opposite Harry's Bar) is a charmer: 80 period-style rooms and suites, with those over the Grand Canal special treats.

Agreeable lobby, bar-lounge, restaurant-cum-canal terrace. *First class*.

Hotel Monte Carlo (Calle Specchierie, just off Piazza San Marco) embraces 64 small but spotless rooms with bath, in a heart-of-town setting, with an exceptional restaurant (Do Forni, see below) in connection. Good value. *Moderate*.

Palazzo del Giglio (Campo Santa Maria del Giglio) is a cluster of venerable houses deftly converted by CIGA Hotels into an apartment house for visitors who would like suites—with bedroom, living room, bath, and full kitchen; they interconnect so that space can be increased. *Luxury*.

Hotel Panada (Calle Larga San Marco) insists, in its brochure, that it is precisely 45 steps from St. Mark's. I haven't counted. But the hotel is scrubby-up spotless, with nifty rooms, many with bath, and an inexpensive restaurant. *Moderate*.

Hotel Petit Palais (Lungomare Marconi, Lido) is a smallish but good beach-front hotel; all 26 rooms have bath; restaurant, bar. *Moderate*.

Hotel do Pozzi (Corte dei do Pozzi) is a find: a lovely, updated old house on a quiet albeit central mini-square. Every one of the 35 spacious rooms has bath and a piece of good contemporary art on the walls. Everything shines. And the Raffaele Restaurant (see below) is in connection. *Moderate*.

Hotel Quattro Fontane (Via Quattro Fontane, Lido) is central to both Casino and beach, with baths in 62 of its 72 rooms. Restaurant, bar. *Moderate*.

Hotel Regina (Corte Barrozi at the Grand Canal) is the 65-room mate to earlier-recommended Hotel Europa. The Regina's rooms, recently redecorated, are to this appraiser so good-looking as to constitute luxury-category rooms in a first-class house. There's a restaurant that has a summer Grand Canal terrace, and the cocktail lounge, all browns and rusts and modern overstuffed furniture, is the best-looking of its kind in town. Facilities of the adjacent Europa are close to hand for Regina customers. A CIGA hotel. *First class*.

Hotel San Marco (Calle del Fabbri) is enviably close to Piazza San Marco, but not quite a dozen of its 55 otherwise okay rooms have their own baths. Restaurant, bar. *Moderate.*

Hotel Savoy e Jolanda (Riva degli Schiavoni) is a nice old waterfront house with 80 spruced-up rooms, 60 of which have bath; and a restaurant-caffè-cum-view. *Moderate.*

Pensione Wildner (Riva degli Schiavoni) is a long-established waterfront spot with a reputation—well deserved—for good value. Sixteen of the 20 neat bedrooms have bath; bar, restaurant. *Moderate.*

Venice: To Eat and Drink

The cuisine of Venice is relatively uncelebrated abroad; Venice appears to have so much else going for it. But Venetians are experienced trenchermen. They claim—with foundation—that it was their ancestors who invented the fork before the rest of the world had given table utensils any thought. With so long a history as middlemen between East and West they are in other ways culinarily sophisticated. Rice, for example, is a staple, and the *risotti* of Venice are quite as delicious—and as popular—as those of Milan. Look for *risotto con i caparozzoli*—a seafood variation, *risi e bisi* (or rice and peas) is everywhere to be seen. *Polenta,* a corn-meal staple beloved also of as diverse peoples as Romanians and American Southerners, is often served as one might potatoes, and is also toasted, grilled, roasted, even boiled. One finds a variety of fish—bream, sole, red mullet, sea bass, eels, sardines—as well as shrimp, lobster, and squid. Meat dishes—veal and lamb especially—are everywhere available. So is liver—*fegato alla veneziana*—a prime specialty. Lucky is the diner who comes upon *torresani*—tiny roast pigeons. The pasta dishes common to all regions of Italy are popular in Venice too, as elsewhere. Wines of nearby Verona—especially Soave (white) and Bardolino and Valpolicella (red) are popular. Restaurants invariably have house wines in carafes; they are the best buys. What follows is a selected group of restaurants that I personally like, in various quarters, in varying price ranges. The presentation is alphabetical, and each is categorized *expensive, moderate,* or *inexpensive.*

Antico Carbonara (Calle Bembo) is as elderly as its name implies, with an interesting near-Rialto location, and as good for *risotto* and seafood as for less local dishes. *Moderate.*

Antico Martini (Campo San Fantin) has been around even longer than neighboring La Fenice opera house—which means early eighteenth century. It is at once posh and popular, thanks to delicious cooking, smiling service, and touches like crystal chandeliers, silk Austrian shades framing the windows, fresh flowers at every table —and amusing frescoes of 1930s flappers for contrast. The *risotta primavera* is sublime; so is the *cannelloni.* And the fresh grilled fish or scampi, and the veal scaloppine. A bonus, for dancing and music, is the restaurant's own night club. *Expensive.*

La Colomba (Piscina di Frezzeria) is a series of plain rooms, tables close together, good contemporary art on walls, and snooty waiters obviously aware that first-rate good food can compensate for their bad manners. Seafood is the thing here—clam or mussel chowder, shrimp in a variety of styles, to start, grilled fresh sardines or lobster thermidor for entrees. Mind, though, the steaks are good too. Depending on your order, *Moderate* to *Expensive.*

Danieli Royal Excelsior Hotel (Riva degli Schiavoni): The city's most beautiful hotel does not disappoint with its restaurant. Taking advantage of its situation, the CIGA management has placed the restaurant on the roof with an adjacent covered terrace, for warm-weather meals. The seafood antipasto is an inspired opener. *Risotto* with seafood accents is equally tasty. Main-course specialties include a remarkable *fritto misto baccalà*—the beloved local cod—with polenta, and a super veal scaloppine. Extraordinary desserts, extraordinary wine list. *Expensive.*

La Fenice (Calle Fenice) is a lovely touch and taste of eighteenth-century Venice, appropriately adjacent to the opera house of the same era, bearing the same name. The look is brocaded walls, Rococo chairs, silk-shaded sconces, mullioned windows. A delightful staff serves good things to eat, such as a seafood antipasto, the traditional *pasta a fagioli* (Venice is as good a place as any to try this beans and pasta combination), *lombatina,* or paillard of veal, or a chicken specialty—*petti do pollo principessa*. Luscious desserts. *Expensive*.

Do Forni (Calle Specchiere) is handsome and robust, with beamed ceilings, copper pots on the walls, big baskets of multicolored fruits and vegetables, oversize crusty breads, and specialties like fish soup, seafood *risotto, fritto misto*. And more prosaic meat standbys, too. Everything is fresh, and the service has style. *Moderate*.

Graspo de Ua (Rialto, near Banco d'Italia) is packed with *ambiente* —busily decorated walls, dazzling displays of edibles, welcoming waiters. And super food. Start with *tar tufi di mare*—big clams or small oysters as you decide, but delicious on the halfshell with a squeeze of lemon. Or the ravishing antipasto to which you help yourself from a groaning table. Little fried soles—*bambinolli,* a grilled shrimp platter, or *baccalà*—the local cod—are all good entree bets. So is *cannelloni*. Cheeses are in abundance. *Moderate*.

Gritti Palace Hotel (Campo Santa Maria del Giglio): One lunches or dines at the Gritti for the exceptional food and the likewise exceptional wines. And, as a warm-weather bonus, a table on the terrace overlooking the Grand Canal. Pasta is a joy, *taglierini verdi gratinati al prosciutto*—green noodles with cheese and smoked ham —in particular. *Risi e bisi*—rice and peas—is commendable here. So are the grilled fish. And beef as well as veal dishes. Sweets are made more of than in many places; consider a blend of chocolate ice cream and lemon sherbet blanketed by hot chocolate sauce. Let the wine waiter make suggestions from the masterfully stocked cellar. *Expensive*.

Harry's Bar (Calle Vallaresso) is understated—smart, populated with a clientele at once affluent and knowing, as regards good food, served with skill. (Downstairs waiters know how to dart in and out of the close-together tables with dispatch and good humor. Upstairs is less frenetic but also less fun.) If you are going to have a dry martini in Venice, Harry's is the place; they're faultless. So is the pasta—ravioli, green noodles, *cannelloni*. The fish soup is super. So is *risotto alla primavera*. Choose from a relatively limited group of fish and meat dishes; *piccatina di vitello all pizzaiola* is a fine veal choice. The steaks are as good as one will find in town. And the bittersweet choc-

olate cake with whipped cream is perfection. Same astute management as the Cipriani and Locanda Cipriani hotels. *Expensive*.

Locanda Cipriani (Torcello Island) is a smart albeit casual inn (see
Venice: To Stay) with a remarkably good restaurant, nicely combined
with a day's excursion to this lagoon island (see The Essential
Venice). Management is the same as Harry's Bar and Hotel Cipriani,
in town, so that one can count on just about everything being good,
most especially homemade pasta, and fresh-caught Torcello fish and
seafood with both the *risotto* and *zuppa di pesce* outstanding. Setting is a garden-framed terrace. Relaxing. Summer only. *Expensive*.

Montin (Fondamenta Eremite) is an away-from-the-center choice
with a slightly saucy, slightly raffish air, big trellis-covered garden
for warm-weather service, and fine fare. Venetians like liver—*fegato*
—and it's popular here. Or how about duck with *polenta?* More con-
ventional are broiled fish, fried scampi, and spaghetti with clam
sauce. For dessert: *zuppa inglese*. *Moderate*.

Caffè-Pasticceria-Bar-Gelateria Paolin (Campo San Stefano) is included at this point only to serve as a sample of the engaging caffès
similar to it and in *campos* and *calles* all over town. The point I make
is that it's a nice fresh change to leave visitor-populated San Marco
for the Venice of the Venetians, and join them for an espresso with
pastry, a drink, or whatever, in the course of one's explorations. Unlike Piazza San Marco caffès—where service is often nasty and tabs
inflated—these places are friendly and the prices are right. They're
all *inexpensive*.

Poste Vecie (Pescherie, near the Rialto Bridge on the side opposite
San Marco) is a neighbor of the fish market, which means that products of the sea are indicated. The antipasto table seems almost to
dwarf this friendly, small-scaled Old Venice-style place. Choose from
it for starters, or have a pasta, with a piece of broiled fish, and cheese
to follow. *Inexpensive*.

Quadri (Piazza San Marco) is the bigger of the caffès on the left, as
you face the basilica. Outdoors, it is little different from its competitors. What makes it special is that it is also a proper restaurant within,
green and gold eighteenth-century in look, with its upstairs room

beneath a painted Renaissance ceiling. The menu is wide-ranging, with *risotto* and a variety of shrimp preparations the specialties. *Moderate.*

Da Raffaele (Ponte del Ostreghe) is busily albeit amusingly over-decorated, with tables on the quiet canal it fronts, for summer meals. The menu is standard, which is not to say unappealing—good soups, pastas, rice dishes, equally satisfactory entrees, which include well-roasted chicken—an agreeable choice for a change. Kind service. *Inexpensive* to *Moderate.*

Rosa Salva (Calle Fiubera) is at first glance a caffè, where one wants to stop for midmorning coffee and a piece of the scrumptious pastry (there is none better in town). It is also, should you be in the market, the town's most distinguished caterer of private parties. For coffee and cake: *Inexpensive.*

Da Romano (Burano Island) is an unpretentious country seafood house with a venerable and well-deserved reputation for quality. Go for lunch on a sunny day and seek out a Lagoon specialty like *rospo* —a fish species good simply grilled with a squirt of lemon, or *canocchi*, a Lagoon variation on the lobster theme. Friendly. *Moderate.*

Al Theatro (just opposite Teatro Fenice) is as good a spot as any in town for a pizza. But it's also a proper restaurant—fresh-caught *rospo* is a fine fish choice and the pasta is first rate. *Inexpensive.*

Da Vinicio (Calle della Regina) is an apt Rialto-quarter choice, warm and cozy, with seafood (especially grilled scampi) and modest tabs its main lures. *Inexpensive.*

San Giorgio (Londra Hotel, Riva degli Schiavoni) is the ideal warm-weather locale for lunch, or dinner for that matter, when one would enjoy a view of the animation along the waterfront. Have *cannelloni San Giorgio,* fish soup, or pork chops *zingara* style. *Moderate.*

Terrazza (Bauer-Grünwald Hotel, Campo San Moisè): Preferred season for a meal here is summer, with a table on the terrace along-side the Grand Canal. There are table d'hôte lunches and dinners, but the à la carte is special, especially if you choose *cozze alla marinara,* an Italian variation of France's *moules marinières; sogliola alla mugnaia,* grilled sole, or a broiled steak out of Tuscany, whose beef is Italy's best. If you order table d'hôte, *moderate;* if you order à la carte, *expensive.*

Venice: To Buy

Venice does not compete with Rome, Florence, or Milan as a shopping center. Which is not to say there are not interesting buys —antiques especially—to be made in interesting places. Herewith, arranged alphabetically, by and within categories, are some personally scouted sources.

ANTIQUES

Though without the quantity of Florence, Venice does indeed have some shops with museum-caliber objects, mostly Italian— Venetian for that matter—in origin, authentic, rare, and extraordinarily expensive. Dealers tend to be correct if cool, rather grand and distant, not nearly as welcoming of questions as their colleagues in other cities. They include:

Arredi d'Arte (Ponte delle Ostreghe): larger pieces but accessories as well.

Pippo Casellati (Via XXII Marzo): frequently with fine old paintings, as well as furnishings.

Salvadori (Via XXII Marzo): good style as well as good quality.

V. Trois (Via XXII Marzo): with fine fabrics as well as fine antiques.

ANTIQUE PAINTINGS

Like the above shops, which emphasize furnishings but frequently have paintings, the following group emphasize paintings and prints but often also have furnishings.

Giocondo Cassini (Via XXII Marzo) specializes in Piranesi prints, as well as antique books, maps, and other graphics.

A. Frezzatti (Via XXII Marzo) usually has handsome art works.

Marco Redolfi (Campo San Maurizio) is full of eighteenth-century paintings and prints, and appealing smallish objects, like old plates.

Pietro Scarpa (Via XXII Marzo) deals only in paintings and drawings of exceptional—usually museum—quality.

FABRICS

Bevilacqua (Campo San Zan Degola): very elegant, very expensive silk brocades.

Ceroni (Calle del Ponte del Lovo, near the Rialto) sells handsome materials for men's and women's suits and coats.

Rubelli (Campo San Gallo) is for damasks and brocades, rich and costly.

V. Trois (Via XXII Marzo) sells antiques (see above) but also Fortuny fabrics, the printed cottons that fans the world over can spot instantly—and covet.

FOOD AND WINE

Mercada Canna Regio (Ponte delle Guglie) is near the railway station and the Ghetto, in the northern part of town; don't miss its open-air fresh fish and other food displays when you're in the neighborhood.

Rialto: The Rialto area has for centuries been a market place—one of the most color-drenched in Italy. Go as early in the morning as you can for strolls through the scattered stalls, most especially the *pescherie* (fish markets) and *erberie* (vegetable markets).

Giovanni Venturini (Ponte delle Ostreghe) is a mouth-watering grocery-wine shop-delicatessen-*salumeria* that is a good source of snacks—especially the salami and cheeses—for cocktails in your room or for train rides, and for wines.

GLASS

The island of Murano, noted over the centuries for its glass, is the site of a hundred and fifty factories, with retail sales generally made from each. If a word to the wise is sufficient, let it be known that the tourist office receives the majority of its complaints from visitors who have ordered—but not received as promised—glass, from Murano sources, that was to be shipped to their homes. Although I note a few reliable sources below, as a convenience, one is advised to purchase from among the more reputable dealers in Venice. Some of the bigger of these, it is worth pointing out, have a series of little shops in and about San Marco, which they use to attract customers to their main showroom, escorting them on foot. Nothing the matter with this high-pressure ploy; go along if you like, but don't feel obligated to buy. There are no bargains; the good stuff is expensive.

Barovier (Fondamente Vetrai, Murano Island) is a long-established Murano glass factory; watch it being blown.

Bortoli (Calle Vallaresso, near San Marco): a good source of glass from various factories; china, too.

Ditta I. Lombardo (Calle Fabbri) is another all-round source, with a good choice of small gift-type pieces.

Pauly (Ponte Corsorzi, near San Marco, with other outlets) is another major factory. Mostly traditional style with quality first rate, and the variety interminable.

Venini (Piazzetta Leoncini in Venice; Fondamente Vetral, on Murano) is one of the better-known factories, with branches and outlets abroad and in other Italian cities, including Rome. The style is smartly contemporary.

Salviati (various Piazza San Marco and other Venice locations,

Fondamente Radi on Murano) is another major-leaguer, mostly traditional style, but with some Mod-look output as well.

GLOVES

Rialto: The open-air stalls in the market have men's and women's leather gloves at good prices.

LACE AND LINENS

Brocchi (Calle Valaresso, off San Marco) is an estimable source of the traditional Venetian lace (it was once a major craft) and of fine hand-worked linens, too.

LEATHER AND REPAIRS

Valigeria Sinigaglia (Calle San Stefano) is fairly typical of many Venice leather and luggage shops, but noteworthy because it is good at quick repairs.

MEN'S CLOTHING

Alta Moda (Calle Vallaresso, near Harry's Bar) is about as *alta moda* as one will find in Venice—both clothes and accessories, with some women's things, too.

Carlello (Campo San Felipo Giacomo) is for traditional-style clothes, shirts, and ties.

Elite (Calle Larga San Marco) has smart custom-tailored suits, sport jackets, and topcoats.

SHOES

Casella (Campo San Moisè) sells men's and women's shoes; good selection, moderate tabs.

Franz (Calle San Stefano, near San Marco) is for beautiful custom-made shoes, both men's and women's, in a variety of styles. They are costly, take about two months to make, and are shipped to you at home, unless you're fortunate to have that long a stay in Venice.

Pedrenzone (Campo San Felipo Giacomo) is a source of handsome men's shoes.

SILVER AND JEWELRY

A. Codognato (Bocca di Piazza San Marco) has long specialized in antique jewelry; you look at it while seated on lovely eighteenth-century Venetian chairs.

Rialto: The market has a concentration of worth-inspecting jewelry shops, under the arcade, on the far side of the bridge.

Sfriso (Campo San Tomà) is a reputed silversmith—largish pieces like trays and bowls, but small carry-aways, too. And other work in gold. It's all made by hand.

WOMEN'S CLOTHES

Missiaglia (Piazza San Marco, next to Caffè Quadri) has modish women's sportswear, accessories, and jewelry; men's furnishings, too.

Patrizia (Ponte dei Greci) is among the more high-style shops for women's clothes and *bibelots;* snappy men's togs, too.

Roberta di Camerino (Calle Ascensione near San Marco) is a Venetian entrepreneur-designer who has opened shops on several continents; locations range from Tokyo to New York. The mother house has a wide selection of sportswear (its light weight makes it a favorite with travelers) and such accessories as umbrellas, handbags, wallets, belts, silk scarves. Expensive but imaginative.

Venice: To Note

Access. Most visitors arrive by *train;* tracks cross between the mainland town of Mestre, on Ponte della Libertà, to Stazione Santa Lucia, the railway terminal on the northwest side of the city; hotels generally have representatives meet guests with advance reservations, and assist them into boats that take them to hotels. Travelers, alone or in groups, in the care of travel agencies, should look for the agent's representatives at the station. Unmet visitors will find porters to take their baggage either to the *vaporetti*—public boats that operate as do buses in ordinary cities—or to the much more expensive—but much more convenient—private motor launches (*motoscafi*) that operate like taxis on land and will transport one directly to the pier of his hotel. Departing train passengers are advised, as in all Italy, to obtain advance specific seat reservations; hotel concierges can do this, or it can be done upon arrival, while one is at the station. *Motorists* (there are *autostrade* from Milan and Rome) arrive in much the same way, crossing the same Ponte della Libertà, to public garages at Piazzale Roma, opposite the train station, from which the procedure into town is similar to that outlined above for rail passengers. There are no direct Venice-North America flights as there are between that continent and Rome and Milan. Inter-European flights to Venice land at the mainland Aeroporto Marco Polo, from which passengers generally are transported on airline-sponsored boats directly to the in-town Air Terminal near Piazza San Marco, from which they may hire private boats to their hotels or ask their hotel to send for their bags. Or a private boat—and this will be costly—may be engaged to take one from the airport directly to one's hotel pier.

Getting About. There are only two ways: on foot and by water. Public water buses—*vaporetti*—operate on a series of half a dozen-odd routes, with the Grand Canal their main artery. Major lines are No. 1 (*accelerato*) and No. 2 (*diretto*). Tickets are cheap (priced according to length of journey) and purchased at stations, which have signs indicating route numbers and stops. Ticket agents are accustomed to queries from tourists and invariably are helpful, as indeed are traveling Venetians. Assuming the weather is fine, these water trips are so scenic that one doesn't mind getting lost or aboard the wrong boat upon occasion. As I indicate at the beginning of this chapter, it is wise to travel with a good map of the city. It is further advisable, before setting out, to go over one's itinerary—whether it be sightseeing, shopping, dining, or a combination thereof—with the hotel concierge; in most cases these men know their city intimately—and intricately. *Gondolas*—of which there are only some 400 in operation contemporarily (in contrast to an estimated 10,000 in the seventeenth century) are expensive, at least for a casual ride. Their high cost can be obviated by group charters, either for sightseeing or evening serenades, complete with schmaltzy music. For an ordinary journey—on which as many as five persons can be accommodated on standard-size gondolas (fewer on the smaller craft called *sandoli*) —one is advised to determine with the gondolier a fee *in advance of boarding—not hesitating to bargain*. There are generally clusters of gondolas at Piazzetta San Marco and Piazzale Roma. Gondoliers are licensed, as would be a taxi driver—worth bearing in mind in case of any misunderstanding or difficulty.

Sightseeing. Trained guides may be hired for help in ambulatory tours of town. There are boat excursions to the Lagoon islands, and bus tours to the celebrated Palladio-designed houses and other attractions of the surrounding Veneto region.

Clothes. Casual during the day in summer and for as long as the weather remains hot; dressier in the better places after dark, and in the cooler months.

Climate. Spring, summer, and fall are much like most of Italy, typically temperate zone. Winter, however, can be rainy and the rain causes floods, at which point one crosses Piazza San Marco by boat!

Local Literature. The crackerjack Ente Provinciale di Turismo publishes current schedules of the open hours of museums and other attractions, and other good gratis material. And watch local dailies, including *Il Gazzettino*.

Further Information. Ente Provinciale di Turismo, Castello, Calle del Rimedio, Venice; Tourist Information Offices, Calle Ascensione 71c, near Piazza San Marco; Stazione Santa Lucia, Piazzale Roma, and the *autostrade* roundabout at Mestre, on the mainland.

VI

Italy: A Mini A to Z

ADDRESSES

Italian Government Travel Offices (ENIT): 630 Fifth Avenue, New York 10020; 500 North Michigan Avenue, Chicago 60611; St. Francis Hotel, San Francisco 94119; Place Ville Marie, Montreal; Via Marghera 2, Rome. *Ente Provinciale per il Turismo di Roma,* Via Parigi 11, Rome. *Ente Provinciale per il Turismo di Firenze,* Via Manzoni 16, Florence. *Ente Provinciale per il Turismo di Milano,* Via Marconi 1, Milan. *Ente Provinciale per il Turismo di Napoli,* Via Partenope 10A, Naples. *Ente Provinciale per il Turismo di Venezia,* Castello, Calle del Remedio, Venice. *Italian Cultural Institute* (Istituto Italiano di Cultura), 686 Park Avenue, New York, and 1200 Rue McGregor, Montreal. *Automobile Club d'Italia,* Servizio Turismo, Via Marsala 8, Rome.

ADVANCE BOOKINGS

Hotels, Package Tours, Transportation—ideally through a travel agent—preferably one who is a member of the American Society of Travel Agents (ASTA), and who knows Italy firsthand; if you like, you may reserve your own hotel or pensione accommodations by writing directly. *Opera and Concert Tickets:* Your travel agent may be able to get tickets for you in advance, through his representatives on the spot in Italy. Or write ahead yourself. Generally, tickets so ordered are held at the box office for you. Italian Government Travel Offices (addresses above) have advance schedules for the major houses. Should you arrive without tickets, ask your hotel concierge for help, if your own visit to the box office has been fruitless. Or, as a last resort, stand out in front an hour or so before curtain, watching for ticket-holders wanting to sell; I've had good luck in this respect. Tickets for Milan's La Scala—concerts as well as opera—are the toughest to obtain.

BREAKFAST

Breakfast is a distinctly minor meal in Italy, usually a *caffè completo*—which means simply a roll or two and coffee, which is lightened by considerable milk. The most common addition to this standard repast is a boiled egg. But bigger hotels will serve bacon, fried or scrambled eggs, toast, fruit, and fruit juices (Italy's oranges, fresh-squeezed, result in delicious juice), all, of course, at additional cost. In hotels, breakfast—which is not included in room rates—is usually served in guests' rooms, although it may be taken in dining rooms or special breakfast rooms. It may also be ordered the night before via the concierge or, in larger places, through room service. If eggs are part of a room-service breakfast, expect only a shaker of salt to accompany them, no pepper unless you specify.

CLIMATE

Expect, roughly, the kind of four-season, temperate-zone weather of the United States, but with milder winters and longer, hotter summers, especially in Rome and Naples, along with excessive summer and early fall humidity in those cities. Generally, spring and autumn are the kindest Italian seasons, late summer the most uncomfortable, with August—when everything is overcrowded, what with so many Italians and other Europeans vacationing—the month to avoid if at all possible. *Average temperatures:*

	Winter (February)	Spring (May)	Summer (July)	Fall (October)
Rome	52	70	82	65
Florence	47	67	81	63
Milan	40	66	75	56
Naples	54	70	83	66
Venice	48	67	77	60

CLOTHES

This is Europe's best-dressed country. No other Europeans—not the French, not the British—have quite the sense of style of the Italians, especially the urban Italians, with Rome and Milan leading. And I'm speaking of men (Italian males are the world's vainest—but with taste) as well as women. Be as informal as you like during the day—especially in summer and early fall—but dressier—in better places at least—after dark. In the case of papal audiences at the Vatican: jackets and ties for the gents, covered heads and arms for the ladies.

CURRENCY

The lira. (Plural: lire). Inquire as to the rates for it from banks and currency-exchange firms in the U.S. or Canada before departure; you may want to buy some in advance. In Italy, best rates are obtained at banks (you absolutely must have your passport with you), and change-offices identified by the word *Cambio,* but hotel cashiers also change money. Take the bulk of your funds in travelers checks—they're the safest—with plenty in twenty-dollar denominations—they're the most convenient, but some ten-dollar checks, too. Denominations of the lira: 500-, 1,000-, 5,000-, 10,000-, 50,000-, and 100,000-lire notes; 5-, 10-, 20-, 50-, 100-, and 500-lire coins. *But,* and there is a big But: Both low-denomination paper and silver are in short supply. Unless and until this odd situation changes, it pays to be a hoarder of small-denomination money, the better to gain admission to museums (which may not have change for bigger notes), tip taxi drivers, make small purchases, or whatever. It is as well to be prepared for this inconvenience, and to expect change, upon occasion, in the form of hard candies, sticks of chewing gum, and postage stamps.

CUSTOMS

Entering Italy: Generally, Italian customs officers assume what you're taking in is your own business; you're allowed personal effects, of course: two cartons of cigarettes, two bottles of wine in addition to a bottle of liquor, a reasonable amount of film for your own use, and gifts and doodads you may have picked up in other countries during the course of your travels, whose final resting place will be your own home base.

Returning to the United States: The current limit on duty-free purchases is one hundred dollars, allowable once every thirty days, providing you have been out of the country at least forty-eight hours. (If you haven't, you're allowed a big, fat ten-dollar exemption.)

Worth noting: You may ship, *duty-free,* without having to declare them, and *not* counting as part of your hundred-dollar allowance, gifts or parcels not exceeding a total value of ten dollars, so long as they are not liquor, perfume, or tobacco. Send *as many as you like* from wherever you like, but not more than one parcel per day *to the same recipient.* Mark each such package "GIFT—TOURIST PURCHASE—VALUE UNDER TEN DOLLARS." Remember, too, that *antiques,* duly certified to be at least one hundred years old, are admitted duty-free, and do not count as part of the hundred-dollar quota; neither do *paintings, sculptures,* and other *works of art,* of any date, if certified as original; it is advisable that certification from the seller or other authority as to their authenticity accompany them. Also exempt from duty, but as a part of the hundred-dollar quota: one quart of liquor. And—this is important—there is no restriction on how much one may bring in above the one-hundred-dollar limit so long as the duty is paid; on many articles the duty is surprisingly moderate.

DRIVING

Take your own car, rent one in advance of your arrival or on the scene, or buy a new car in Italy; U.S. and Canadian licenses are valid if you're operating your own car; an international license is necessary if you're driving a rented car. Reduced-price gas coupons are available, to drivers of cars registered outside of Italy, from Banco Nazionale del Lavoro, 25 West 51st St., New York 10019, or Automobile Club of Italy (address above).

ELECTRIC CURRENT

Confusing. There are two types of voltage, 110-115 AC and 220-230 AC. You never know what voltage your hotel is on until you get there (unless you are well-organized enough to write ahead!) so that the adapter you may have brought along for your shaver, hair dryer, or whatever may or may not work. Additionally, many of the newer hotels have plugs into which the prongs on the appliance-converters sold in the U.S. do not fit. *Buona fortuna!*

LANGUAGE

Italians, especially urban Italians, have become extraordinary linguists in recent years, with fluency in English high, in hotels, caffès, restaurants, shops, transport terminals. Where the Italian you encounter does not speak your language, he welcomes whatever Italian you have at your command. That, together with sign-language, makes communication not only possible, but frequently enjoyable. There is a good deal of French, some German, too. And it is worth remembering that Italians can understand Spanish with little difficulty.

MUSEUM PASSES

By no means are all of the museums you'll want to visit operated by the Italian Government. But many are, especially in Rome, with a sprinkling in the other cities. A museum pass, good for the nationally-run museums, is sold in selected offices of Alitalia Airlines in the United States and Canada for a pittance—one dollar at the time of writing (subject to change). At that price, you can't afford to be without one, even though you will have to sign your name carefully and add the number of the pass, in a special register, at every museum where you use the pass. Those Alitalia offices selling the museum card are in Boston, Buffalo, Calgary (Alberta), Chicago, Cleveland, Dallas, Hartford, Houston, Miami, Milwaukee, Minneapolis, Montreal, New York, Philadelphia, Toronto, Vancouver, and Washington D.C. (For a list of the museums at which the card is valid, inquire at Italian Government Travel Offices.)

OPEN HOURS

Except for hotels, restaurants, and transport terminals, Italy closes down for lunch. In other words, you shop between 8:30 and 9 A.M. through to about 1 P.M., resuming at 3:30 or 4 P.M., on into early evening—7:30 or 8 P.M. Museums operated by the Italian Government have tended, in recent years, to close for the day at the infuriatingly early hour of 2 P.M., during the week, even earlier—1 P.M.—

on Sundays, and to observe a completely shuttered day as well. Other museums—those run by municipalities or privately—are more generous with hours. Most churches keep roughly the same hours as shops. All of which is by way of saying that getting about, day by day, in Italy requires careful advance planning, with the aid of hotel concierges—who should be up-to-the-minute on hours and open days, and the gratis what's-on booklets they have on hand for clients.

TELEPHONING

To use a public phone, you need a token, obtainable, for 50 lire, from someone working in the bar, restaurant, newsstand or tobacco shop wherein is located the phone. Until you get the hang of the system, ask for help from locals on the scene; they're usually happy to oblige.

TIPPING

One has the feeling that this is where it all began and where it will never end. For so long as the shortage of change and small-denomination notes persists, and you are without the wherewithal to give a tip, simply throw up your hands and so indicate. It is not, after all, your fault that the Italian Government is not minting enough currency. Although restaurants add a 15 per cent service charge, waiters expect 5 per cent, or at least the amount of the bill rounded out, in addition. Hotel bellmen expect 150 lire per bag. Station porters get about the same, plus the set fee per bag. (In Naples, no matter what you give will not be considered enough.) Chambermaids look forward to about 150 lire per day but, I suspect, rarely get it. Room service waiters like tips, too, but first look to see how much service charge for them has been tacked on to your check. Hotel concierges should get 300 lire per day, but only if they have been of special service, beyond handing you your key or your mail. Service is included at caffès, but leave a bit extra, anyway. Washroom ladies—they are inescapable—get 50 to 100 lire ransom; bootblacks the same. Theater ushers get 100 lire. I could go on and on, but suffice it to say that taxi drivers get 15 per cent (not less than 150 lire), and in Naples will complain bitterly—nay, hysterically —that neither that amount or even double it is adequate.

Acknowledgments

I am grateful to many kind friends and colleagues on both sides of the Atlantic for co-operation in connection with the preparation of this book. Dottore Emilio Tommasi, the Italian Travel Commissioner in New York, has been enthusiastic and helpful from the start of the project, and so has Amelia Medweid, public relations director at the Italian Government Travel Office in New York, who has never been too busy to come to my aid. Neither, for that matter, has Conte Dottore Sigmundo Fago Golfarelli, Direttore Generale Stampa Estera e Pubblicità, Ente Nazionale Italiano per il Turismo, Rome. I thank them very much indeed, and am most grateful, as well, to Max Drechsler, my research editor and, like myself, a long-time Italy enthusiast; Louise M. Fisher, who typed the final manuscript with her usual expertise; and cartographer Rafael Palacios for the endpaper maps he designed especially for this book.

I want also to thank, alphabetically, for their personal kindness and professional co-operation: Elizabeth R. Adams, Marguerite Allen, Piera Francioni Anziano, Pierre Barrelet, Angelo Bettoja, Lis Brewer, Graziano Catinella, Giuseppe Cecconi, Francesco Chiais, Andrea Ferrara, Roberto Furco, Joseph A. Giacoponello, Nico Girolla, Luciano Giudetti, Josephine Inzarillo, Raymond G. Kitchener, Egidio Lis, Martha Morano, Dottore Nico Pasante, Renato Patessio, Dottore Giovanni Pini, Luigi Richard, Dottore Massimo Rosati, Dottore Natale Rusconi, Elio Sica, Elio Terrazzini, Franco Tortora, Giorgio Valentini, and Mario Varnier.

Whatever errors crop up are mine, as are, of course, the opinions expressed.

R.S.K.

Index

Advance booking, 209–10
Air travel to: Florence, 107
    Milan, 140
    Naples, 170–71
    Rome, 70
    Venice, 206
Amalfi, 151
    hotels, 151
    restaurants, 151
Amalfi Drive, 150–52
Arno River, 75
Auto travel. See Driving in Italy

Barano, 160
Bellagio, 118
Breakfast in Italy, 210
Business hours, 213–14

Caesar, Julius, 2
Canzone del Mare, 158
Capri, 157–58
    hotels, 158–59
    restaurants, 159
Car rentals, 171
Caruso, Enrico, 145
Casamicciola, 160
Caserta, 156–57
Castel Gandolfo, 30

Castellammare, 150
Castelli Romani, 30
Cavour, Camillo, 4
Cernobbio, 118
Churches. See under individual
    cities
Clement III, Pope, 4
Climate, 210. See also under indi-
    vidual cities
Clothing, 211. See also under indi-
    vidual cities
Cocteau, Jean, 12
Colonno, 118
Como, 117–19
    hotels, 117–18
    Lake, 117–18
    restaurants, 118
    shopping, 118
Concerts
    Florence, 89
    Milan, 123–24
    Naples, 161
    Rome, 38
    tickets, obtaining, 209–10
    Venice, 190–91
Constantine, Emperor, 3, 110
Convention facilities, Rome, 40
Cosimo the Elder, 76

Council of Ten, The, 173
Currency, 211
Customs
    entering Italy, 211–12
    returning to the U.S., 212

Driving in Italy, 212
    Naples, 171
    Rome, 71

Electricity, 212–13
Ercolano, 150
Este, Ippolito d', Cardinal, 13
Etruscans, 2, 75

Fields, Gracie, 158
Fiesole, 75, 83
    restaurant, 83
Florence, 74–108
    air access, 107
    Angelico, Fra, 80, 81
    Annunziata Church, 86
    Apostoli Church, 86
    Bartolommeo, Fra, 80
    Botticelli, Alessandro, 80, 84, 88
    Bronzini, Agnolo, 76, 82
    Brunelleschi, Filippo, 78, 81, 82
    Buonaiuto, Andrea di, 82
    buses, 108
    Carmine Church, 86
    Casa Buonarroti, 85
    Castagno, Andrea del, 87–88
    Cenacolo di Santa Apollonia, 88
    churches, 86–87
    Cimabue, Cenni, 80, 82
    clothing, 108
    concerts, 89
    Credi, Lorenzo, 87
    Daddi, Bernardo, 84
    Donatello, Donato, 79, 82, 84
    Duomo Complex, 78
    festivals, 89
    Forte Belvedere, 88
    Galleria dell'Accademia, 83–84

Galleria delle Spedale degli In-
    nocenti, 88
Ghiberti, Lorenzo, 78
Ghirlandaio, Domenico, 82, 86–
    87, 88
Giambologna, 79
Giardini de Boboli, 77
Giotto di Dondone, 78, 80, 82
Gozzoli, Benozzo, 76
history, 74–76
hotels, 90–94
information sources, 108
Lippi, Filippo, 80, 82, 84, 86, 87
Loggia della Signoria, 77
Longhi, Pietro, 85
major sights, 78–83
Masaccio, 84, 86
Masolino da Panicale, 86
Michaelangelo   (Buonarroti),
    78, 79, 80, 82, 83–84, 85
Michelozzo   di   Bartolommeo,
    81, 85
Monaco, Lorenzo, 84
Museo Archeologico, 84
Museo Bardini, 84
Museo dell'Opera del Duomo,
    84–85
Museo di San Marco, 80–81
Museo Horne, 84
Museo Nazionale Bargello, 79
Museo Stibbert, 85
museums, 84–85
newspapers, 108
Ognissanti Church, 86–87
opera, 89
Orsanmichele Church, 87
palaces, 85–86
Palazzo Davanzati, 86
Palazzo Medici-Riccardi, 85–86
Palazzo Strozzi, 86
Palazzo Vecchio, 77, 79
Perugino, Pietro, 80
Piazza della Signoria, 77
Piazzale Michelangelo, 77, 88

Piero di Cosimo, 88
Pitti Palace, 80
Ponte Vecchio, 79
Raphael, 80, 84
restaurants, 94–98
Robbia, Luca della, 79, 81, 84,
    86, 88
San Lorenzo, 82–83
San Marco, 87
San Miniato al Monte, 87
Santa Croce, 81
Santa Firenze, 87
Santa Maria Novella, 82
Santo Spirito, 87
Sarto, Andrea del, 80, 86
shopping, 99–107
sightseeing, 108
Sinagoga, 88
taxis, 107–8
Teatro Comunale, 89
Teatro della Pergola, 89
Teatro Verdi, 89
theaters, 89
Tiepolo, Giovanni Battista, 85
Titian, 80, 85
train access, 107
Uccello, Paolo, 80, 87, 88
Uffizi Gallery, 79–80
Vasari, Giorgio, 81
Via Tornabuoni, 77
villas, 88–89
Vinci, Leonardo da, 79, 80
walking tour, 76–78
wine estates, 87
Fontana, 160
Forio, 160

Garibaldi, Giuseppe, 4
Ghibellines, 75
Gregory I, Pope, 3
Guelphs, 75

Hadrian, Emperor, 2
Herculaneum, 156

Holy Roman Empire, 3
Horse racing
    Naples, 161
    Rome, 40
Hotels
    Amalfi, 151
    Bellagio, 118
    Capri, 158–59
    Como, 117–18
    Florence, 90–94
    Ischia, 160–61
    Milan, 118, 124–28
    Naples, 162–63
    Positano, 151
    Rome, 40–50
    Sorrento, 152
    Venice, 192–97
Hours of business, 213–14

Information sources
    Florence, 108
    Italian Government Travel Of-
        fices, 209
    Milan, 141
    Naples, 171
    Rome, 73
    Venice, 208
Innocent VIII, Pope, 4
Ischia, 159–61
    hotels, 160–61
    restaurants, 161
Ischia Ponte, 160
Ischia Porto, 159–60

John XXIII, Pope, 178

Keats, John, 15

Lacco Ameno, 160
Language, 3, 213
Lecco, 119
Leo X, Pope, 4
Lorenzo the Magnificent, 76
Ludovic the Moor (Sforza), 110

Manin, Daniele, 174
Marcus Aurelius, Emperor, 2
Marina Grande, 158–59
Marina Piccola, 158–59
Martelli Chapel, 82
Medici, Lorenzo de', 76
Medici family, 75, 76, 83, 85
Mestre, 174
Meta, 150
Milan, 109–41
    Abbazia di Chiaravalle, 122
    air access, 140
    Ambrosiana Gallery, 115
    Antico Ospedale Maggiore, 122
    Arco della Pace, 112, 122
    Bassano, Jacopo, 115
    Bellini, 116, 119
    Botticelli, Alessandro, 115, 116
    Bramante, Donato, 121, 122
    Bramante Cloisters, 122
    Brera Gallery, 115
    Bronzini, Agnolo, 115
    Canaletto, Giovanni, 119
    Caravaggio, Michelangelo, 115
    Certosa di Pavia, 121–22
    churches, 112–13, 121–22
    Cimitero Monumentale, 122
    Civico Museo del Risorgimento
        Nazionale, 120
    Civico Museo di Milano, 119–20
    Civico Museo di Storia Contem-
        poranea, 119–20
    clothing, 141
    concerts, 123–24
    Correggio, Antonio, 116
    Duomo, the, 111, 112–13
    excursions, 118–19, 121–22
    Galleria d'Arte Moderna, 116
    Galleria Vittorio Emanuele II,
        117
    Ghirlandaio, Domenico, 115
    Giardini Pubblici, 112, 123
    Giordano, Luca, 115, 119
    Guardi, Francesco, 119

    history, 109–11
    hotels, 124–28
    information sources, 141
    international Fair, 124
    La Scala. *See* Teatro alla Scala
    Lippi, Filippo, 115, 116
    Longhi, Pietro, 119
    Lotto, Lorenzo, 116
    Luini, Bernardino, 115, 121
    major sights, 112–19
    Mantegna, Andrea, 116
    Manzù, Giacomo, 116
    Marini, Marino, 116
    Modigliani, Amedeo, 116
    Museo Archeologico, 119
    Museo d'Arte Antica al Castello
        Sforzesco, 116
    Museo del Duomo, 120
    Museo Poldi Pezzoli, 115–16
    Museo Teatrale alla Scala, 120
    museums, 115–16, 119–20
    newspapers, 141
    nightlife, 124
    opera, 114–15, 123–24
    Palazzo Clerici, 122
    Piazza della Repubblica, 112
    Piccola Scala, 124
    Piccolo Teatro, 124
    Pinacoteca di Brera, 119
    Pollaiuolo, Antonio, 116
    Reni, Guido, 115
    restaurants, 128–33
    San Lorenzo Maggiore, 121
    San Maurizio, 121
    San Satiro, 121
    Santa Maria delle Grazie, 111,
        117
    Sant' Ambrogio, 121
    Sant' Eustorgio, 121
    shopping, 133–40
    sightseeing tours, 141
    Stadio San Siro, 123
    Stazione Centrale, 112
    Stazione Nord, 112

taxis, 141
Teatro alla Scala, 113–15, 123–24
Tecnica Leonardo da Vinci, 120
theater, 124
Tiepolo, Giovanni Battista, 115, 116, 119
Tintoretto, 116, 119
Titian, 115, 119
train access, 140–41
Triennale, The, 124
Vinci, Leonardo da, 112, 115, 117
Vivarini, 115
walking tour, 111–12
Moltrasio, 118
Monte Epomeo, 160
Munthe, Axel, 158
Museum passes, 213
Museums. *See under* individual cities
Mussolini, Benito, 4

Naples, 142–71
air access, 170–71
Aquarium, 155
Banco di Napoli Galleria di Arte, 153
Bellini, 147
Botticelli, Alessandro, 147
buses, 171
Cappella, Banco di Napoli, 153
Cappella di Sansevero, 154–55
car rentals, 171
Castel Nuovo, 155
catacombs, 155
Certosa di San Martino Museo Nazionale, 152–53
churches, 148, 153–55
climate, 171
clothes, 171
concerts, 161
Duomo, the, 148, 153–54
excursions, 149–52, 156–61

Ferelli, Giacomo, 154
Galleria Umberto I, 145
Garibaldi, Giuseppe, 144
Gesù Nuovo, 154
Giordano, Luca, 147, 148, 153, 154
Giotto di Dondone, 155
history, 143–46
horse racing, 161
hostility to foreigners, 142–43
hotels, 162–63
information sources, 171
Kingdom of the Two Sicilies, 144
Lippi, Filippo, 147
Luini, Bernardino, 147
major sights, 146–52
Mergellina (area), 145
Museo Capodimonte, 146–47
Museo Civico Filangieri, 153
Museo Nazionale, 146
Museo Nazionale Duca di Martina, 153
museums, 146–47, 152–53
newspapers, 171
opera, 161
Palazzo Reale, 147
parks, 155
Piazza Municipio, 145
Piazza Plebiscito, 145
Piazza Trento e Trieste, 145
Raphael, 147
restaurants, 163–67
San Domenico Maggiore, 154
San Fernando di Palazzo, 154
San Francesco di Paola, 145, 154
San Gregorio Armeno, 148
San Lorenzo Maggiore, 154
Santa Brigida, 154
Santa Chiara, 148
Santa Lucia, 145
Sant' Angelo a Nilo, 154
Sant' Anna dei Lombardi, 148

Sarto, Andrea del, 147
shopping, 167–70
sightseeing, 171
soccer, 161
Sodoma, Il, 147
Spaccanapoli (old Naples), 149
Stanzione, Massimo, 154
taxis, 171
Teatro di San Carlo, 147–48, 161
theater, 161
Titian, 147
train access, 170
trolleys, 171
Via Roma, 146
walking tour, 145–46
zoo, 155
Napoleon, 110, 143–44
Nero, Emperor, 2
Nesso, 118
Newspapers, 73, 108, 141

Octavian Augustus, Emperor, 2
Odoacer, 3
Opera
Florence, 89
Milan, 113–15, 123–24
Naples, 161
Rome, 37–38
tickets, obtaining, 209–10
Venice, 190–91

Paestum, 156
Pius IX, Pope, 4
Polo, Marco, 173
Pompeii, 149–50
Porta Marina, 149
Porto Marghera, 174
Positano, 151
hotels, 151
restaurants, 151

Railways
Florence, 107
Milan, 140–41

Naples, 170
Rome, 70–71
Venice, 206–7
Ravello, 151–52
Restaurants
Amalfi, 151
Bellagio, 118
Capri, 158–59
Como, 118
Fiesole, 83
Florence, 94–98
Ischia, 160–61
Milan, 128–33
Naples, 163–67
Pompeii, 150
Positano, 151
Rome, 50–60
Sorrento, 152
Tivoli, 13
Venice, 197–202
Risorgimento, The, 110, 144, 174
Rome, 1–73
air access, 70
American Embassy, 7
Angelico, Fra, 19, 20
Arco di Constantino, 30
auto access, 7
basilicas, 8, 9–10
Bassano, Jacopo, 19
Baths of Diocletian, 10
Bellini, 15, 16, 19
Bernini, Pietro, 4, 15, 22, 25,
      27–28, 30, 32, 33, 34
Borghese Gardens, 6
Bordone, Paris, 19
Botticelli, Alessandro, 15
Bramante, Donato, 28
Bronzini, Agnolo, 15
buses, 71
business hours, 73
Canaletto, Giovanni, 18
Capitoline Hill, 6
Caravaggio, Michelangelo, 15,
      18, 19, 22, 25, 26

Carpaccio, Vittore, 15
Castel Sant' Angelo, 14
catacombs, 30–31
churches, 20–29
climate, 72
clothing, 72
Colosseum, 9
concerts, 38
contemporary architecture, 31, 35–36
convention facilities, 40
Cortona, Pietro da, 27
Croce, Baldassar, 29
currency, 72
Domenchino, 25, 27
Donatello, Donato, 25
flea markets, 61
Fontana di Trevi, 12
forums, 31–32
fountains, 12, 32
Galleria Borghese, 14–15
Galleria Farnesina, 15
Galleria Nazionale d'Arte, 10–11
Galleria Nazionale d'Arte Moderna, 15
Gesù de Roma, Il, 24
Goethe Museum, 15
history, 1–5
horse racing, 40
hotels, 40–50
information sources, 73
Isola Tiberina, 32
Keats-Shelley Memorial House, 15
Landini, 32
Lotto, Lorenzo, 11
Maderno, Carlo, 27, 29, 30, 31
major sights, 7–13
maps of, 6
Michelangelo (Buonarroti), 8, 12, 25, 28
movies, 38–39
Musei Capitoline, 16

Museo Barracco, 15–16
Museo dei Conservatori, 16
Museo Nazionale d'Arte Orientale, 16–17
Museo Nazionale delle Arti e Tradizioni Popolari, 17
Museo Nazionale Romano, 10–11
museums, 10–11, 13–20
newspapers, 73
opera, 37–38
Ostia, 33
palaces, 11–12, 17–19, 33–34
Palatine Hill, 32
Palazzo Barberini, 7, 11
Palazzo Braschi, 17
Palazzo Corsini, 17–18
Palazzo Doria Pamphili, 18
Palazzo Farnese, 11–12
Palazzo Spada, 18–19
Palazzo Venezia, 6, 19
Pantheon, 9
Papal audiences, 30, 39–40
parks, 34
Piazza del Popolo, 6
Piazza Navona, 12
Piero di Cosimo, 11
Pincio Hill, 6
Pintoricchio, 23, 26
Piombo, Sebastiano, 26, 28
Quattro Coronati, 28
rail access, 70–71
Raphael, 4, 11, 14, 15, 19, 22, 25, 26
restaurants, 50–60
St. Peter's Basilica, 7–8
San Agostino in Campo Marzio, 22
San Andrea al Quirinale, 22
San Antonio de Portoghesi, 22
San Bernardo alle Terme, 22
San Carlo al Corso, 23
San Carlo alle Quattro Fontane, 23

San Clemente, 23
San Giovanni in Laterno, 24
San Girolamo della Carità, 24
San Luigi dei Francesi, 24–25
San Paolo Fuori le Mura, 9–10
San Pietro in Montorio, 28
San Pietro in Vincoli, 28
San Rocco, 28–29
San Silvestro in Capita, 29
Sant' Agnese in Agone, 22
Santa Brigida, 22
Santa Cecilia in Trastevere, 23
Santa Maria d'Aracoeli sul
    Campidoglio, 25
Santa Maria degli Angeli, 25
Santa Maria dell'Anima, 25
Santa Maria dell'Umiltà, 27–28
Santa Maria della Vittoria, 27
Santa Maria del Popolo, 26
Santa Maria in Cosmedin, 26
Santa Maria in Traspontina, 26–
    27
Santa Maria in Trastevere, 27
Santa Maria in Vallicella, 27
Santa Maria Maddalena, 26
Santa Maria Maggiore, 9
Santa Maria Nova, 26
Santa Pudenziana, 28
Santa Susanna, 29
Santa Trinità dei Monti, 6, 29
San Teodoro, 29
Sarto, Andrea del, 19
shopping, 60–70
sightseeing tours, 40, 71–72
Sistine Chapel, 8–9
Sodoma, Il, 15
sound and light shows, 39
Spanish Steps, 6
squares, 34–35
SS. Cosma e Damiano, 23
Stazione Termini, 7
street markets, 64
subway, 71
taxis, 71

theater, 39
Tintoretto, 11, 19
tipping, 72–73
Titian, 11, 14–15, 16, 19
Triton fountain, 7
Vatican City, 4, 7–9, 19–20, 36–
    37
Veronese, Paolo, 15
Via del Corso, 6
Villa Giulia, 20
Vinci, Leonardo da, 19
Vittorio Emanuele Monument, 6
worship, non-Catholic, 73
Romulus Augustulus, Emperor, 3

Sant' Angelo, 160
Serenissima, The (Venice), 174
Sforza family, 110
Shopping
    Florence, 99–107
    Milan, 133–40
    Naples, 167–70
    Rome, 60–70
    Venice, 202–6
Sightseeing tours. *See under* indi-
    vidual cities
Sixtus IV, Pope, 4
Soccer, 161
Sorrento, 152
    hotels, 152
    restaurants, 152
Sound and light shows, 39

Telephones, 214
Theater
    Florence, 89
    Milan, 124
    Naples, 161
    Rome, 39
Tipping, 214
    Rome, 72–73
Tivoli, 12–13, 37
    restaurant, 13

Tours, 209–10
Traffic, 142, 145
Tremezzo, 118

Urban VIII, Pope, 8

Vatican City, 4, 7–9, 19–20, 36–37
  St. Peter's, 7–8
  Sistine Chapel, 8–9
  Vatican Museum, 8, 19–20
Venice, 172–208
  air access, 207
  Arsenal, 187
  Bassano, Jacopo, 179, 180
  Bellini, 178, 180, 184, 185
  Biennale, 191–92
  Bordone, Paris, 182
  Bridge of Sighs, 179
  Burano Island, 176, 188
  Carpaccio, Vittore, 178, 182, 183, 184
  Canale di San Marco, 176
  Canaletto, Giovanni, 180
  Ca' Rezzonico, 181
  Carmini Church, 184
  Casino Municipale, 191
  churches, 177–78, 184–87
  climate, 208
  clothes, 208
  Collezione Peggy Guggenheim, 183
  concerts, 190–91
  Degli Scalzi Church, 184–85
  Doges' Palace, 176, 178–79
  Donatello, Donato, 180
  festivals, 191–92
  Galleria Giorgio Franchetti, 182
  Galleria Internazionale d'Arte Moderna, 182
  Gallerie dell'Accademia, 177, 179–80
  Gesuati Church, 185
  Ghetto, The, 187–88

Giordano, Luca, 184
Giorgione, 180
Giudecca Island, 176
gondolas, 188, 207–8
Grand Canal, 176
Guardi, Francesco, 180, 182
history, 173–75
hotels, 192–97
information sources, 208
Libreria Vecchia, 189
Lido, 176, 188–89
Longhi, Pietro, 183, 184
Lotto, Lorenzo, 180, 183, 184
major sights, 177–81
Mantegna, Andrea, 182
Murano Island, 176, 188, 203
Museo Correr, 182–83
Museo di Icone dell'Istituto Ellenico, 183
Museo Storico Navale, 183
museums and galleries, 179–80, 181, 182–84
newspapers, 208
opera, 190–91
palaces, 189
Palladio, Andrea, 177, 179
Palma Il Vecchio, 184
panoramas, 189–90
Piazzale Roma, 176
Piazza San Marco, 176, 187
Pinacoteca della Fondazione Querini Stampalia, 183–84
Ponte di Rialto, 177
rail access, 206–7
Redentore Church, 176, 185
restaurants, 197–202
St. George's, 185
San Francesco della Vigna, 185
San Giorgio Maggiore, 177, 185
San Marco, 176, 177–78
San Martino, 186
San Maurizio, 186
San Moisè, 186
San Nicolo dei Mendicoli, 186

San Pantalon, 187
San Sebastiano, 187
San Sovino, 180
San Stefano, 187
San Zaccaria, 187
Santa Maria del Giglio, 186
Santa Maria della Salute, 186
Santa Maria Formosa, 186
Santa Maria Gloriosa dei Frari, 180
Scuola di San Giorgio degli Schiavoni, 184
Scuola Grande di San Rocco, 180–81
shopping, 202–6
sightseeing tours, 208
Stazione Santa Lucia, 176
SS. Giovanni e Paolo, 180

Teatro La Fenice, 190–91
Tiepolo, Giovanni Battista, 180, 181, 184, 185
Tintoretto, 179, 181, 184, 185
Titian, 179, 180
Torcello Island, 176, 181, 188
Veneziano, 179, 180
Veronese, Paolo, 179, 180, 185
Vivarini, 180, 182, 185
walking tour, 175–77
Vesuvius, Mount, 143, 146, 155
Victor Emmanuel II, King, 4
Victor Emmanuel III, King, 4–5
Villa Adriana, 37
Villa d'Este, 12–13, 118–19
Visconti family, 110

Wagner, Richard, 151–52

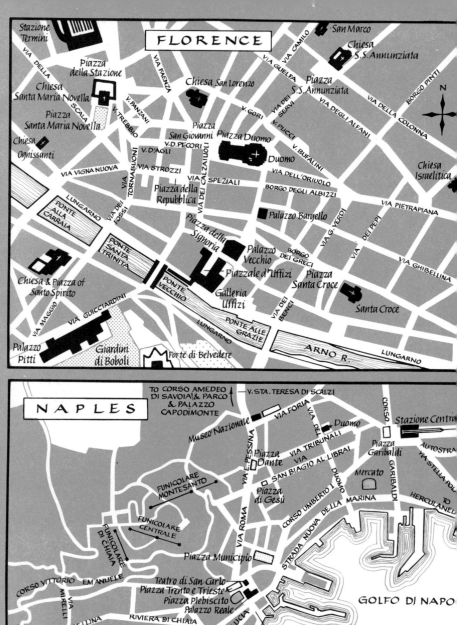

FLORENCE

Stazione Termini
VIA DELLA SCALA
Piazza della Stazione
Chiesa Santa Maria Novella
Piazza Santa Maria Novella
Chiesa Ognissanti
VIA VIGNA NUOVA
V. PANZANI
V. FAENZA
V. TREBBIO
Chiesa San Lorenzo
VIA DEI SERVI
V. GORI
Piazza San Giovanni
V.D.PECORI
Piazza Duomo
V. D'AGLI
VIA STROZZI
VIA DEI TORNABUONI
VIA DEI FOSSI
Piazza della Repubblica
VIA DEI CALZAIUOLI
SPEZIALI
Duomo
VIA DELL'ORIUOLO
BORGO DEGLI ALBIZZI
VIA PIETRAPIANA
Palazzo Bargello
VIA G. VERDI
VIA DEI PEPI
VIA GHIBELLINA
San Marco
Chiesa S.S. Annunziata
Piazza S.S. Annunziata
VIA DEI SERVI
V. PUCCI
V. BUFALINI
VIA DEGLI ALFANI
BORGO PINTI
VIA DELLA COLONNA
Chiesa Israelitica
N
LUNGARNO
PONTE ALLA CARRAIA
PONTE SANTA TRINITA
PONTE VECCHIO
Piazza della Signoria
Palazzo Vecchio
Piazzale d'Uffizi
Galleria Uffizi
Piazza Santa Croce
BORGO DEI GRECI
VIA DEI BENCI
Santa Croce
Chiesa & Piazza of Santo Spirito
VIA MAGGIO
VIA GUICCIARDINI
Palazzo Pitti
Giardini di Boboli
Forte di Belvedere
PONTE ALLE GRAZIE
LUNGARNO
ARNO R.
LUNGARNO

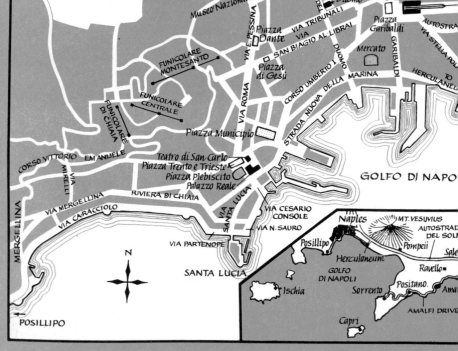

NAPLES

TO CORSO AMEDEO DI SAVOIA & PARCO & PALAZZO CAPODIMONTE
V. STA. TERESA DI SCALZI
VIA FORIA
Museo Nazionale
VIA E. PESSINA
FUNICOLARE MONTESANTO
FUNICOLARE CENTRALE
FUNICOLARE DI CHIAIA
CORSO VITTORIO EMANUELE
VIA MIRELLI
VIA MERGELLINA
VIA CARACCIOLO
MERGELLINA
POSILLIPO
N
Piazza Dante
VIA TRIBUNALI
SAN BIAGIO AL LIBRAI
VIA ROMA
Piazza di Gesù
Piazza Municipio
Teatro di San Carlo
Piazza Trento e Trieste
Piazza Plebiscito
Palazzo Reale
RIVIERA DI CHIAIA
VIA SANTA LUCIA
VIA CESARIO CONSOLE
VIA N. SAURO
VIA PARTENOPE
SANTA LUCIA
Duomo
Piazza Garibaldi
CORSO UMBERTO I
STRADA NUOVA DELLA MARINA
CORSO
Stazione Centrale
AUTOSTRA
VIA STELLA POL
Mercato
VIA GARIBALDI
TO HERCULANEU
GOLFO DI NAPO
Ischia
Naples
Posillipo
Herculaneum
GOLFO DI NAPOLI
Sorrento
Capri
MT. VESUVIUS
AUTOSTRAD DEL SOLE
Pompeii
Sale
Ravello
Positano
Ama
AMALFI DRIVE